Leading Issues in Business Research Methods

Edited by

Antony Bryant

Leading Issues in Business Research Methods
Volume One.
First published March 2011
Second Print March 2012

Copyright © 2011 The authors

ISBN: 978-1-906638-87-0

All rights reserved. Except for the quotation of short passages for the purposes of critical review, no part of this publication may be reproduced in any material form (including photocopying or storing in any medium by electronic means and whether or not transiently or incidentally to some other use of this publication) without the written permission of the copyright holder except in accordance with the provisions of the Copyright Designs and Patents Act 1988, or under the terms of a licence issued by the Copyright Licensing Agency Ltd, Saffron House, 6-10 Kirby Street, London EC1N 8TS. Applications for the copyright holder's written permission to reproduce any part of this publication should be addressed to the publishers.

Disclaimer: While every effort has been made by the editor, authors and the publishers to ensure that all the material in this book is accurate and correct at the time of going to press, any error made by readers as a result of any of the material, formulae or other information in this book is the sole responsibility of the reader. Readers should be aware that the URLs quoted in the book may change or be damaged by malware between the time of publishing and accessing by readers.

Note to readers.
Some papers have been written by authors who use the American form of spelling and some use the British. These two different approaches have been left unchanged.

Published by: Academic Publishing International Limited, Reading, RG4 9AY, United Kingdom, info@academic-publishing.org

Printed by Good News Digital Books in the UK

Available from www.academic-bookshop.com

Leading Issues in Business Research Methods

Contents

List of contributors... iii
About the Editor... iv
Introduction to Business and Management Research: Business and
Management Research – Concepts and Issues...v
   Antony Bryant, Editor

Towards a Second Order Research Methodology 1
   Jim Brown and Petia Sice

Grounded Theory: Its Diversification and Application Through two
Examples from Research Studies on Knowledge and Value Management 22
   Kirsty Hunter, Subashini Hari, Charles Egbu and John Kelly

Interpretivism and the Pursuit of Research Legitimisation: An Integrated
Approach to Single Case Design.. 45
   Felicity Kelliher

Applying a Behavioural Simulation for the Collection of Data................... 63
   Kristina Risom Jespersen

Individualised Rating-Scale Procedure: A Means of Reducing Response
Style Contamination in Survey Data? 79
   Elisa Chami-Castaldi, Nina Reynolds and James Wallace

Pragmatic Research Design: an Illustration of the Use of the Delphi
Technique 101
   Trevor Amos and Noel Pearse

Googling Companies - a Webometric Approach to Business Studies..... 116
   Esteban Romero-Frías

The Factors that Influence Adoption and Usage Decision in SMEs:
Evaluating Interpretive Case Study Research in Information Systems..... 141
   Japhet Lawrence

Strategies for Gaining Access when Doing Fieldwork: Reflections of two Researchers 164
Satirenjit Kaur Johl and Sumathi Renganathan

Taking Stock of Research Methods in Strategy-as-Practice 183
Ramya T Venkateswaran and Ganesh N Prabhu

Using Focus Groups in Studies of ISD Team Behaviour 196
Colm O'hEocha, Kieran Conboy and Xiaofeng Wang

List of contributors

Trevor Amos, Rhodes University, Grahamstown, South Africa
Jim Brown, Northumberland College, UK
Elisa Chami-Castaldi, School of Management, University of Bradford, UK
Kieran Conboy, Business Information Systems Group, NUI Galway, Galway, Ireland
Charles Egbu, Glasgow Caledonian University, Glasgow, UK
Subashini Hari, University of Wolverhampton, UK
Kirsty Hunter, Glasgow Caledonian University, Glasgow, UK
Satirenjit Kaur Johl, Universiti Teknologi PETRONAS, Malaysia
Felicity Kelliher, School of Business, Waterford Institute of Technology, Ireland
John Kelly, Nottingham Trent University and Axoss Ltd, UK
Japhet Lawrence, University of Kurdistan-Hawler, Erbil, Kurdistan Region of Iraq
Colm O'hEocha, Business Information Systems Group, NUI Galway, Galway, Ireland
Noel Pearse, Rhodes University, Grahamstown, South Africa
Ganesh N Prabhu, Indian Institute of Management Bangalore, India
Nina Reynolds, School of Management, University of Bradford, UK
Sumathi Renganathan, Universiti Teknologi PETRONAS, Malaysia
Kristina Risom Jespersen, Aarhus University, Department of Economics, Denmark
Esteban Romero-Frías, University of Granada, Spain
Petia Sice, Northumbria University, School of Informatics, Newcastle Upon Tyne, UK
Ramya T Venkateswaran, Indian Institute of Management Bangalore, India
James Wallace, School of Management, University of Bradford, UK
Xiaofeng Wang, Lero, the Irish Software Engineering Research Centre, Limerick, Ireland

Leading Issues in Business Research Methods

About the Editor

Antony Bryant is Professor of Informatics at Leeds Metropolitan University, Leeds, UK.

His research includes investigation of the ways in which the Open Source model might be used more widely, and in particular how it can be de-veloped as a contributory feature for the re-constructed financial sector in the wake of the economic melt-down; coining the term Mutual-ity 2.0 and developing the concept in various contexts, for example, http://www.opendemocracy.net/article/email/mutuality-2-0-open-source-the-financial-crisis.

He has written extensively on research methods, being Senior Editor of The SAGE Handbook of Grounded Theory (SAGE, 2007) – co-edited with Kathy Charmaz with whom he has worked in the area of Grounded Theory and research methods in general.

He has developed and taught a wide range of post-graduate courses in The Netherlands, South Africa, Malaysia, and China. He is ASEM Professor at the University of Malaya, and Visiting Professor at the University of Amsterdam.

Introduction to Business and Management Research: Business and Management Research – Concepts and Issues

The Electronic Journal of Business Research Methods started publication in 2002. There was no general introduction to the journal at its inception, but Dan Remenyi's paper in the first issue began with the observation that '[W]hen reflecting on what is often said by those who write about research in Business and Management Studies one is left with the feeling that there is sometimes an incomplete understanding in our community of what constitutes research processes'. In the ensuing years the papers presented in the journal have sought to offer a range of perspectives and issues 'on topics relevant to research in the field of business and management' with the aim of increasing levels of such understanding. (See EJBRM 'Aims and Scope' – http://www.ejbrm.com/page?ident=scope)

Exactly what constitutes the domain of research in the field of business and management might itself seem to be a topic for research and discussion, but rather than seek some precise characterization or definition, it is preferable to be able to point to a range of examples that are encompassed by this term. The papers constituting the eight volumes published to date go some way towards this, and it is hoped that the selection offered here provides an accessible and substantive introduction, as well as a fairly representative cross-section.

The term 'business and management' refers to a wide-ranging and overarching domain covering topics such as businesses as organizations, business models, management models and practices, marketing and branding, and financial models; as well as the widespread applications of ICT (information and communications technology) that provide the basis for concerns such as knowledge management, customer relationship management, and distributed or virtual organizations. Given this spectrum it is not surprising that the methods used in 'business and management research' constitute a microcosm of research methods in general.

One issue for publications such as EJBRM is the extent to which they provide a showcase for research by academics in universities and research centres, but also seek to appeal to a wider, non-academic audience with interests in the ways in which business-related topics and issues might be examined and analysed through research. It is tempting to look for 'quick wins' in this regard, but the business of research does not lend itself to this model despite attempts to force it to do so by those who fund research and related activities. Recent developments in the UK in the context of the Research Excellence Framework [REF] exemplify the ways in which ideas about 'research impact' need to be enhanced to take account of a wide range of factors and a protracted time-frame (15-20 years in case of the REF). Given that EJBRM has only been in existence since 2002, choosing papers for this selection was not a case of looking for those which had had any obvious impact.

So what criteria were most suited in selecting a small number of papers from the existing volumes of the journal? I have deliberately avoided papers where the authors sought to delve too deeply into epistemological issues. Any course on research methods must certainly cover epistemological topics, differentiating between various positions such as positivism, interpretivism, constructivism, and the like. But ultimately students must be brought to a realization that research should be judged on the outputs and insights, regardless of the stated or imputed epistemological position of the researcher(s). This is not an easy position to adopt, and I will readily admit that in some of my teaching and writing on research methods, I have sometimes put too much emphasis on the former at the expense of the latter. Moreover I can point to many instances in which a student outlined a research proposal based on what I would regard as an erroneous epistemological position, but which led to a rigorous and imaginative output, and the literature is replete with many other examples of this.

Researchers and students requiring overviews and analyses of research-oriented epistemological issues can choose from a wide and impressive array of sources including key collections such as Denzin and Lincoln's

Leading Issues in Business Research Methods

Handbook of Qualitative Research (various editions), or Silverman's Qualitative Research (various editions and titles); also texts such as those by Miles and Huberman (1994), Blaxter et al (2007). Those unfamiliar with this literature should be encouraged to gain some acquaintance as a matter of standard grounding in the research arena.

In thinking about and planning research, it is crucial that epistemological issues are brought into consideration, even if it is to discount ideas and arguments that run counter to one's assumptions or predispositions. Those who favour qualitative approaches should always be able to explain why they have not favoured quantitative ones; and vice-versa. Similarly if one adopts a positivist or neo-positivist position, one should also have some understanding of the interpretivist-constructivist stance; and again the converse applies. In both cases this implies that researchers have some familiarity with assumptions, methods and techniques that they do not share, or which they do not intend to use. It is important that academic researchers have a rounded view and thus understand that there are often many ways of investigation a research question. Subsequently, in actually carrying out or performing research, it is also important that issues concerned with types and quality of data, the nature of evidence, processes of analysis, and reliability of resources and sources are understood. On the other hand when it comes to reporting on research findings and outcomes, in journals and other outlets, these issues should take something of a back seat; with the underlying processes of investigation and analysis, the findings themselves, and their potential import taking pride of place.

In the light of this, when selecting papers for this collection I looked for those which demonstrated an imaginative and insightful use of a variety of methods; contributions that will supplement the many 'how to' textbooks, handbooks, and papers that are now so readily available. This necessarily resulted in a slant towards papers that centre on issues of day-to-day research activities such as gaining access to research sites, gathering data, performing interviews, using the internet and Web as a research resource, performing rigorous analysis, evaluation and so on. The standard texts of necessity have to focus on the broad issues around research methods and techniques, whereas papers that report on actual projects can often shed a more detailed light on specific practices and processes themselves.

The selection encompasses preparatory issues – such as gaining access to research sites for fieldwork and case studies – as well as operational ones focusing on survey design, responder bias, and relationships between researchers and other participants. The papers cover a variety of techniques including well-established ones such as focus groups, as well as introducing innovative ones for web-based research. Given the preponderance of interpretive approaches, several of the papers were chosen for their arguments and suggestions about the validation and rigour of such methods.

One way of discussing current research practice in general is to focus on the multi-faceted characteristic of 'openness'. The research literature is replete with constant reminders that research projects should be undertaken in an open-minded manner, and that the research process itself should be open-ended; both in terms of the application of specific research techniques, and the way in which results are presented. In other words, when using research techniques or methods, the researcher should constantly be aware that the instruments themselves may obstruct the development of the research itself – the obvious example being use of a closely structured questionnaire obscuring some detailed and far more interesting issues. Similarly when reporting the outcomes, care must be taken to ensure that any claims above-and-beyond the results themselves have some firm conceptual and evidential basis. It is often justifiably claimed that the media are responsible for exaggerating or misconstruing research findings, but in far too many cases the fault lies in the research papers or reports themselves, with authors making claims that exceed the bases of the actual findings – a feature of both qualitative and quantitative research. (Anyone looking for examples would be well advised to begin by perusing Ben Goldacre's 'Bad Science' website – http://www.badscience.net/)

In addition to these aspects of openness, there is the issue of open-access. Far too many research papers are available only to those with access to institutional libraries with subscriptions to the relevant journals. With the predominance of on-line publication there are strong arguments for this to be replaced with open-access, perhaps in some cases with a delayed publication model; for instance giving immediate access only on some premium basis, but general availability one month later. EJBRM is an exemplar of an open-access journal, with a swift route from submission to publication, and a wide range of different contributions and topics.

Leading Issues in Business Research Methods

The selection that follows amounts to a total of sixteen papers, covering a range of issues, methods and techniques, with a preponderance of articles reporting on qualitative research; but this reflects the general trend in the journal itself. Many of the papers make reference to epistemological issues, but mostly simply in the form of briefly stating a position from which the specific argument then develops. My own view of this aspect of research derives from the Pragmatist position based on the work of John Dewey and William James, and the more recent writings of Richard Rorty. In essence Dewey's view was that all forms of our knowledge are provisional, and rather than aiming at some idea of universality and truthfulness in the abstract, it would be better to judge our ideas in terms of their practical usefulness. Dewey's argument was there are no fixed points from which to observe reality, and no appeals to 'raw experience'; hence no universal and context-free claims to truth. All knowledge is provisional, and has to be judged in terms of its usefulness within some set of confines – Dewey termed this 'instrumentalism'. Rorty takes this further, rejecting the view that there is any hierarchy of forms of knowledge: i.e. science or philosophical insight has no greater status than do other forms of knowledge such as common-sense or practical wisdom. Our knowledge of the world is best seen as a web or a network of statements rather than an edifice, and the value of any form of knowledge is its usefulness and applicability which may be constrained in terms of time and place and user. Rorty approvingly quotes Nietzsche's dictum that what passes for truth—or more poignantly 'The Truth'—is in fact 'a mobile army of metaphors, metonyms, and anthropomorphisms' (quoted by Rorty, 1991, p.3).

Many academic papers on research often adopt an almost apologetic stance with regard to 'practice', implying that the latter is somehow more valuable, insightful, or 'relevant'. In many instances this may well be the case. Posing the question 'So what?' too many research reports often demonstrates this all too clearly. Yet on the other hand far too much 'practice' amounts to no more than simply a form of muddling-through, itself often based on some poorly understood or inadequately popularized research or model. Keynes elegantly made this point by noting that 'Practical men, who believe themselves to be quite exempt from any intellectual influence, are usually the slaves of some defunct economist.' (Keynes, 1936, ch. 24 'Concluding Notes')

Here again Pragmatism offers a useful feature in terms of what Dewey and others term 'the difference principle' – i.e. 'given my research findings what practical differences do they make with regard to currently accepted ideas?' This is not to imply that all research has to have an immediate and far-reaching impact, but it raises the issue for consideration, and in the context of the papers presented here this should be something that readers take into account.

A final note: Several of the papers address the ways in which research methods and techniques need to take account of the emergence of the internet and Web, but none of them actually mentions Wikipedia. Wikipedia cannot be ignored in the context of research. At its inception in 2001 it was looked upon either as a quirky novelty or as something of a 'health hazard', since the entries were un-moderated and so open to creation, revision or updating by anyone regardless of expertise or qualification. People compared it unfavourably to long-standing and well-respected encyclopaedias such as Britannica, pointing out that anyone visiting a Wikipedia page was in the same position as someone visiting a public convenience (i.e. washroom) where one might wonder who had used the facilities immediately beforehand! In practice Wikipedia has dispelled such scepticism, and in recent years a comparison of its entries with those in Encyclopaedia Britannica has demonstrated that not only are errors to be found in both to roughly the same extent, but that those in Wikipedia are usually corrected far more speedily.

What does need to be grasped, however, is that Wikipedia encapsulates many important issues with regard to use of resources in research – e.g. provenance of data, nature of evidence, currency of information, alternative viewpoints and interpretations. Users of Wikipedia are now clearly alerted to pages that are either insufficiently referenced, contain only partial information, appear to be the subject of antagonistic editing, or are likely to be affected by current events. So rather than warning researchers and students away from Wikipedia, it is in fact far better to direct them there with the understanding that all the warnings found at the top of various entries apply not only to Wikipedia, but to all sources of information. In this sense Wikipedia is a critical resource for research, albeit as an exemplar and starting point rather than as a sole and exclusive one.

References

Blaxter, L., Hughes, C., Tight, M. (2010) How to Research, 4th edition. Open University Press: Milton Keynes

Bryant, A. (2009). Grounded Theory and Pragmatism: The Curious Case of Anselm Strauss [113 paragraphs]. Forum Qualitative Sozialforschung / Forum: Qualitative Social Research, 10(3), Art. 2, http://nbn-resolving.de/urn:nbn:de:0114-fqs090325

Bryant, A. & Charmaz, K. (2007a). Editors' introduction: Grounded theory research methods and practices. In Antony Bryant & Kathy Charmaz (Eds.), The Sage handbook of grounded theory (pp.1-28). London: Sage.

Bryant, A. & Charmaz, K. (2007b). Grounded theory in historical perspective: An epistemological account. In Antony Bryant & Kathy Charmaz (Eds.), The Sage handbook of grounded theory (pp.31-57). London: Sage.

Denzin, N. K. and Lincoln, Y. S. (1994, 2000, 2005) Handbook of Qualitative Research, 1st, 2nd, 3rd Editions. SAGE: London

Keynes, J.M., (1936) The General Theory of Employment, Interest and Money

Miles, M., and Huberman, M. (1994) Qualitative Data Analysis. SAGE: London

Rorty, R. (1980). Philosophy and the mirror of nature. Princeton NJ: Princeton University Press.

Rorty, R. (1991). Essays on Heidegger and others. Cambridge: CUP.

Silverman, D. (2004) Doing Qualitative Research. SAGE: London

Silverman, D. (Ed) (2010) Qualitative Research. SAGE: London

Antony Bryant, Editor
Professor of Informatics
Faculty of Arts, Environment, & Technology
Leeds Metropolitan University, UK
a.bryant@leedsmet.ac.uk
March 2011

Leading Issues in Business Research Methods

Towards a Second Order Research Methodology

Jim Brown[1] and Petia Sice[2]
[1] Northumberland College, UK
[2] Northumbria University, School of Informatics, Newcastle Upon Tyne, UK
Originally published in EJBRM (2005) Volume 3, Issue 1.

Editorial Commentary

At first sight this paper might appear to be one of those discussions about research that agonises too much about the epistemological and philosophical foundations of varying research orientations and methods – or methodologies; hence failing to understand that valuable research insights can and do arise from all manner of possibly misplaced, incoherent, or ill-conceived philosophical starting points (see Editor's introduction above). The reason for its inclusion, however, is that it offers a useful introduction to many important issues and writings that should certainly be part of any well-read researcher's intellectual background; whether or not one agrees with their overall import.

Not all researchers will wish to get deeply immersed in the seemingly endless miasma of epistemological discussions around topics such as positivism, interpretivism, critical realism and the like; let alone trying to grapple with the term 'autopoieisis'. On the other hand, if challenged to explain their use of terms such as systems, information, communication, metaphor and the like, they should certainly be able to demonstrate some knowledge of differing accounts of language and communication, with reference to the work of Russell Ackoff, Stafford Beer, C W Churchman, Jurgen Habermas, and Ilya Prigogine amongst others (detailed references are given at the end of the paper itself).

Jim Brown and Petia Sice offer a useful introduction to these authors and topics, couched in the context of research centred on organizations and systems. They take the phrase 'second order' from the work of Beer; but the explication that follows owes more to Checkland's SSM, a sensible choice since this work is likely to be better known to the target readership of the original paper and this reprint.

The missing dimension to this paper, as far as I am concerned, is that of Pragmatism; particularly as developed in the writings of Richard Rorty (see Editor's introduction). One of the key features of Pragmatism as espoused by John Dewey was that theories need to be understood in terms of being tools for understanding. As such they should be evaluated and assessed in terms of their usefulness in specific and constrained contexts, rather than in terms of their fundamental and possibly universal truthfulness. This tool-oriented yardstick should be applied to all 'theories' and models, including those referred to in this paper.

Abstract: This paper addresses the need for re-examining the cognitive perspective on the role of language in social research. From the autopoietic perspective, language is not a tool to reveal an objective world; rather language is a venue for action, coupling the cognitive domains of two or more agents. Responsible research enquiry would seek to create systemic communication practices that allow the co-existence of differing understandings within. Creating a dialogue for exploring and emerging meaning is essential in developing understanding and validating the research results.

Keywords and Key phrases: autopoiesis, social systems, language, dialogue, research method, systems thinking.

1 Introduction

The application of any research methodology without reflection on the underpinning assumptions is flawed. What is more, such an approach is bound to lead us to an incomplete understanding of the situation under consideration, since it places 'restrictions' on the ways we question the validity of the knowledge unearthed in the application of the methods. Thus, creative interpretation becomes limited. The paper considers this problem. It emphasises the importance of theoretical reflection and an epistemological perspective in exploring the assumptions underlying research designs. The discussion focuses in more detail onto the role of language in the research process.

Crotty (1998) suggests that the basic elements of any research process include methods, methodology, theoretical perspective(s) and epistemology. Thus, it is essential for any rigorous research attempt to clarify and explore the answers to the questions:

- What methods (techniques, procedures, i.e. interviews, observations, etc.) are to be used?
- What methodology (strategy, plan of activity, process of design, i.e. ethnography, action research, etc.) governs our choice of methods?
- What are the theoretical (philosophical) perspective(s) of looking at the world and making sense of it (i.e. systemic thinking, complexity theory, theory of language, etc.) that influence our logic and criteria and provide context for applying the methodology?
- What epistemology grounds the theoretical perspective(s)?
- The above questions and any proposed answers are interlinked and are best considered as mutually determined.

The intention of this paper is to go beyond simple answers and explore epistemological and other theoretical perspectives within the context of research design, based on a rigorous understanding of the human condition (that is, our way of being human) in both its biological and social embodiments. It is the theory of autopoiesis that offers such an understanding. The paper focuses on an autopoietic perspective on knowing, the role of language, and the systems approach.

2 Autopoiesis, experience and knowledge

It is through our particular way of being that we act as observers. Thus, everything we say (even to ourselves), is said by one observer to another. Consequently, our capacity to distinguish and therefore, our knowledge, depend upon the make-up of the particular observer.

Since the observer is a living entity, a 'true' insight into the domain of knowledge requires an understanding of cognition that takes into consideration the biological phenomenon and is mindful of the observer's role within it. The theory of autopoiesis is based on explaining the generative process of the living. Autopoiesis is the mechanism that defines the manner in which a living system exists as a distinguishable entity (Varela, 1996).

An autopoietic system is a network of processes for production of components that:

- Through their interaction and transformations continuously, regenerate the network of processes that produced them;
- Constitute the entity as a concrete unity in the space by specifying the topological domain of its realisation as such a network (Maturana and Varela, 1980).

Consequently, an autopoietic system that exists in a physical space can in general be thought of as a living system.

Autopoiesis is basic to the living individual. What happens to the individual is subservient to its autopoietic organisation, for as long as it exists the autopoietic organisation remains invariant (Varela, 1979). What this means, is that the living individual is an autonomous entity that actively maintains its identity. Its identity and therefore its emergent global properties are generated through a process of self-organisation within its network of components. A two-way process of local-to-global and global-to-local causation (Figure 1) conditions this process of self-organisation.

Internal Dynamics ↔ Autopoietic Entity ↔ Environment
(Local) (Global) (World)

Figure 1: The mutual embeddedness of component dynamics, autopoietic entity and its environment.

Firstly, there is the local-to-global determination ('upward' causation) through which the entity, with its properties, emerges. Secondly, however, there is global-to-local determination ('downward' causation), where global characteristics constrain or direct local interactions between the components (Varela, 1979). For example, in organisms with a nervous system, the rules of interactions within the neuronal network are in reciprocal relationship with the overall activity of the autopoietic entity. Largely, behaviour is a regulator of perception. That is to say, what the organism senses is a function of how it behaves, and how it behaves is a function of what it senses. Situated behaviour, thus, takes the form of coupling (often referred to as 'structural coupling') with the environment, where environmental perturbations trigger changes in the entity but do not determine them, because changes in autopoietic systems are necessarily subservient to conservation of identity.

The dialectics of the living are based on the necessary emergence of a meaning relevant to the perspective of the cognitive self (for example one's perception), and on a coupling with the environment which refers to the necessary dependence of the self on its environment (for example socio-linguistic interactions). Consequently, the contents of human experience (how the world appears to us); depend crucially on the mutual embeddedness of the neuronal dynamics (included in the overall physical and chemical dynamics), the human agent as a unity with global properties (body, mind, consciousness, self and so on) and, the environment. Thus, human experience is personal but not private. Experience is clearly a personal event, but that does not mean it is private, in the sense of some kind of isolated subject that is parachuted down onto a pre given objective world. This irreducibility of human experience, from the duality portrayed by the embodiment and the situatedness of the human agent, cannot be underestimated when developing approaches or methodologies for research (Varela, Thompson and Rosch, 1991).

3   Autopoiesis and the role of language

The coupling of a living organism with its environment may include interacting with other organisms and if the interacting organisms reciprocally select each other, their respective paths of ontogenic structure changes, generating a domain of communicative interactions. The individual ontogenies of the participating organisms occur as part of the network of co-ontogenies that comes about in constituting higher order or social unites.

'As observers we designate as communicative those behaviours which occur in social coupling and as communication that behavioural co-ordination which we observe as a result of it'. (Maturana and Varela, 1987)

This consensual domain of communicative interactions in which behaviourally coupled organisms orient each other with modes of behaviour, whose internal determination has become specified during their coupled ontogenies, is a linguistic domain. The name 'linguistic domain' was chosen because such learned communicative behaviours constitute the basis for language, although they are not identical with it. The conduct of each organism is internally determined by its autopoietic structure; however, the conduct of one organism is a source of perturbations for the others while the coupling lasts. The linguistic domain, therefore, is intrinsically non-informative, although the observer may describe it as if it were so. What determines the interaction is the dynamics of structural coupling of the interacting organisms.

Such a view contradicts the more traditionally established metaphor of 'the transmission of information', in which, communication represents something generated at a certain point, carried through an information channel and delivered to a receiver. This metaphor is not correct, since biologically there is no transmitted information. (Krippendorff, 1997) Moreover, it presupposes that what happens to the receiver (listener) is predetermined only by the perturbing agent (sender). In fact, however, communication depends on not only what is transmitted, but also what happens in the organism that receives it. Communication, therefore, is a matter of mutual orientation, primarily with respect to each other's behaviour, and secondarily with respect to some subject (Maturana and Varela, 1980).

Therefore, language is a venue for action, coupling the cognitive domains of two or more actors. Language should not be regarded as a system of symbols that are composed into patterns that stand for things in the world and thus reveal our 'objective' knowledge of it. Words are tokens for linguistic co-ordination of actions and not things we move from one place to another. Thus, it is appropriate to discuss languaging as an act rather than language as a symbolic notation. Since we exist in language, the domain of discourse that we generate becomes part of our domain of existence and part of the environment in which we conserve identity and adaptation. As observers, we live in a domain of recursive discourse. Thus, the unity of the human society is generated through the network of conversations that language generates and which through its closure generates language itself. Social systems exist, for their members, in co-creating reality. Where language agreements decide what is true and what is false:

'Human agreements decide what is true and what is false? It is what human beings say that is true and false; and they agree in the language they

use. That is not agreement in opinions but in form of life'. (Wittgenstein, 1967)

Thus, meaning becomes fundamentally social and language becomes part of everyday being in the world. The world is continuously innovated generating new possibilities through communication. Thus, by its design the communication structure needs to be open to evolution in order that it can accommodate and promote new opportunities. Autopoietic theory reintegrates the individuals as the fundamental creators of the communication structure.

It is through languaging that we coordinate our actions and create our world. Because of this, we have a responsibility to create communication practices that will allow, at least transiently, the coexistence of different understandings as we develop and explore our language together. Bohm (1987) suggests that a new type of dialogue is needed in human communications. The basic idea of this dialogue is to be able to talk while suspending your opinions, holding them in front of you, neither suppressing nor insisting upon them, not trying to convince but simply to understand. We must perceive all the meaning of everybody together, without having to make any decisions or saying who is right or who is wrong. It is more important that we all see the same thing.

In this way, an organisation is able to take conversations and collective practices to a deeper level. The form of dialogue, suggested by Bohm (2000), encourages opening up and engaging in listening without a particular purpose, listening for the sake of hearing what other thoughts and opinions there are, what is being said, whilst trying consciously to suspend our assumptions and judgements. It is building awareness of what there is to be heard without focusing on it through the lenses of our judgements and assumptions. This 'listening' increases our chances of becoming sensitive and thus, able to hear the prejudices of agents outside ourselves.

This form of dialogue should be seen as a core element within any human enterprise, as it creates the context for all activities, rather than (as may be suggested by more traditional communication approaches) being merely part of the chain of activities. Dialogue is about involvement, about cocreation and communication. Therefore, a generative dialogue process in organisations will enhance their capability of developing a meaningful language providing a valid venue for action and continuous learning.

4 The systems approach, autopoietic epistemology and language

Insights from the systems thinking tradition are considered helpful in providing a holistic perspective. The systems thinking approach makes conscious and formal use of the concept of wholeness, as captured in the word system. The concept of a 'system' embodies the idea of a set of elements dynamically related in time. Each of which can affect the performance of the whole (Beer, 1979) however, none of which can have an independent effect overall (Ackoff, 1994). The system exhibits as a single whole, emergent properties which have no meaning in terms of the parts of the whole (Ashby, 1956).

'The system concept, the idea of a whole entity which under a range of conditions maintains its identity, provides a way of viewing and interpreting the universe as a hierarchy of such interconnected and interrelated wholes'.(Checkland, 1981)

These definitions embody an approach that, unlike the reductionist methodologies, encourages an exploration of the relationships between elements, rather than concentrating on the properties of the individual elements themselves, therefore considering performance in terms of the systems structure (Senge, 1990). Further, there is an implication that systems are governed by the dynamic interactions of their components, a system's conduct is classified and analysed through the 'patterns of its behaviour', or its 'trends', rather than through seeking to predict events. This systemic perspective encourages 'closed loop thinking', where we are looking for continuing interrelated processes, rather than one way relationships (Ackoff, 1978).

The Systems Approach includes a set of theories that attempt to rigorously explore, analyse and diagnose systems behaviour, i.e. Viable Systems Model (Beer, 1979), Soft Systems Methodology (Checkland, 1981), Systems Dynamics (Senge and Sterman, 1992; Forrester, 1994), complexity and emergence (Nicolis and Prigogine, 1989).

The Systems Approach has proven its merits (Flood and Jackson, 1987). It is not the purpose of this paper to discuss them. What is important to reflect on in order to clarify our theoretical stance is, the observer has to be included as part of the system.

The most basic cognitive operation we perform as observers is the operation of distinction. It is through the operation of distinction that we specify a unity as an entity distinct from its background (Maturana and Varela, 1987). We characterise both the unity and the background with the properties with which the distinction endows them and specify their separability. If the observer applies the operation of distinction recursively and, thus, distinguishes the components within the unity, he redefines it as a 'composite unity', i.e. a system. It is through our human way of being that we perceive the world in terms of systems. The autopoietic epistemological perspective suggests that cognition (the distinctions we make) is conditional to embodiment. The act of cognition is a matter of interacting with the world, in the capacity in which one is able to interact, and not simply the act of processing what is objectively to be 'seen'. Thus, systems are epistemological qualities and not definitions of how things actually are or occur. Different observers perceive or describe systems, and therefore, their boundary and their structure differently. The observer has to be accounted for as part of any explanation. Nevertheless, systems have become the means by which we explore and describe the consistency of situational behaviour. Therefore, descriptions of system structures are useful tools and, if some form of agreement can be reached about 'what a system does' then it is possible to communicate about its structure and boundaries with greater (in relative terms) coherence. Language needs to take account of a systemic vocabulary.

The definition of a system is a dynamical activity. It involves both objective and subjective reality and the cycle of perception and action, that unites them. Indeed, the definition of the system is likely to change in a whole host of ways when new distinctions are identified and become relevant. Thus, any attempt to freeze the definition of any system stifles creativity. It constrains knowing by forcing new explanations to be built on frozen categories, as though these were absolute truths given in nature rather than specified by us. Systemic language should continuously evolve and reinvent itself.

5 A second order research methodology

Having realised that perceptions of the same observation vary between observers and that systems themselves are dynamic and therefore changing. A second order research methodology is required to understand any given situation. This second order methodology seeks to understand the perceptions and opinions of the actors within the system under investigation as a primary activity, in this way developing understanding of the dynamics of the systems under investigation. Such a methodology is show in (Figure 2).

Second order methodology follows the recursive systems principles of Beer (1979). It is important that as many levels of recursion are considered as needed to encompass the organisation as a whole. Use of the process is in second order situations, where understanding of others understanding is required.

The process outlined is iterative. It is a closed cycle of exploring, reflecting and developing language in dialogue. It requires that employee's participate in the process as researchers in their own right. In fact, the principle of employee's participation is crucial to the success and continuation of the process.

The individual stages 1-6 (Figure 2) are developed below:

5.1. Listen for situations of concern; develop awareness

Developing awareness is essential and the starting point of the process. Awareness' can spring from many sources. Activates considered prime candidates for developing awareness include meetings of all descriptions, organisational reviews, quality audits, reports, customer and employee surveys to name but a few.

Observing, experiencing, sensing, informal and formal communication practices (meetings, conversations, dialogue groups). These can feed into the emergence of situations of concern; this may be facilitated by managers and/or academics.

Leading Issues in Business Research Methods

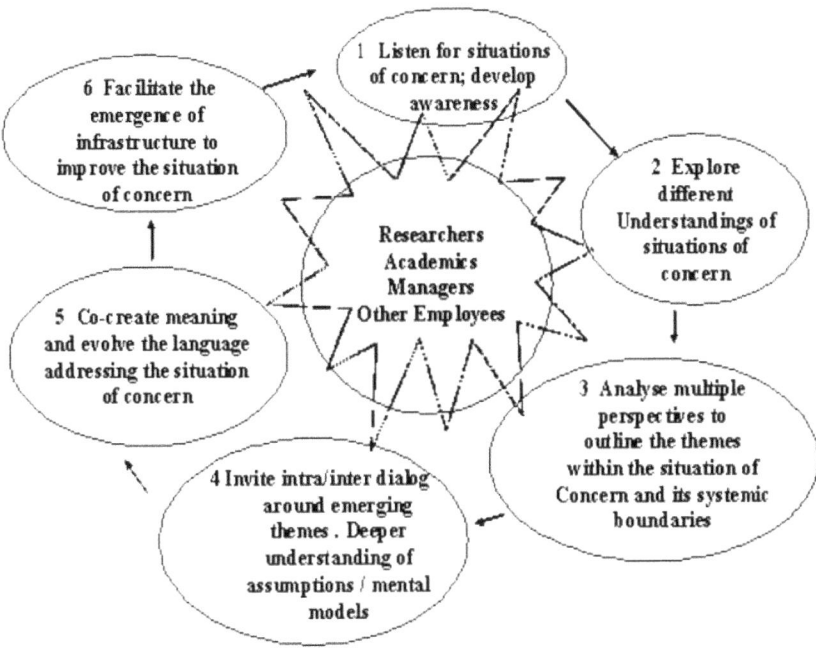

Figure 2: A 'second order' methodology

'Volunteer' researchers (employees, managers and or academics) meet key actors in the situation of concern (senior management and/or middle management, senior sponsorship is sought). A volunteer steering team emerges with a project leader that can facilitate effective communication within team and with other stakeholders. A project plan is outlined with regard to exploration, interviews, observations, meetings, and updated on a short-term basis.

5.2. Explore different understandings of situation of concern

Within stage 2, the research explores differing understanding of the situation. People base their thinking and therefore conclusions and subsequent actions on preconceived beliefs. No matter how strange those beliefs seem to others' (Fish 1985). The team undertakes an examination of their varying views of reality, neither accepting nor rejecting them. Looking without judgment, accepting the views of others' exist and for them constitute reality.

Several recognised research methods can be employed within stage 2 these could include semi-structured interviews. For this, two researchers are more effective with one leading the interview with general questions and the other concentrating on peripheral matters arising from the main questions. In this way with few main topics, a richer picture can emerge allowing exploration and further analysis.

Dialogue groups with stakeholders are another approach; these sessions can be conducted by members of the project team or with the help of professional facilitation. Informal conversations and formal organisational meetings are also sources of research data. Intranet discussion forums allow individuals to partake in virtual discussion groups at time and place that suit themselves. A mixture of the above methods suited to the situation and system can be employed to provide research material that is used to develop an initial awareness and understanding of the situation(s) of concern.

5.3. Analyse multiple perspectives to outline the themes within the situation of concern and its systemic boundaries

Cross analysis of interviews by at least two researchers and if the subject is of high importance three is used to identify emerging themes of concern and identify the system boundaries as seen by the interviewees. Software tools such as Nudist or Atlas may be used to contribute to the language analysis however such tools are an assistance rather that a necessity. Whatever form of analysis is employed the outcomes should be an emergence and agreement within the organisation members of the theme(s) of concern and the system boundaries. Once emerged a recursive structure such as the Viable System Model Beer (1979) may be used to give a holistic systems approach.

Analysis of the multiple perspectives held by the team allows the underlying themes and varying concerns to be established. Churchman (1970) maintains that a wide analysis will produce a rich and complex picture. However, Ulrich (1983) points out that the purpose of the analysis will impose restrictions.

5.4. Invite intra/inter dialogue around emerging themes. Deeper understanding of assumptions/mental models

This stage seeks to deepen and increase shared understanding. The aim is to arrive at a view of reality shared by the team that incorporates, while clarifying varying realties.

Section 4 may include systems thinking development workshops to share insight into systemic analyses and issues for dealing with complexity

Reflective dialogue is also a useful method if utilised around assumptions and insights from stage 3, representing a shared understanding not individual feedback.

It may be necessary to utilise professional facilitation within dialogue groups (Bohm's dialogue practices) in order to develop the focus to explore underlying assumptions and creation of shared meanings.

An important part of this stage is exploring and bringing into the open mental models, beliefs and assumptions. This is not an easy task but can be achieved with the use of influence diagrams (from systems dynamics), storytelling, narratives, art, etc to bring into the open mental models beliefs and assumptions. Simulations models can be used as what-if micro worlds. The outcome from Section 4 is a deeper understanding of others and the system dynamics including underlying or hidden beliefs, assumptions and factors that affect the system

5.5. Co-create meaning and evolve the language addressing the situation of concern

As human beings, we communicate and conduct our lives through language.

Organisationally we use many languages, the language of the boardroom, the workshop, technical languages, etc. Most are full of terminology unknown to people outside the particular discipline. For the development of meaning leading to understanding, a common language understood by all is required.

Habermas (1976, 1984a, 1984b) discussing language and speech acts, points out that a shared language makes communication possible, that

Leading Issues in Business Research Methods

people then pass information and reveal their inner thoughts, while establishing interpersonal relationships.

Section 5 utilises dialogue sessions in order to gain deeper an understanding of developing beliefs and insight primarily to identifying and bring to the surface issues that need addressing. In addition, section 5 is used to evolve a common organisational language to deal with the situation(s) of concern (Krippendorff, 1997).

5.6. Facilitate the emergence of infrastructure to improving the situation of concern

Section 6 concentrates on facilitation to develop the emergence of infrastructures, strategies and implementation teams based on insights and recommendations from section 5. One approach that may be utilised is 'Deep Slice', whereby both a vertical and horizontal element gives a departmental as well as an organisational approach to section 6.

Table 1: 'Deep Slice' approach
(Source Knowledge Management Workshop Presentation given by Professor David Weir at Draeger Safety UK, 3rd & 4th August 2004)

Department A	Department B	Department C	Department D
Department Head	Department Head	Department Head	Department Head
Supervisors	Supervisors	Supervisors	Supervisors
Specialists	Specialists	Specialists	Specialists
Implementers	Implementers	Implementers	Implementers

As can be seen from Table 1 deep slice teams have a vertical departmental based element. Vertically each team has members from all levels of the departmental championed by the departmental head. Members of other departments can be utilised as consultants if and when appropriate. The horizontal or organisational element is formed from teams at similar organisational levels such as departmental heads etc. The horizontal element brings the cross-departmental communication and exchange of ideas and opinions allowing an organisational wide holistic view. Thus, 'Deep Slice' provides the means of developing teams to address the outcomes of section 5 in a manner best suited to the organisation and situation(s) of concern.

The research process is an ongoing learning process. Stages 1-6 do not necessarily follow in order often being interlinked in multiple ways.

This methodology is based on insight from theory and practice. It has and will be continually revised and amended, as understanding grows. Developing and evolving in pace with the changing systems

This framework recognises and promotes organisations as evolving structures and looks at order as dynamic rather than static.

6 Setting the context for the proposed methodology, structure and order

This section outlines our understanding of the nature of organisations and thus provides the context for the use of the methodology.

It is vitally important to set up the context and reveal the assumptions in relation to understanding the nature of organisations as they condition our thinking. To gain understanding, researchers must be aware of the underlying assumptions and beliefs that drive the system that is the organisation.

Organisations are evolving structures; there is a need to clarify the interplay between structure and order.

Structure suggests some order. Order broadly speaking is related to recognised distinctions, arrangements and linkages between elements within one or many dimensions. Could this be the reason why implicitly we refer to structure as something static? However, a much deeper set of questions are, how is it that structure originates and grows, how is it sustained, and how does it finally dissolve? That is, how is the order sustained, changed, created or destroyed? Structure is dynamic and should be better referred as structuring, while relatively stable products of this process are structures (Bohm & Peat, 2000).

Recognising that it is structuring that is important rather than structure in itself is a revealing insight. What follows is a realisation that order is also dynamic and that our perceptions of order change in the continuous cycle of interaction between the subject and the object of knowing.

The problem, however, is that in practice we often act as if the order that we perceive is a given or absolute reality. Very often social groups and societies work with categories of distinction upon which they implicitly agree, and because these categories are valid for the majority, they are accepted as if they have some sort of objective existence. This is dangerous because when the context of inquiry changes and new perceptions of order are needed, the mind tends to cling to these old perceptions since these are what have been accepted. Such implicit conventions of order, when held fixed, stifle creativity. Moreover, they can lead to a breakdown in communication between the supporters of the new emerging perceptions of order and the stabilised or well-accepted perceptions of order. This, of course, is because we tend to reinforce our concepts and beliefs as though they are absolute and in so doing we choose to fragment 'the world' from ourselves, without recognising that, we are participants in its creation.

What we need to remember is that our concepts and their meanings are moulded by the activities of our everyday life within our social group or society. When the context of this society changes new, categories are needed. Thus, working with the old set of concepts within the new context will more often than not result in inappropriate behaviour. In essence, our ordering of 'reality' influences how we live and our way of life gives meaning to our concepts. It becomes clear, therefore, that we should adopt fluid rather than fixed perceptions of structure and order.

Our Western culture embraces the perception of static order. Consequently, we implicitly believe that we can find an order (or a structure) that explains the behaviour of the system; or that we can conjure and implement an order that generate the behaviour that we want to achieve. It is the assumed position that the world is governed by orders that we call laws. Moreover, if we discover these laws we can explain, manage, control and even create systems to obey them: God has created the universe according to his order, thus, it is the job of the managers to create and govern organisations according to their understanding of order. Authors such as Nicolis and Prigogine, however, consider such a premise to be a misconception (Prigogine & Nicolis, 1989). They contend that man must have looked for the power of creation in the wrong place and, because of this, created the domination of one person's will over the others; and an order of human enterprise where control and rigid structures are the norm. The power of creation, as studies in deterministic chaos have shown, lies within what is being created, within the building blocks and their communication with each other. 'As there is no one to build nature we must give to its very elements the microscopic activity, a description that accounts for the building process' (Prigogine & Stangers, 1984).

The phenomenal domain of human enterprises is realised through the network of interactions between the human actors. Stacey, in interpreting the impact of chaos theory on management paradigms argues that such networks through local agent interactions are capable of spontaneous self-organisation, to produce emergent orderly, evolving patterns of behaviours of the network without any prior comprehensive system wide blueprint for the evolution of the system (Stacey, 1992). It is clear, therefore, that bestowing on managers the sole responsibility for the design of the rules and structures of their organisation is a perilous route based on a fragile illusion. The dynamics are determined by the pattern and nature of the actor's relationship. What's more, the response to any perturbation is determined by these very dynamics. Stabilising the behaviour of the network means simply repeating the past. When operating in the chaotic region, however, the network is capable of rapidly recognising fluctuations in the environment and generating flexible behaviours in response. The 'tuning' of the network in response to these perturbations is accomplished through continuous evolution of the structure. This is what Maturana and Varela (Maturana and Varela, 1987) define as adaptation and learning. The flexibility to learn and innovate in turbulent environments is essential. Far from equilibrium, organisations begin to perceive the smallest changes in the environment or, indeed, inside themselves. Further, since only variety absorbs variety, organisations respond by self-organising themselves to react to fluctuations and to adapt to the environment. There are multiple paths from which to choose. Dissipative structures emerge that promote alignment with the environment. New order and possibilities for future development arise from amplification and exploitation of fluctuations.

Indeed, the concept of the dissipative structure has thrown light on the role of the manager, as one of a conductor of communication, promoting coherence in the enterprise activities and the exploration of new horizons. It is by organising the system to work in the chaotic region that high sensitivity to perturbations in the environment can be achieved and orderly behaviours can emerge and evolve through mutual re-enforcement. Managers can exploit the chaotic characteristic of behaviour by looking for conditions that will allow small efforts to produce a significantly variable spectrum of appropriate behaviours. The future emerges through spontaneous self-organisation and there is no alternative but to make the change and see what happens, to discover where you are going as you are getting there. We are looking for order that allows change and flexibility. We are looking for meditative organisations that promote listening and continuous tuning with the environment. In chaotic systems, the issue is not simply one of finding the answers, but in general one of knowing the questions. In the face of uncertainty, we cannot know what we do not know. Therefore, any study should be conducted according to which institutional form (or forms) is best able to contend with the unknowable future. The institutional form, thus, needs to be able to match the ever-changing variety of the environment. If the environment is changing quickly, and we cannot predict these changes well in advance, we need autonomous and spontaneously self-organising systems. In a chaotic world, there is no knowledge of either future problems or their possible solutions. Therefore, our management policies should be concentrating on the means rather than the end (Sice, Mosekilde and French, 2000). In addition, as the operation of coherence in social systems, is realised through communication, special attention should be given to the linguistic domain, to variety of the language and to the patterns of the conversation network of organisations.

7 Concluding remarks

Research into social systems inevitably involves and relies on human communication.

The communication process involving the researcher and other actors that are the object of research inevitably changes to a lesser or larger degree the initial perspective, assumptions and opinions of all those involved. It is ethically and practically important that this communication process is a focus of reflection in the research enquiry.

Although social scientists communicate in numerous ways, interviewing their subjects, engaging discursively with others, publishing their work, and thus continuously engaging in language, self- reflection on the application of language theory is surprisingly rare in the literature.

Languaging surely affects our perceptions, how we create a world, and in that world what becomes real to us. Without an awareness of our languaging we are, as Heinz von Foerster (1979) noted, double blind: We do not see (certain things that other language uses could bring forth) and we do not see our not seeing this.

The cure for such blindness lies in consciously deviating from established linguistic practices, for example, by inventing a new vocabulary, by introducing new metaphors or by creating different communities to language. 'Second order' research methodologies are needed to bring into consideration the importance of 'second-order' understanding and the role of language in creating reality. In a second order philosophy the employees are engaged as researchers, it is not action research conducted by a third party but research conducted by the individuals involved with input from a third party. Research that can be carried on by the employees, providing the innovative drive and continued improvement, enlisting the help of consultants and academics as and when required to fill the role of facilitator with the required fields of expertise identified by the employees themselves. It is the act of turning employees into researchers, who understand the dynamics of their own organisation. Along with input from academia acting in the role of consultants and facilitators, that brings the second order and the innovation to this approach. It is the members (managers and employees) of the organisation that define the area of concern, develop the language, analyse the findings and develop the action plans that from the solutions.

Organisationally it must always be remembered that evolution is a continuous process as already stated in section 6, structure and order are not static they adapt themselves to changing environmental conditions, reacting to the perturbations received from the external environment. To think of structure and order as static is a mistake, stifling adaptation by clinging to outmoded order and structure can only cause standstill in organisational evolution. With the speed of external environmental change allied with the growing unpredictability of change, the realisation that organisations should be considered as evolving systems is important. For organisations, the saying "evolve or die" is more important today than ever before.

References
Ackoff, R.L., (1978) *Art of Problem Solving, accompanied by Ackoff's Fables*, Wiley.
Ackoff, R.L., (1994) "Systems Thinking and Thinking Systems", *Systems Dynamics Review*, Vol. 10.

Leading Issues in Business Research Methods

Ashby, W.R., (1956) *Introduction to Cybernetics*, Chapman and Hall.
Beer, S., (1979) *The Heart of Enterprise*, John Wiley & Sons, Chichester.
Bohm, D., (1987) *Unfolding Meaning*, Routledge, London.
Bohm, D., (2000) *On Dialogue*, Routledge, London.
Bohm D and Peat D (2000) *Science, Order and Creativity*, Routledge, London.
Checkland, P.B., (1981) *Systems Thinking Systems Practice*, John Wiley & Sons.
Churchman, C. W. (1970) "Operations Research as a Professional", *Management Science* Vol 17, p37-53.
Crotty M. (1998) *The Foundations of Social Research*, Sage Publications, London.
Fish, S. (1985) "Consequences", in *Against Theory* (ed) Mitchell W. J. T, University of Chicago Press.
Flood, R., and Jackson M, (1991) *Creative Problem Solving, Total Systems Intervention,* Wiley, Chichester.
Forrester, J.W., (1994) *Policies, Decisions, and Information Sources for Modelling, in Modelling for Learning Organisations.*
Habermas, J. (1984a) *The Theory of Communicative Action, Volume 1 Reason and Rationalisation of Society*, Polity Press, Cambridge.
Habermas, J. (1984b) *The Theory of Communicative Action, Volume 2 Reason and Rationalisation of Society* Polity Press, Cambridge.
Habermas, J (1976) *Communication and the evolution of Society*, English edition 1979, Heinemann, London
Krippendorff K. (1997) "Human-Centeredness: A Paradigm Shift Invoked by the Emerging Cyberspaces" Keynote address prepared for a symposium on Connected Intelligence: Human Beings in Information Systems at the Zentrum für Kunst und Medientechnologie, Karlsruhe, Germany 1997, October27-28.
Maturana, H., Varela, F.J. (1980) *Autopoiesis and Cognition*, D. Reidel, Dordrecht, Holland.
Maturana, H., Varela, F.J., (1987) *The Tree of Knowledge*, New Science Library, Boston, Mass.
Nicolis, G., Prigogine, I., (1989) *Exploring Complexity*, W. H. Freeman and Company, New York.
Prigogine I and Stangers I (1984) *Order out of Chaos: Man's New Dialogue with Nature*, Heinemann, London
Senge, P.M., (1990) *The Fifth Discipline: the Theory of the Learning Organization*, John Wiley & Sons.
Senge, P.M., and Sterman, J.D., (1992) "Systems Thinking and Organisational learning: Acting Locally, Thinking Globally in the organisation of the Future", *European Journal of Operational Research*, Vol 59, No 1, p 137-150.
Sice P, Mosekilde E and French I (2000) "Using System Dynamics to Analyse Interactions in Duopoly Competition", *System Dynamics Review*, Vol. 16, N, pp. 113-133.
Stacey R (1992), *Managing Chaos*, Kogan Page, London.

Ulrich, W (1983) *Critical Heuristics of Social Planning: A New Approach to Practical Philosophy*, Haupt Berne.
Varela F. (1979) *Principles of Biological Autonomy*, Elsevier, New York.
Varela F, Thompson E. and Rosch E. (1991) *The Embodied Mind: Cognitive Science and Human Experience*, The MIT Press, Cambridge, Massachusetts.
Varela F. (1996) "Neurophenomenology: A methodological remedy to the Hard Problem" *Journal of Consciousness Studies* (Special Issue on the Hard Problem) June 1996 pp 330-350.
von Foerster, H. (1981) *Observing Systems*, Intersystems.
von Foerster, H. (1979)"Cybernetics of Cybernetics" in Krippendorff, K. (ed.), *Communication and Control in Society*, Gordon and Breach, New York, pp. 5-8.
Wittgenstein, L., (1967) *The Philosophical Investigations*, Blackwell, Zettel.

Grounded Theory: Its Diversification and Application Through two Examples from Research Studies on Knowledge and Value Management

Kirsty Hunter[1], Subashini Hari[2], Charles Egbu[1] and John Kelly[3]
[1]Glasgow Caledonian University, Glasgow, UK
[2]University of Wolverhampton, UK
[3]Nottingham Trent University and Axoss Ltd, UK
Originally published in EJBRM (2005) Volume 3: Issue 1.

Editorial Commentary

The Grounded Theory Method [GTM] is far and away the most widely claimed method in qualitative research. By some counts it exceeds all other qualitative methods combined. Such popularity is both an achievement and blight, since in too many cases researchers claiming use of the method do so in name only, using this as a covering for inadequate research designs and practices. Indeed many editors of research journals readily admit that they tend to discount papers claiming use of GTM since so many are not worthy of serious consideration.

The consequence of this is that research reports claiming use of GTM can take far less for granted than might be the case for other methods. One aspect of this is that reference is often made to the founding ideas in the work of Glaser and Strauss, as well as their individual and divergent paths in subsequent years.

The paper itself is now somewhat dated, and perhaps even at the time of its publication did not take account of recent developments in and around the method itself. This is not to criticize the authors as such, but simply to use this opportunity to point readers to writings on GTM that go beyond those of Glaser and Strauss. In particular what is now referred to as the constructivist approach to GTM as exemplified in the work of Kathy Charmaz and some of my own writings (REFS); also to the range of work encompassed by the Handbook of Grounded Theory (Bryant and Charmaz, 2007).

Hunter et al offer an interesting overview of the method, with useful discussion of issues around GTM, including the split between Strauss and Glaser, the problem of dealing with a plethora of data, the process of coding, saturation, and the potential use of software support. I would, however, advise anyone with an interest in GTM to start with Charmaz' primer (2006) before delving into the method itself,

Bryant, Antony & Charmaz, Kathy (Eds.) (2007c) *The Sage handbook of grounded theory*, London: Sage.
Charmaz, Kathy (2006) *Constructing grounded theory: A practical guide through qualitative analysis*, London: Sage.

Abstract: The grounded theory research method has been adopted by researchers across a range of different disciplines. Two different examples that are currently using the method as part of individual research programmes are explained. These two examples form part of two separate PhD programmes that are currently at similar stages of development making for a timely comparison of the different applications of the grounded theory research method. Both examples involve research conducted in the construction related fields of knowledge management (KM) and value management (VM). A background is provided for each study and the similarities and differences between each application are outlined as well as the process and stages involved in the research investigations undertaken. The use of computer software packages is explored and a case for and against using such a tool is made to the effect that this will largely depend on the nature of the problem under investigation. The paper concludes with the suggestion that grounded theory is a method that can be adapted to suit the nature of the research problem provided that the fundamental aspect is adhered to which is to ensure that the theory derived is 'grounded' in the data.

Keywords: grounded theory, knowledge management, value management, software packages

1 Introduction

This paper explores grounded theory by reviewing the key characteristics of the research method, the founders of the method as well as how the method has changed over time. The paper responds to the work of Blismas and Dainty (2003) who called for an open debate on the merits and demerits using computers in inductive research. The research work outlines a case for and against the use of computer software packages which involves one example using such a package and the other adopting a manual approach. The two examples are explained which differ in approach and outcome. For the purposes of this paper these approaches will be labelled 'Approach A' and 'Approach B.' Approach A investigates the role of knowledge management in small and medium enterprises (SMEs) and approach B explores the commonality of project issues using value management workshop reports.

The paper is structured as follows; a background on the two PhD research areas; knowledge management and value management followed by a general review of grounded theory and the different approaches it encapsulates. A summary of both approaches which form part of the two individual PhD research programmes distinguishes between the two approaches before an in depth explanation of Approach A; the theoretical model and Approach B; theory generation is offered. Succeeding this, a review of the usage of software packages is given to corroborate with the researchers different approaches to addressing the data. Finally, the paper concludes with challenges and recommendations with the aim of transferring lessons learned for the grounded theory researcher.

2 Background on the research areas

Knowledge management and value management are two construction-related disciplines that have both become more established in the UK in the last ten years. Approach A contributes to knowledge through the exploration of knowledge management in SMEs where there has been little evidence of implementation in knowledge management practices. Approach B's contribution to knowledge is the investigation of value management in an area which is not familiar with value management; that of the public service sector. Therefore, both approaches are exploring new ground for implementation (SME's and the public service sector) for the two management disciplines.

2.1. Knowledge management

Malhotra (1998) suggested that, "Knowledge management caters for the critical issues of organisational adaption, survival and competence in face of increasingly discontinuous environmental change. Essentially, it embodies organisational processes that seek the synergistic combination of data and information processing capacity of information technologies and the creative and innovative capacity of human beings".

The economic crisis of the early 1990's led to downsizing in many organisations, as well as mergers and acquisitions. This led to "corporate memory" losses in some organisations as key knowledge workers were forced to leave their employment. The crises of the early 1990's, to some extent helped to focus minds on the need and importance of knowledge management.

The review of literature indicates that some of the large organisations in the construction industry have adopted and reaped the benefits of KM, but there is very little evidence of KM in SMEs in the construction industry. Denzin et al. (1998) suggest that when there is a high degree of unpredictability, a pilot study is a good means to add value to the research. In this PhD study, prior to the main study, a pilot study was undertaken which helped the investigator to refine their data collection plans with respect to both the contents of the data and the procedure to be followed.

The pilot study explored the main challenges in knowledge management process in construction SMEs. Eleven organisations involving twelve professionals in Glasgow, Scotland, were interviewed. The result from the study indicated that knowledge capture seemed to be the main challenge associated in knowledge management process. The main study involves qualitative research methods using a grounded theory analysis in a case study context.

2.2. Value management

Value management came from the term value analysis which was developed from the work of Lawrence Miles, a purchase engineer for General Electric Company in the 1940's. Miles questioned, 'if I cannot obtain the product I must obtain an alternative which performs the same function,'

Kelly and Male (1993). The 'Job Plan' was used to provide a logical sequence of activities to achieve a value that would satisfy the client. Value engineering followed value analysis and is currently in use in the manufacturing industry. It became popular in the UK construction industry in the early to mid 1990's, Kelly and Male (2002), where it became known as value management. Value management is viewed in the UK as the encompassing term for value engineering, value analysis, value planning, value review, value methodology and value management reviews, Male et al. (1998). In the US, the term value engineering is used more widely.

Kelly and Male (2002) believe that, 'value management has reached a level of maturity within manufacturing and construction whereby the style and content of the various workshops is reasonably predictable.' This suggests that the application of VM should be further explored to develop new ground for implementation, such as that of the service sector. The grounded theory method is being used to determine if there is commonality of issues at different stages in the project life cycle and if these issues are generic in nature. If the issues are found to be generic this would suggest that the same tools and techniques used in value management could be applied regardless of sector or project type.

3 Grounded theory: Glaserian and Straussian approach

Glaser and Strauss first described the method of grounded theory in 1967 as a means of enabling the 'systematic discovery of theory from the data of social research'. Since then two different approaches have emerged; the Straussian and the Glaserian. It should also be noted that a number of other adaptations have developed identified in Heath and Cowley (2003), however, this particular research focuses on the founders of grounded theory and how their approaches diversified over time. It was not until the publication of Strauss (1987); Strauss and Corbin (1990), and Glaser (1978, 1992) that differences in approach and meaning was recognised. Glaser's approach remained faithful to the original joint description of the grounded theory method whereas Strauss's approach was referred to by Glaser (1992) cited by Heath and Cowley (2003) as 'full conceptual description.'

Heath and Cowley (2003) describe the difference between the two approaches being methodological which involves a different focus on induction and deduction processes. Glaser's being simply an extension of the original whereas Strauss's incorporates analytical techniques. According to Strauss and Corbin (1990) theory denotes a set of well-developed categories (e.g. themes, concepts) that are systematically interrelated through statements of relationship to form a theoretical framework that explains some relevant social, psychological, educational or other phenomenon.

3.1. Literature review

Strauss and Corbin (1990) suggest that a researcher does not begin a project with a preconceived theory in mind. The researcher begins with an area of study and allows the theory to emerge from the data. Theory derived from data is more likely to resemble the "reality" than is theory derived by putting together a series of concepts based on experience or solely through speculation. However, Smith (1997) suggested that general reading of the literature may be carried out to obtain a feel for the issues at work in the subject area, and identify any gaps to be filled using grounded theory. The researcher is able, therefore to approach the subject with some background knowledge, but it is important that the reading is not too extensive as the theories should evolve from the data itself, producing a grounded theory. In these particular studies both researchers have acquired background knowledge on the areas under investigation, however, the literature for both studies will be used to confirm or challenge the theory after the point at which theoretical saturation is reached.

Glaser (1978) argued that everything is data. Thus, the researcher would perhaps be unwise to carry out reading that provides him/her with anything more than, as Glaser & Strauss (1967) term, a partial framework of local concepts, which designate a few principal or gross features of the situations that he / she will study. If the researcher is concerned with factor relating theory, it could be advantageous to carry out the literature review in order to stimulate the interactive processes of data collection and analysis. Glaser believes that the literature should be used to gain an overall picture of the research problem and afterwards to confirm the theory. Glaser's approach also involves induction initially followed by deduction once the theory emerges.

Strauss's approach involves using the literature to identify phenomenon. Strauss analyses the data predominantly through deduction. This has been criticised by Glaser (1992) cited in Heath and Cowley (2003) who suggests that the researcher would be making assumptions about what is in the data as opposed to what actually exists. Robrecht (1995) cited by Heath and Cowley (2003) puts forward the view that there is a chance of 'forcing' which involves looking for data rather than at the data set as a whole.

The other issue regarding literature reviewing in grounded theory is determining when the second review of the literature should occur. Strauss & Corbin (1994) argue that selective sampling of the second body of literature should be woven into the emerging theory during the third stage on grounded theory induction, the stage they term concept development. However, in contrast to these arguments, Glaser (1978) asserts that the researcher should refrain from accessing this second body of literature until the theory has emerged from the data.

3.2. Analysis

The aim of using grounded theory is the identification of core categories achieved by the grouping and integration of coded concepts under a single cover term. Grounded theory is a repetitive process; the analyst is required to return constantly to data sources, to check aspects of the emerging interpretation and to gather new data, as and where appropriate. Smith (1997) refers to grounded theory as a process of constant comparative analysis. The main features of the area of interest are mapped through repeated comparison of the data.

In terms of obtaining a suitable sample size in grounded theory, the grounded theorist does not decide on the size of the sample population before the study begins. Sample size is deemed to be satisfactory only when the key concepts that have been identified from the collected data have reached saturation point, in other words, when no new data emerges.

3.3. Validation

An important aspect of grounded theory often misinterpreted to suggest that qualitative research never "validates" theory. This is not entirely the case, some qualitative studies do and some do not, but even those that do validate theory do not do so in the sense of testing as in quantitative research. Rather, it is a process of comparing concepts and their relationships against data during the research process to determine how well they stand up to such scrutiny.

4 The two approaches to grounded theory

The literature review has highlighted the diversification of the research method from its initial introduction over thirty years ago. The following sections focus on the two individual PhD research programmes to illustrate the similarities and differences between the two approaches applying grounded theory. Table 1 encapsulates the differences prior to an explanation of each offered in the subsequent sections.

Table 1: The Two Approaches

| Characteristics | Approach A
KM in SMEs | Approach B
VM and Project Issues |
|---|---|---|
| Research Strategy | Case Study | Case Study |
| Research Technique | Interview | Archival records |
| Use of Software Package | Yes | No |
| Outcome of Approach | Theoretical Model | Theory Generation |
| Inductive / Deductive | Inductive | Inductive |
| Assumptions Made | No | Yes |
| Prior Knowledge | literature and pilot study | literature and experience |
| Approach Chosen | Strauss and Corbin | Combination of Glaser and, Strauss and Corbin |

The two grounded theory focused PhD programmes reported have been chosen for their distinct approaches in using the grounded theory method as evident in the characteristics breakdown in Table 1. The two approaches are different in the outcome expected and the techniques employed to reach this. The combination of the two approaches provides a comprehensive overview of the implementation of the grounded theory method in practice.

5 The theoretical model and theory generation

Two outcomes will be derived from the individual PhD investigations. Approach A will involve the development of a theoretical model which will facilitate knowledge management initiatives in small and medium enterprises in the construction industry. Approach B will involve the generation of a theory to be applied by value management practitioners to support the facilitator in VM workshop preparation and ultimately to benefit the project team.

5.1. Approach A: Theoretical model

The discovered grounded theory is generally called a theory (Chen, 1996) or a model (Backman & Hentinen, 1997). Work done by Turner (1976), Locke and Golden-Biddle (1997), have led to the development of a theoretical model in management research using grounded theory which have focused on process within an organisation. Approach A investigates the process of knowledge capture along with the main challenges associated with implementing knowledge capture initiatives / programmes in SME's, efficacy of different technologies and techniques and the nature of training provisions that will be of benefit to SME's with their knowledge capture initiatives. The model developed will provide insight or a perspective on phenomena and will also focus an individual on one perspective or set of ideas for facilitating KM initiatives.

The objectives of the study are:
- To investigate the main challenges associated with implementing Knowledge capture initiatives/ programmes in SMEs.
- To investigate the efficacy of different technologies and techniques.
- To examine and document the nature of training provisions that will be of benefit to SMEs with knowledge capture initiatives.
- To develop, implement and validate an Information Technology (IT)-based framework for raising awareness for knowledge capture.

To achieve the above objectives it is intended to use the case study approach as a research strategy and semi-structured interviews as the research technique. The method of analysis for the interviews would follow the grounded theory approach of Strauss and Corbin. The outcome of this will be the theoretical model.

Backman and Kyngas (1999) suggest that the researcher should follow one particular author i.e. Glaser or Strauss and then develop their own method using one of these as a foundation. If the researcher was to apply a combination of applications of grounded theory from different texts this would undoubtedly result in confusion and the resulting findings would be lacking in substance. Hence Approach A chooses the Strauss and Corbin methodology for analysis of data obtained through semi structured interview. The research strategy adopted will be case studies in construction SMEs where the number of employees in an organisation is less than 250. The analysis is through constant comparisons of codes, concepts and categories till the saturation point in reached.

Approach A has chosen the Strauss and Corbin method which follows:
- The development of analytic techniques with the provision of guidance to novice researchers.
- Research questions that take the form of identifying the phenomenon to be studied and what is known about the subject.
- A micro analysis (word-to-word) adopted for the data obtained through interviews.
- A constant comparison method of data analysis (deductive and inductive) involves:
- Open coding: The researcher forms initial categories of information about the phenomenon being studied from the initial data gathered.
- Axial coding: This involves assembling the data in new ways after coding. A coding paradigm is developed which incorporates:
- identifying a central phenomenon
- exploring causal conditions
- specifying strategies
- identifying the context and intervening conditions
- Selective coding: This involves the integration of the categories in the axial coding model. In this phase, conditional proposition/research questions are typically presented. The essential idea is to develop a single storyline around which categories are formed.

The result of this process of data collection and analysis is substantive level theory relevant to a specific problem, issue or group under study.

5.2. Approach B: Theory generation

Grounded theory has been used as the methodology in this study for the analysis of data through the constant comparative method. This research approach principally adopts the Strauss and Corbin version as Glaser's approach predicates that there should not be a pre-conceived theory in mind which is not the case in this research. This research forming the basis for this paper was inspired by the research question which is 'do similar issues appear at similar project stages and are these generic in nature?' Strauss and Corbin (1998) highlight the requirement for a theoretical statement to enable an explanation or prediction of theory. The theoretical statement for this research is that similar issues occur at similar project stages irrespective of project type. The grounded theory as used in this research enables theory to be drawn from the data and not from speculation or preconceived ideas. A theory is built as opposed to being tested and offers an explanation of phenomena rather than just a set of findings (Strauss and Corbin, 1998).

The project objectives for this particular strand of the research focusing on project issues are:
- To determine the scope for being able to predict issues prior to a workshop and analyse what advantages this would have to the value management practitioner, the construction industry and the client.
- To establish whether different projects e.g. construction and service related, at comparable intervention points have similar issues and thus establish if these issues can be predicted prior to a VM workshop.

Table 1 indicates that a combination of approaches is used. This is in terms of adopting Glaser's original approach to grounded theory which refers to substantive and formal theory. This study forms a substantive theory which borders on formal theory. Although the majority of the case studies are construction industry focused there is theory that may be applied to other areas such as the manufacturing and service sectors. The analysis has been done using comparative analysis which has been described as, 'a strategic method for generating theory,' Glaser and Strauss (1967). And finally, the constant comparative method is used. Glaser and Strauss (1967) state that the rule is to maximise the comparison groups which has been done by ensuring that as many case studies as possible have been used to generate the theory.

6 The use of a software package

Software packages may be used by the researcher to support the research study. In the two PhD research studies, the research work on knowledge management in SMEs (Approach A) has used a software package due to the nature of the research problem, whereas the research work on value management and project issues (Approach B) identified that the use of a software package would only serve to hinder the progress of the research. The case for use of such a package has been presented by the researcher using it to investigate interview data relating to knowledge management in SMEs and the case against the adoption of software has been constructed by the researcher investigating commonality of issues in value management studies.

Blismas and Dainty (2003) made a number of significant points with regards to the use of software which are acknowledged:
- The restriction of the study imposed by a software package
- Importance of understanding how the package operates and what the weaknesses are so these can be addressed
- To remember that the computer is only to aid the process
- Advantage of a software package is that all the data is contained 'within a single analytical environment.'
- A lot of work is required on the part of the researcher despite use of a software package
- Difficulty in analysing qualitative data, particularly huge amounts in a PhD timescale
- Importance of making any prejudices of the researcher apparent in the research explanation

One of the benefits outlined by Blismas and Dainty (2003) is that 'they help the researcher to investigate more lines of thought in a shorter period than would normally be possible manually." However, it is also stated that 'the intuitive steps required within the manual process can never be replaced.'

6.1. Approach A: The case for a software package

Qualitative research usually means the collection and analysis of unstructured textual material in order to develop concepts, categories, hypotheses and theories. Most of the time during 'qualitative data analysis' is spent on reading, re-reading, interpreting, comparing and thinking on texts. Thereby the analysis of thousands of text segments in hundreds of interviews seems an insurmountable task with or without a computer. There are a large number of computer programs available as an enabler for qualitative analysis, such as NUD*IST, ATLAS/ti, Decision explorer and Code-A-Text, to mention a few. Dainty et al. (2000) reflected on the use of computer-aided qualitative data analysis software (CAQDAS) tools within an industry-led research project. The CAQDAS aids data management, allowing text or discourse to be edited, visually coded, contextually annotated, hyperlinked to other texts or multimedia data, and searched according to parameters specified by the user. Software programs which are based on these principles have been called 'code-and-retrieve' programs (Kelle, 1995).

The data-handling and manipulation capability of CAQDAS proves a great benefit to the research by significantly increasing the rate at which data could be accessed, retrieved, and viewed. Additional features such as colour coding of documents in managing the coding and analysis status of documents are available. It is difficult to foresee an occasion where analysis of textual data or interview transcripts would not benefit from such data-handling and manipulation capabilities. The CAQDAS represents a strong metaphor for systematic, objectivity and rigour, but also optimistic forecasts that computer software would make the qualitative research process more transparent and rigorous (Richards and Richards, 1991). The program NUD*IST contains extensive features which support the construction of hierarchies of codes and categories. But linkages between codes may not only take the form of hierarchical relations but can form whole networks of categories, containing chains or loops. Since a theory can be regarded as a network of categories the idea itself suggests that tools for connecting codes to each other could be helpful for displaying the structure of the emerging theory and that software which facilitates the connection of categories can make a major contribution towards theory building.

Lee and Fielding (1996) have found that the median sample size, even in qualitative studies that use software for data management, is about 40 which seems feasible if one bears in mind that 'representativeness' in the statistical sense is usually not regarded as the crucial purpose of qualitative sampling. In this research, for main study, 41 professionals were interviewed in the construction industry SMEs. Researchers are primarily guided by their research objectives and analysis strategies, and not by the software they use.

Approach A has adopted the software – QSR N6, for analysis of the data obtained through semi-structured interview (Figure 1). N6 is selected for the research as it exhibits advanced data-handling and manipulation features being the sixth version of NUD*IST (Non-numerical Unstructured data Indexing Searching and Theorizing).

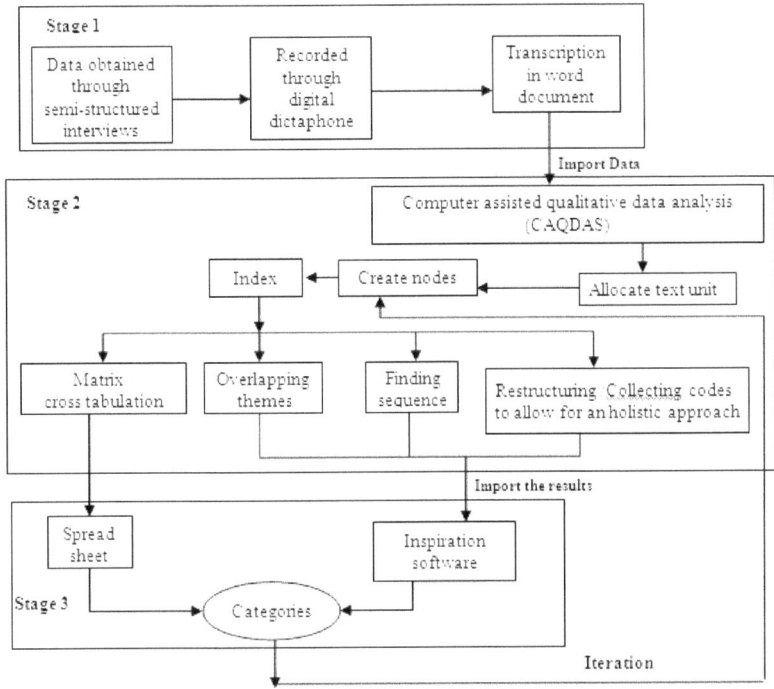

Figure 1: **Process diagram for analysis**

The software aids data management, allowing text or discourse to be edited, contextually annotated, hyperlinked to other text, import and export to statistics packages and search text according to parameters specified by the user. N6 also contains matrix "cross tabulation" of coding to show and discover patterns in data, which can be exported as text report or table. As suggested by Blismas and Dainty (2003) coding and subsequent analysis require intensive input by the researcher, regardless of the mode to achieve them. However the use of software allows limitless manipulation on the data without altering the original data set, data- handling capabilities significantly increase the rate at which data could be accessed, retrieved and viewed. This provides a great advantage over the manual method. One of the limitations of using computer software packages for coding text documents is that only a small section of the data is visible at any instant, making data scanning very difficult.

6.2. Approach B: The case against a software package

Nissan and Schmidt (1995) highlight the fact that words can mean so many things and have different meanings when used in conjunction with other words. This was evident in the case study data where some project issues were one-worded, some a phrase and some a sentence therefore making it difficult to attach meaning by using other words for a software package to pick up on.

Coffey and Atkinson (1996) highlight that there are no computer software packages that are capable of doing an analysis on their own and that there is '... no great conceptual advance over manual data sorting.' The process of using such a package involves coding the text; however, the coding process does not differ a great deal from the manual method. In addition to this, coding is not the same as analysing and therefore the data has still to be analysed manually. Scott et. al. (2002) recognised that data could be programmed although it was felt that this approach would act as a 'filter between the researcher and the data,' as it was feared that the richness would be lost from the data. This is supported in Cronholm (2002), who suggests that only a general analysis can be conducted using computer software. It is also suggested that manual coding permits the researcher to become more familiar with the data, Scott et al. (2002). This is an important feature in this study as the researcher has been able to identify and understand the project issues expressed in different forms by reading each one individually through the constant comparative method.

In this approach a significant factor also making it difficult to use a computer package is the manner in which the issues are expressed in words as various forms have been used to communicate the issues. These include clichés, adages, colloquialisms, figures of speech, questions, words or phrases, various terminology such as technical phrases or institutional terms and acronyms. Tables 2 and 3 give an example of some of the comparable issues that have been highlighted to differentiate the similar issues.

It is evident from the way some of these issues have been expressed where confusion may result from the use of a computer software package.

Leading Issues in Business Research Methods

Table 2 and Table 3: Comparable issues

Hotel	Housing Association	Towers refurbishment	Secure project websites
Budget	Cost	Finance	Funding
Contingencies (1B)	Aggregate tax	Cost reflecting design	£200 per month for a site
Cost (1B)	Funding availability (7B 3R)	Inflation	Currently on shoestring
Cost in design terms	Cost in use to X (4B)	Life cycle of materials (0, 1)	Funding of web sites
Cost plan (1B)	Cost in use to tenant (1B)	No nasty surprises - open and honest (2, 4)	Outside funding to cover operating costs (1, 0)
Final account procedure	Cost limits (1B)	Openness	
Preliminaries (3B)	Costs in use (1B)	Process to manage out turn cost	
Provisional sums – what's included?	Inflation due to X programme	Quality promise	
Recovery of costs		Require cost certainty (0, 3)	
		Right price for job	
		Sufficiency of tender (5, 3)	

Hospital	Town Hall	Integrated Group People System
Risk	Risk	Risks
£20m Budget Dictates Size in m2 (1B)	Changes in scheme (0, 1)	Be forward looking - not an inhibitor (1, 0)
Affordability of Specialist Equipment (1B)	Communications (1, 4)	Business will keep changing - selling off / merger / acquisition
Capacity Management by Strategic Health Authority	Condition of existing building	Compensation agreement with service providers
Consumerism	Conflict between conservatism and business plan	Do not create further level of bureaucracy
Content	Conflicting specialist advice	Driver to integrate stops
Current Budget £20m	Fear of risk taking	Integration driver support removed

Hospital	Town Hall	Integrated Group People System
NHS Estates Involvement	Impact of lack of funding on scheme (0, 3)	Internal politics (1, 1)
Procure 21 this is the First	Interpretation of information	Not co-locating HR until 2003
Section 106 Planning (1B)	Managing expectation (1, 3)	Overselling the product
Status of FBC	The organ	Risk - integrity of data / compromising data
Trust Commissioning		Risk of losing corporate support by lack of resource at implementation
Validation of Information Requirements (1B)		Risk of not resourcing procedure at the start
		Risks - possible to implement with number of IT departments
		Risks - system being too rigid
		Service provider robustness
		Support from the top of the organisation (4, 4)

6.3. Synopsis on the use of software packages

Computer packages can never replace the intuition of the researcher or the need to make judgments, which are a key characteristic of qualitative research. There are no ways of avoiding these time-consuming but essential aspects. Simister (1995) pointed out that one of the problems inherent within the richness of interview data is that analysis is impractical without a reduction in the form of data. Yet, this reduction must be balanced with general intelligibility and must also convey the deep meanings that have emerged from the analysis (Miles and Huberman, 1994). Coding and subsequent analysis require intensive input by the researcher, regardless of the mode used to achieve them.

7 Challenges of the grounded theory method

In both studies, the researchers have had to overcome a number of challenges of using the grounded theory method. Any research method has specific characteristics associated with it that have to be addressed. The following is a condensed list of the challenges faced using this particular method to inform the researcher employing a grounded theory approach.

- The general management of the data i.e. sorting and coding.
- Dealing with a huge amount of data and prevention of getting 'lost' in the data.
- Ensuring the theory is grounded by standing back from the data to prevent prior assumptions; knowledge and experience influence the process. Therefore there is a requirement to have an open-mind: An open-minded approach to the data is something that can operate at a variety of levels. It is not possible to start a research study without some pre-existing theoretical ideas. Approach A is based on a literature review and pilot study, while approach B is based on literature review and experience.
- The unknown factor of when data saturation is going to occur. With other methods i.e. questionnaire the researcher normally has a pre-defined period of time in which to obtain the data from respondents and has an idea how long it will take to analyse the results from the nature and length of the questionnaire. This is not feasible with grounded theory as it is not possible to predict in advance the size of the sample that will be used.
- For analysing data there are various methods suggested by Glaser, Strauss and Corbin, Glaser and Strauss, and other authors, which can cause a considerable amount of confusion amongst researchers. It is the researcher's decision to choose the path that suits them for analysis of their data.

In terms of challenges specific to the typical construction-industry researcher, the following was found:
- With regards to data gathering; it is a challenge to collect data across units in the SMEs and to have unrestrained, long term access to their organisations (Approach A).
- Some of the issues uncovered used specific construction terms and acronyms that would not easily transfer to the development of a formal theory outside the scope of the construction industry (Approach B).
- A level confidentiality had to be retained when reviewing the project issues which resulted in wording referring to projects and companies being removed from the data (Approach B).

Finally, it is important to consider some of the advantages of choosing to use the grounded theory method. First of all, it captures complexity, in the sense that if the data is very detailed and difficult to make sense of, the process of categorisation in grounded theory will start to organise the data into a sensible order so that the properties can be examined and coding can commence. Grounded theory also links very well to practice as the derived theory can be tested outside the research paradigm to investigate the applicability of the new theory. In addition to this, it supports the theorizing of 'new' substantive areas which can then be further explored to develop a more formal theory.

8 Recommendations to the grounded theorist

Having engaged in the aforementioned grounded theory studies the researchers are able to make some recommendations for others to consider prior to starting their individual studies:

- It is important to have a good background and understanding of the differences between approaches to prevent confusion and bias to specific methods.
- Development of a method to best suit the nature of the data being explored is important as well as a method which suits the researchers preferred style of investigation. However, it is important to adhere to the grounded theory principles to ensure that any theory derived is 'grounded.'
- A software package should only be used if it will support the study and not influence the researchers approach in anyway, for instance, by changing the direction of the research to suit the package chosen or the package available.

It is important to remember that provided the rules of grounded theory are adhered to, the researcher may adapt the method to suit their own research project as no research studies can be compared like for like. The literature on grounded theory provides the background, principles and rules, however it does not provide the researcher with a step-by-step guide to structure a study as there are too many variables involved. Therefore, the researcher has to be original when configuring their own approach.

9 Synthesis

This paper has highlighted two examples of the application of grounded theory in the construction industry in the areas of knowledge management and value management. Background on each research area has been given as well as valuable points with reference to grounded theory which have been picked up through the course of a comprehensive literature review. In addition to this, the research has highlighted the case for and against the use of a software package which has left the use of such a medium open for debate, following on from the work of Blismas and Dainty (2003).

Although, the grounded theory method has been used in both research studies, the two approaches are different in the techniques employed and the outcome expected, making for an interesting comparison on how this method can be adapted to suit the nature of the study. The researchers have outlined the challenges faced which are mainly general with regards to the use of grounded theory but differ in terms of the techniques and sources of data obtained which pose specific challenges in themselves. A series of recommendations have been made to the wider research audience and not specifically to the construction industry researchers which have been developed from the researchers experience from engaging in grounded theory studies that will be of use to those researchers who may be considering using grounded theory in their area of work.

10 Conclusions and Further Work

This study has illustrated the benefits and pitfalls of the use of software packages and has highlighted that use of these must suit the type of problem under research and not make the mistake of adapting the research problem to suit the capabilities of the software packages available.

Blismas and Dainty (2003) opened a debate on whether software aids qualitative data analysis or if it inhibits a multiplicity of approaches for qualitative data analysis. Since Approach A uses software and Approach B does not, this paper has succeeded in exploring the pros and cons of each and a more thorough review can be made in the later stages of investigation through subsequent comparative studies. It is anticipated that more research work on the use of software packages in research will be reported as a response to the work of Blismas and Dainty.

It is clear that grounded theory is very diverse in its application and can be modified and applied to suit the nature of the research problem and the particular research style of the investigator. This opens up the approach to wide audience of researchers who will use the method in different ways to analyse their sources of data which will also differ depending on the particular research techniques employed.

The two research studies have shown that the use of grounded theory can vary considerably, however, the fundamental aspect which must be adhered to is to ensure that the theory derived is 'grounded' in the data. It would be interesting to read more on these kinds of studies that use the grounded theory method to make cross comparisons and to highlight the scope for the grounded theory approach.

Further work in the two ongoing PhD research programmes will be reported both individually with the possibility of another joint paper to identify the approaches taken for coding and categorising the data as well as generating the framework and theory.

References

Backman K, Hentinen M. (1999), "Model for the self-care of home dwelling elderly", *Journal of Advanced Nursing*, 30 (3), 564-572.

Backman Kaisa and Kyngas Helvi A. (1999), "Challenges of the grounded theory approach to a novice researcher", *Nursing and Health Sciences*, 1, 147-153.

Blismas Nick G and Dainty Andrew R. J (2003),"Computer-aided Qualitative Data Analysis: Panacea or Paradox?" *Building Research and Information*, 31(6), 455-463.

Chen YL (1996), "Conformity with nature: A theory of Chinese American elder's health promotion and illness prevention processes", *Advanced Nursing Science*, 19, 17-26.

Coffey, Amanda and Atkinson, Paul (1996), *Making Sense of Qualitative Data*, Sage.

Cronholm, Stefan (2002), *Grounded Theory in Use – A Review of Experiences, European Conference on Research Methodology for Business and Management Studies*, Reading University, UK (29-30 April, 2002), Edited by Dan Remenyi.

Dainty, A.R.J., Bagilhole, B.M. and Neale, R.H. (2000), "Computer-aided analysis of qualitative data in construction management research", *Building Research and Information*, 28(4), 226–233.

Denzin, Norman K., Lincoln, Yvonna S. (1998) *Strategies of qualitative inquiry.* Sage Publications.

Glaser, B. (1978) *Theoretical Sensitivity: Advances in the Methodology of Grounded Theory*. Mill Valley: The Sociology Press.

Leading Issues in Business Research Methods

Glaser, Barney. G and Strauss, Anselm L. (1967), *The Discovery of Grounded Theory: Strategies for Qualitative Research,* Aldine, Chicago.

Heath, Helen and Cowley, Sarah (2003), Developing a Grounded Theory Approach: A Comparison of Glaser and Strauss, *International Journal of Nursing Studies,* Article in Press, Elsevier Ltd.

Kelle, U. (editor) (1995) *Computer-Aided Qualitative Data Analysis: Theory, Methods and Practice.* London: Sage.

Kelly and Male (1993), *Value Management in Design and Construction, The Economic Management of Projects,* E & FN Spon.

Kelly and Male (2002), *Best Value in Construction,* Edited by Kelly, John., Morledge, Roy and Wilkinson, Sara., Blackwell Publishing.

Lee, R. & Fielding, N. (1996) *"Computer-Assisted Qualitative Data Analysis: The User's Perspective",* in F. Faulbaum and W. Bandilla (editors) SOFTSTAT '95: Advances in Statistical Software 5. Stuttgart: Lucius.

Locke, K and Golden-Biddle, K (1997), "Construction opportunities for contribution: structuring intertextual coherence and problematizing in organisation studies", *Academy of Management Journal,* 40, 1023-62.

Male, S., Kelly, J., Fernie, S., Gronqvist, M., Bowles, G. (1998), *The Value Management Benchmark, A Good Practice Framework for Clients and Practitioners,* Thomas Telford.

Malhotra, Y, (1998), "Deciphering the knowledge management hype", *Journal for Quality and Participation,* Vol. 21, No.4, pp. 58-60.

Miles, M.B and Huberman, A. M (1994), *"Qualitative Data Analysis,"* 2nd Edn. Thousand Oaks, CA: Sage.

Nissan, Ephraim and Schmidt, Klaus (1995), *From Information to Knowledge, Conceptual and Content Analysis by Computer,* Intellect Ltd.

Richards, L. and Richards, T. (1991) *"The Transformation of Qualitative Method: Computational Paradigms and Research Processes",* in R. Lee and N. Fielding (editors) Using Computers in Qualitative Research. London: Sage.

Scott Malcolm, Davidson Jean and Edwards Helen (2002), "Application of Template Analysis in Information Systems Research: A Technique for Novice Researchers", *European Conference on Research Methodology for Business and Management Studies,* Reading University, UK (29-30 April, 2002), Ed Dan Remenyi.

Simister, S (1995), *"Case study methodology for the construction management research,* in Proceeding of the 11th Annual Conference ARCOM, Vol. 1, pp. 21-32.

Smith, K. (1997) Understanding grounded theory: Principles and evaluation, *Nurse Researcher,* Vol. 4.

Strauss, A and Corbin J (Eds), (1994), *"Grounded theory methodology: an overview",* in J.S. Lincoln (ed), Handbook of Qualitative Research, Thousand Oaks, CA: Sage. pp. 273-86.

Strauss, A. and Corbin, J. (1990) *Basics of Qualitative Research: Grounded Theory Procedures and Techniques.* Thousand Oaks: Sage.

Strauss, Anselm and Corbin, Juliet (1998), *Basics of Qualitative Research, Techniques and Procedures for Developing Grounded Theory,* 2nd Edition, Sage.

Turner, B.A. (1976), "The organisational and interorganisational development of disasters", *Administrative Science Quarterly,* 21, 378-97.

Interpretivism and the Pursuit of Research Legitimisation: An Integrated Approach to Single Case Design

Felicity Kelliher
School of Business, Waterford Institute of Technology, Ireland
Originally published in EJBRM (2005) Volume 3: Issue 2.

Editorial Commentary

This paper uses the experience gained from a longitudinal study to explain how issues of 'research legitimisation' can be dealt with in such contexts where an interpretive approach has been employed. Felicity Kelliher offers a particularly clear and useful account of her research from initial design, through data collection and analysis, to eventual presentation and evaluation of outputs. She draws on a good deal of relevant and important literature from a wide range of areas, including key texts such as those by Geertz, Zuboff, and Klein and Myers (detailed references are given at the end of the paper itself).

Her account is not only useful for researchers using or seeking to justify and explain similar research strategies, but also provides a useful source for those who regard interpretive research as somehow less amenable to processes of legitimisation such as reliability, validity, and generalization.

Abstract: While interpretive research is recognised for its value in providing contextual depth, results are often criticised in terms of validity, reliability and generalisability, referred to collectively as research legitimisation. This paper explores the criticisms levied on interpretive case studies and presents a research design that seeks to address these criticisms. The paper describes the research template developed by the author and applies it to a longitudinal case study carried out on a micro firm in the Republic of Ireland. Following some detailed evaluation and analysis the author concludes that legitimisation of an interpretative case study is improved when an integrative approach involving the combination of specific research techniques to relevant and appropriate standards is adopted.

Keywords: Interpretive case study, qualitative research, legitimisation

1 Introduction

Interpretivists believe that reality is not objectively determined, but is socially constructed (Husserl, 1965). The underlying assumption is that by placing people in their social contexts, there is greater opportunity to understand the perceptions they have of their own activities (Hussey & Hussey, 1997). By its nature, interpretivism promotes the value of qualitative data in pursuit of knowledge (Kaplan and Maxwell, 1994). In essence, this research paradigm is concerned with the uniqueness of a particular situation, contributing to the underlying pursuit of contextual depth (Myers, 1997). However, while interpretive research is recognised for its value in providing contextual depth, results are often criticised in terms of validity, reliability and the ability to generalise, referred to collectively as research legitimisation. These concerns are amplified in the single case scenario (Eisenhardt, 1989; Perry, 1998). In reality, all these issues are interdependent and reflect on the layered complexity of the phenomenon at hand:

Reliability refers to the consistency or stability of a measure. Denzin (1970) states that multiple and independent methods should, if reaching the same conclusions, have greater reliability than a single methodological approach to a problem. This combination of methodologies in the study of the same phenomenon is known as triangulation. From an interpretive perspective, Eisenhardt (1989) recommends that the researcher start with a broad research question, establish systematic data collection and ensure case access to create strong triangulated measures. Qualitative research findings can be strengthened in this way by combining participant observation with interviews and documentary sources (Hammersley and Atkinson, 1983) in a single case.

Validity: In terms of validation, qualitative research depends on the presentation of solid descriptive data, so that the researcher leads the reader to an understanding of the meaning of the experience under study (Stake, 1995). In essence, validation is an interpretive understanding of truth (Angen, 2000). Thus, triangulation is not a tool or a strategy of validation, but an alternative to validation in this context (Denzin & Lincoln, 2003). In a single case, data triangulation is particularly important in order to fortify validation in the absence of cross case comparison. Remenyi et al (1998) suggest using multiple data sources, establishing an identifiable chain of evidence, and having a draft reviewed by the key informants to strengthen construct validity in this regard. Generalisability refers to the extent to which the findings of the enquiry are more generally applicable outside the specifics of the situation studied (Robson, 2004). In qualitative terms, the research goal is to offer a case description (including data collection procedures) that would allow the reader to repeat the research process in another case (Kidder & Judd, 1986; Vaughan, 1992). Although a single case may not provide sufficient evidence to make robust generalisations, it can establish the existence of a phenomenon (Van Maanen, 1988), which is adequate for the purposes of exploratory research (Remenyi et al., 1998). Thus, a case can be generalisable to theoretical propositions (Yin, 1984), creating a distinction between analytical and statistical generalisability (Yin, 2003).

The remainder of this paper is broken into four. Section one presents a research design that seeks to address the criticisms levied on the single interpretive case study. Section two describes the research template developed by the author and applies it to a longitudinal case study carried out on a micro firm in the Republic of Ireland. The concluding sections offer a perspective on interpretive data analysis and single case design evaluation. Following some detailed analysis, the author concludes that legitimisation of an interpretive case study is improved when an integrative approach involving the combination of specific research techniques to relevant and appropriate standards is adopted.

2 Case design

A research design is "an action plan for getting from here to there, where 'here' is the initial set of questions and 'there' are the set of answers" (Yin, 1994:19). In this study, the underlying research question sought to assess the learning impact of a critical incident on employees (both individually and collectively) in a micro enterprise. The longitudinal interpretive case was deemed the most appropriate method to facilitate a valid response to the proposed research question. For clarity, a case study can be described as the investigation of a contemporary phenomenon within a real-life context (Yin, 2003), while in-depth case studies are often the vehicle for interpretive investigations, where research involves frequent visits to the field site over an extended period of time (Walsham, 2002). Justification for the suitability of the chosen research instrument is founded on Hill and McGowan's (1999) work which suggests that small company research may be best done using a qualitative approach that includes participant observation, case studies, in-depth interviewing and the use of documentation. Considering learning is not a single event, but rather a phenomenon to be studied in past, present and future terms, observational evidence offered the most appropriate means of assessing the level of adjustment in this context (Sutton & Callahan, 1987). By applying this research method, causal assessment could be established through depth and time series analysis (Kidder, 1981; Kratochwill, 1978) rather than as a single point in time, offering the greatest potential for legitimisation of the research results.

Having established the primary research question, the resultant objectives and the research design ethos, the researcher prepared for data collection by developing a research protocol as recommended by Yin (2003). This research blueprint focused on what questions to study, what data were relevant, what data to collect, and how to analyse the results. It also encompasses the management criteria relating to the case, and the researcher's role as the primary research instrument (Trauth, 2001). The protocol allows for a chain of evidence, ensuring increased reliability and reduced misperception at every stage of the research process.

Following an initial literature review, an IS implementation was selected as an appropriate critical incident in order to investigate its anticipated impact on employee learning, an impending outcome supported by Zuboff's (1988:13) findings that "people who are working with technology for the first time are ripe with questions and insights regarding the distinct qualities of their experience".

Table 1: Research protocol (Adapted from Klein & Myers, 1999:80).

Activity	Description	
Research Question	Assess the learning impact of a critical incident on employees (both individually and collectively) in a micro enterprise.	
Research Method	A longitudinal case study	09/01-08/04
Critical Incident	Information System (IS) implementation in a micro firm	
Case Selection Process	Environmental Criteria: Micro firm influenced by dominant supplier IS requirements and industry regulation. Internal Criteria: Micro firm, whose owner is in the pivotal managerial role as primary employee influencer and has an imminent/recent, IS implementation within the firm.	
Case Access	Identify cases fulfilling the criteria in the research protocol.	06/2001
	Negotiate full access to the case	09/ 2001
	Meet to establish researcher/ employee rapport prior to the in-store IS implementation.	10-12/2001
Research Instrument	Researcher as the primary research instrument in the application of research methods	
Boundary device	Micro firm learning framework	
Research Techniques	On-site observation and semi-structured interviews supported by reflective diaries independently generated by the case business owner and researcher, informal conversations, completion of learning questionnaires and focus groups, and the perusal of internal documentary evidence over a three year period.	
Data Management	Audit trail of data, collection methods and process, including control of the research instrument's influence on the studied environment, specifically the balance of observation/ participatory action.	

As longitudinal case studies can offer a broader understanding of the ways in which people adapt technological systems for their own purposes, particularly over time, a three-year case duration was set in order to determine the causality links more explicitly in this context. Subsequently, the setting of case criteria offered the contextual landscape required to successfully test the research question and internal and external criteria were specified to assist in the identification of acceptable case candidates in this regard.

In order to successfully perform the case study, full and complete company access was vital. In this context, "random selection is neither necessary, nor even preferable" (Eisenhardt, 1989:537). Thus, following the identification of suitable cases, access was negotiated via personal contact with the owner. While negotiation took some time before access was granted, this process was invaluable in ensuring both parties were satisfied with the research terms of reference. Of particular importance was a mutual understanding about the amount of access being requested and the length of the study in elapsed time: three years is a significant investment, not only on the part of the researcher but also in terms of the case participants. In addition, a clear appreciation of the research objectives and the direct contribution in tangible and intangible terms that the research could make to the studied case should clarify boundaries relating to the research before it commences.

An overriding concern of the author's was that the mere collection of in-depth case data does not provide theory concepts in and of themselves. This point is articulated by Zuboff (1988) who states that while observation could be considered first order constructions, researchers rely on good theory and insightful analysis for second order concepts in order to induce theory. Miles & Huberman's (1994) suggest that conceptual frameworks can be used as boundary devices in this context, while Janesick (2002) recommends the development of working models and theories in action that explain the behaviour under study. Therefore, variables were identified early in the case and incorporated into a loose conceptual framework to focus the case investigation. Notably, Crossan et al. (1999) suggest that these tools can help define context and promote the move toward theory in the employee learning research milieu. Thus a framework's latent legitimacy value is significant, particularly if the underlying case purpose is to provide a basis for theoretical replication.

3 Data collection template

A clear schedule of data collection activities was discussed with the micro firm owner at this point in the research process. The author also outlined a schedule of site visits, detailing each visit's likely duration with the micro firm owner. A variety of data collection techniques allowed for a greater possibility of anomalies to be noted, and sought to accommodate limitations relating to individual techniques (Gallivan, 1997).

Table 2: Data collection activities

Activity	Description	Time line
Observation	Sporadic on-site observation over a three-year period (see details below)	10/01 - 09/04
Literature review	Evolutionary process completed in tandem with the case study	2002 - 2004
In-depth interviews/ conversations	Owner interviews Shop floor manager interviews Employee conversations Employee focus groups	6/8 week intervals Quarterly 6/8 week intervals Annual
Diary maintenance	Researcher reflective diary Case owner reflective diary	10/01 - 09/04 12/01 to 06/04
Internal Document review	Complete review at the start of 2002 and subsequent review at the end of 2002, 2003 and June 2004.	01/02 - 06/04
Industry review	Complete review in 2004	2004

Observation: In order to comprehend the employee learning impact, it was deemed important to observe the micro firm and its employees over an extended period. One of the noticeable benefits of longitudinal observation was that general relations were often discovered in vivo, an advantage alluded to by Glaser & Strauss (1967). Thus, the longer the period spent in the field, the better (Gomm et al., 2002) in order to gain true insight into the workings of the micro enterprise in the context of the research question. This point is particularly compelling in the single case scenario. It should be noted that longitudinal cases, even those that require periodic rather than continuous involvement are labour intensive (Mumford, 2001) and the basic ethos behind the interpretive epistemology necessitates the researcher's direct involvement in all stages of the research process in order to allow the researcher the level of empathy required.

With reference to this case, the researcher was present for an initial two week period, encompassing the week directly preceding and the week directly following the IS implementation. The IS installation and upgrade process took eight to twelve hours daily, during which time the researcher was present for observation purposes, taking detailed field notes as required. Each 'working' day was followed by evenings documenting and interpreting the day's observations in order to establish new lines of inquiry for the following day's work. Subsequent two-day observation sessions at pre-defined six to eight-week intervals in year one and two, and at eight to ten-week intervals in year three allowed the researcher to document employee progress over a three year period providing substantial insight into organisational and social perspectives in the studied case over time. Setting the balance between participation and observation can be difficult. In this research, observer as participant (sometimes identified as interrupted involvement) was deemed the most beneficial. This decision was based on the fact that complete detachment would not create the necessary subject trust to realise the research objectives while complete participation could create conflict of interest. In terms of temporal interconnection, the goal was to establish learning in past, present and future terms. The underlying assumption is that learning causation is neither linear nor singular [founded on Pettigrew's (1990) argument] but rather continual in the context of ongoing change.

Finally, observation invariably raises ethical dilemmas, particularly when conducted in a covert way. This dilemma was considered by the researcher prior to commencing the study and was discussed with the micro business owner at length. It was agreed that the researcher would be introduced, as a management consultant to the case employees, employed to establish the best means of optimising IS operation within the case organisation. The researcher's particular interest in learning was explicit, having been raised at several staff meetings and documented in relevant meeting minutes throughout the observation period. Issues of privacy, confidentiality and the relationship between individual cost and scientific benefit were also discussed with both the business owner and the researcher's peers in order to establish an appropriate balance in this regard. The primary tool used for dealing with risk was an informed consent form. The owner was provided with a simple written statement detailing the study's research objectives, potential benefits and risks, rights to confidentiality, and termination procedures, in acknowledgement of relevant ethical aspects of the research process.

Literature Review: A thorough literature review combined with initial case observations provided a number of potential dependent variables in the context of micro business IS adoption and the resultant impact on employee learning. These findings provided the basis for relevant environmental, organisational and individual employee variables when developing the learning framework.

Interviews: Personal in-depth interviews were carried out with the case owner and Shop Floor Manager at pre-defined intervals throughout the case study. As the case sought to establish protocol, the interview schedule was revised as required based on participant feedback and researcher observation (as suggested by Glesne & Peshkin, 1992). These interviews were not recorded or directly transcribed as requested by the case participants, however, extensive notes were taken during the meeting and written up immediately (as recommended by Zuboff, 1988) to ensure optimum recall regarding the interview content. The goal was to 'document carefully the practical contours of interaction in the varied circumstances in which they unfolded' (Gubruim & Holstein, 2003: 229). It should be noted that recording the meaning of what is being said rather than the exact words of the respondent is more important in this context (Perry, 1998; Stake, 1995). These interviews were enhanced by periodic informal face-to-face conversations with each employee when the researcher was on-site, and supplemented by annual group sessions conducted by the author. These interactions allowed employees to voice their individual opinions regarding the IS implementation and its impact on their work.

Diary Maintenance: To achieve dialogical reasoning (Klein and Myers, 1999), researchers must confront the preconceptions that guided the original research design (Janesick, 2002) with the data that emerge through the research process. Underlying philosophical assumptions should be transparent in this regard. Specifically, that the researcher is predisposed to factors of perception and prior theories, as well as prior expert knowledge (Yin, 1994), all of which influence what we take to be factual observations. Geertz (1973: 9) articulated this issue as thus: "what we call data is really our own constructions of other people's constructions of what they and their compatriots are up to". To help overcome these issues, Trauth (1997: 241) recommends, "Self-conscious questioning of [the researchers] own assumptions [to] bring into consciousness the emotional and intellectual reactions to experiences and observations". In the case study, diaries were used as a supplementary research tool valuable in the pursuit of reliable research by providing an essential audit trail in the research context. Several writers advocate the maintenance of a reflective diary as a rigorous documentary tool in this context (for example: Glaser & Strauss, 1967; Janesick, 2002; Stake, 1995). Thus, the researcher maintained a reflective diary separate to the non-reflective recording of observations throughout the case study. This amounted to a personal journal of the research process, specifically the recording of emergent ideas and results, reflections on personal and case participant learning, and an ongoing examination of personal attitude that proved invaluable when analysing the case data. Separately, the micro firm owner maintained an IS related diary throughout the case duration. Here, the diary provided a simple record of events and sought to assist in the identification of certain activities and the frequency of occurrence. Unexpectedly, the owner diary offered new perspectives that were not articulated in either the interview or the observation process.

Internal document review: Having agreed access with the owner, the author carried out a thorough review of the case site's internal documentation including internal quality manuals, IS training documentation and user manuals, 2002 to 2004 business diaries, IS vendor correspondence, wholesale supplier literature, and a review of all historic staff meeting file notes and notes included by the owner in the staff's monthly pay packet. Each record provided valuable data relating to the culture of the organisation and its relationship with the IS vendor and dominant industry suppliers. They also offered supplementary knowledge relating to employee learning focus over time.

Industry review: Separate to the case site data collection, the researcher interviewed an industry expert to establish the case's external environment in terms of political, legal and industry pressures placed on a micro firm operating within the sector. Three in-depth interviews were carried out at the start of the case, each lasting approximately two hours, in order to establish relevant criteria relating to the environmental aspect of the learning framework. A thorough review of all relevant public documentation relating to the sector was also completed in this context. Documentary evidence sought to 'corroborate and augment evidence from other sources', (Yin, 2003:81). In essence, documentary evidence provides context, particularly in a complex environment, creating greater validity and reliability of the research and the resultant framework.

4 Data analysis and interpretation

The philosophical links remain at the data analysis stage of the research process. Considering this research's interpretive stance, the ultimate goal is to describe the context in which events occur. The analytical goal is to make sense of the whole [situation] and the relationship between people, the organisation and technology (Myers & Avison, 2002). Therefore, the underlying philosophy dictates an iterative process of data collection and data analysis (Eisenhardt, 1989; Walsham, 2002), which are tested and modified through cycles of additional data collection and analysis until an adequately coherent interpretation is reached (Glaser & Strauss, 1967). Consequently, the researcher sought to overcome the temptation to convert qualitative data into numbers once it had been collected, in order to preserve the richness of the data and give a holistic view of the research context. While interpretive research does not subscribe to the idea that a pre-determined set of criteria can be applied in a mechanistic way, it does not follow that there are no standards at all through which interpretive research can be judged (Klein & Myers, 1999). Therefore, data analysis was based on Lacity and Janson's (1994: 146) four-step 'intentional analysis' procedure:

a) In the first step of intentional analysis, the researcher describes the "facts" of the phenomenon. "Facts" are socially shared realities agreed upon by all participants. For example, in this case, the owner, shop floor manager and employees may all attest to the "fact" that the IS implementation caused a change to their working environment.
b) In step two, the researcher determines the way participants ascribe meaning to their separate realities by how they perceive cause and effect. For example, in the case study, the owner may attribute the IS implementation as a necessity created by dominant supplier influence in the industry, whereas the employee may believe the IS purchase and installation

was based solely on the owner's preference for an IS solution above a manual system.

c) In step three, the researcher identifies themes (or invariants) that emerge from the research and these are then used to develop common interpretations. Considering the large amounts of non-standard data produced by this qualitative study, data analysis consisted of the identification and development of themes, rather than analysing data based on an external, pre-defined structure. This process was supported by the early conception of the learning framework to guide research focus and data management. As analysis progressed, the researcher identified relationships that connected portions of description, verified through field notes, with explanations offered in the working model.

d) In step four, the researcher abstracts the essences from the text. Essences are wholly subjective gestalts of what is learned from studying the phenomenon, and requires creativity, intuition and reflection. Thus, analysis depends on an investigator's own style of rigorous thinking (Yin, 2003). The pre-mentioned reflective diary proved invaluable in this context, not only in terms of the resultant content, but also in the process of reflective thought required to complete the diary task. Finally, evidence is presented in a narrative form, supported by evidence from the statements and behaviours recorded in field notes, diaries and interviews (a process supported by Janesick, 2002; and Kidder & Judd, 1986).

Internal validity is established where several pieces of information from the same case point to a theoretical proposition (Stake, 1995) or empirical assertion (Janesick, 2002). Therefore, insights are validated with rich descriptions, direct quotes from participants, and practitioner review of the interpretation (Lacity & Hirschheim, 1993) in order to build the thick description (Geertz, 1973) sought under this analytical ethos.

With reference to the research report, it can be linear-analytic, comparative, chronological or theory-inducing (Yin, 1994) dependent on the research philosophy and underlying assumptions adopted. In this instance, chronological reporting provided the greatest insight into the evolving impact of the critical incident on learning over the case duration. Specifically, a chronological record over a prolonged period should offer greater insight into learning as an evolving phenomenon. As this action is founded in the intentional research process detailed above, the researcher planned for the final report creation from the start of the investigation (as advised by Yin, 2003). This iterative approach to data collection and analysis created an important cycle of discovery within the case. Finally, it was important to establish a strategy whereby the micro firm could gain from the research without impeding on the research reliability and validity from an academic standpoint. Academic rigour had to be acknowledged in this context. Thus, once documented, the micro firm owner reviewed a draft copy of the case study to ensure the document contents were complete and accurate from her perspective. It was also agreed that the author would perform an IS audit as part of the observation process and produce a feedback report on the impact of the learning plans and training programmes on each employee from an individual and collective perspective in this context.

5 Design evaluation

The chain of evidence provided by the established research protocol, the subsequent research template and the integrated application of appropriate research techniques discussed in the preceding sections of this paper sought to legitimise the research results throughout the duration of the case.

As previously stated, complete case access was paramount and its importance cannot be over-emphasised in the context of this paper. The researcher's presence at the IS implementation and subsequent upgrades proved vital as it offered contextual knowledge relating to employee learning. Specifically, the researcher observed and documented the individual employees' initial reaction to the information system during the installation and directly following its implementation. This initial investigation sought to identify the relationships and interdependencies between individual learning and collective learning within the micro enterprise, in the context of the external environmental influences and how these elements shape such relationships; culminating in the creation of the learning framework. Having established that the IS implementation required significant adjustment in the employee's knowledge, observational evidence, combined with internal interviews, focus groups and informal conversations, offered the most appropriate means of assessing the level of employee adjustment in context. The value of multiple perspectives over the initial observation period established broad themes and provided for greater data reliability when analysing the case results.

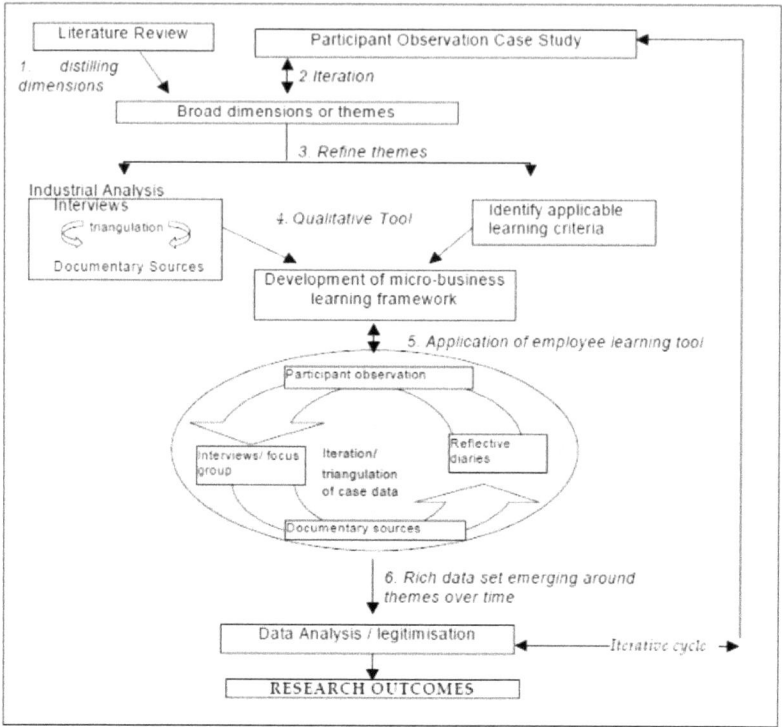

Figure 1: Chain of Evidence

Building staff/researcher empathy proved valuable in terms of mutual comfort with individual employees during the study. The ambition here was to get as close as possible to the world of the micro firm's decision catalyst and IS implementation and to interpret this world and its problems from the inside in order to describe both the unique and typical experiences and events within this environment as bases for theory (as argued by Dalton, 1959). Observed data was documented throughout the case study and periodically checked by participants and research colleagues to reinforce objective reporting. The goal was rigorous and systematic data collection, without excluding serendipitous information (Kaplan & Maxwell, 1994).

The complementary data collection techniques used throughout the case proved particularly valuable in the pursuit of research legitimisation. Reviewing the firm's internal documentation provided greater insight into the firm's internal culture. It also afforded an appreciation of the micro firm's ongoing relationship with both the IS vendor and dominant industry suppliers, while the industry expert interviews gave a holistic view of the micro firm's external business environment.

Maintaining reflective diaries as a complimentary research tool throughout the research process offered an additional audit trail in relation to theme development. Specifically, the researcher's reflective diary acknowledged and identified personal reference frames on a continuous basis while the owner's diary offered individual perspective without the imposition of the researcher's own reference frame during data collection. Lastly, informal conversations with individual staff members and focus group discussions sought to identify individual employee's interpretation of the IS implementation and subsequent learning needs, rather than being restricted to those of the business owner alone. In this context, the principle of multiple interpretations is of heuristic value because it leads to probing beneath the surface; a benefit alluded to by Hussey & Hussey (1997) and Kaplan & Maxwell (1994) in the introduction.

6 Conclusion

This case study sought to establish a typical case supported by a detailed research protocol (Yin, 1994). The underlying purpose of the case design was to provide a basis for theoretical replication alluded to by Yin (1984). The multiple research techniques applied in this case offered reliability via triangulated results. Finally, the pre-established data collection template provided for a standard approach to data collection and analysis in pursuit of research validation. As a note of caution, this form of research is not just a matter of observing the subject matter and analysing the results at a distance at some later date. It involves observing, participating, talking, checking, understanding and making interpretations over an extended timeframe, all of which are required if the observer is to share and understand important parts of the employee's experience. In addition, case participants can be seen as interpreters and analysts in their own right, whose horizon is changed by the researcher's interaction with them (Klein and Myers, 1999). It is inevitable that as the researcher establishes mutual comfort over time, and that they interact with the case subjects at a social as well as professional level. In consequence, reporting on the case participants impartially can prove to be a difficult task. Thus, pre-established standards in each aspect of the case design, protocol, data collection, analysis and interpretation provide for greater legitimisation of research outcomes in this regard.

References

Angen, M.J., 2000, "Evaluating interpretive enquiry: reviewing the validity debate and opening the dialogue", *Qualitative Health Research*, 10(3), p378-95.

Crossan, M.M., Lane, H.W. & White, R.E., 1999, "An organizational learning framework: from intuition to institution", *Academy of Management*, 24(3): 522-37

Dalton, M., 1959, *Men who Manage*, NY: Wiley

Denzin, N., 1970, *The research art in sociology*, London: Butterworth

Denzin, N.K. & Lincoln, Y.S., 2003, *Strategies of qualitative research*, CA: Sage Publications Inc.

Eisenhardt, K.M., 1989, "Building Theories from Case Study Research", *Academy of Management Review*, 14(4), 532-50

Gallivan, M.J., 1997, "Value in triangulation: a comparison of two approaches for combining qualitative and quantitative methods; In: A.S. Lee, J.Liebenau, and J. DeGross (eds.), *Information Systems and Qualitative Research* (p 417-443), London: Chapman & Hall

Geertz, C., 1973, *The interpretation of Cultures*, New York: Basic Books

Glaser, B.G. & Strauss, A.L., 1967, *The Discovery of Grounded Theory*, Chicago: Aldine

Glesne, C. & Peshkin, A., 1992, *Becoming Qualitative Researchers: An introduction*, NY: Longman

Gomm, E., Hammersley, M. & Foster, P., 2000, *Case Study Method*, Sage Publications Surrey

Gubrium, J.F. & Holstein, J.A., 2003, "Analyzing Interpretive Practice". In: Denzin, N.K. & Lincoln, Y.S. (eds.), *Strategies of Qualitative Research*, 2nd ed., CA: Sage Publications Inc.

Hammersley, M. & Atkinson, P., 1983, *Ethnography: Principles in Practice*, London: Routledge.

Hill, J. & McGowen, P., 1999, "Small Business and Enterprise Development: Questions about Research Methodology", *International Journal of Entrepreneurial Behaviour and Research*, 5(1), 5-18.

Husserl, E., 1965, *Phenomenology and the Crisis of Philosophy*, New York: Harper Torchbooks.

Hussey, J. & Hussey, R., 1997, *Business Research: A Practical Guide for Undergraduate and Post-graduate Students*, London: MacMillan Press Ltd

Janesick, V.J., 2002, "The Choreography of Qualitative Research design, in: Denzin, N.K. & Lincoln, Y.S. (eds.), Strategies of qualitative research, 2nd edition, CA: Sage Publications Inc.

Kaplan, B. & Maxwell, J.A., 1994, "Qualitative research methods for evaluating computer information systems", in *Evaluating Health Care Information Systems: Methods and Applications,* J.G. Anderson, C.E. Aydin, and S.J.Jay (eds), CA: Sage, p.45-68.

Kidder, T., 1981, *The soul of a New Machine*, Boston: Little, Brown

Kidder, L. & Judd, C.M., 1986, *Research Methods in Social Relations*, 5th Ed., New York: Holt, Rinehart & Winston.

Kincheloe, L.J. & McLaren, P., 2000, "Rethinking critical theory and qualitative research"; In: Denzin, N.K. & Lincoln, Y.D. (eds.), *Handbook of Qualitative Research*, 2nd ed., Sage Publications, p.279-313.

Klein, H.K. & Myers, M.D., 1999, "A set of principles for conducting and evaluating interpretive field studies in information systems", *MIS Quarterly*, 23(1), 67-94.

Kratochwill, T.R., 1978, *Single Subject Research*, New York: Academic Press.

Lacity, M. & Hirschheim, R., 1993, Information *Systems Outsourcing: Myths, Metaphors and Realities, UK:* Wiley

Lacity, M. & Janson, M., 1994, "Understanding qualitative data: a framework of test analysis methods", *Journal of Management Information Systems*, 11(2), 137-155

Miles, M.B. and Huberman, A.M., 1994, *Qualitative Data Analysis – an Expanded Sourcebook*, CA: Sage

Mumford, E., 2001, "Action research: Helping Organizations to Change in Qualitative research" in *IS: Issues and Trends*, Trauth, E.M. (ed.), London: Idea Group Publishing, p46.

Myers, M.D., 1997, Qualitative research in information systems, MIS Quarterly, 21(2): 241-2.

Myers, M.D. and Avison, D.E. (eds.), 2002, Qualitative research in Information Systems, London: Sage Publications.

Perry, C., 1998, A structured approach to presenting theses, Australian Marketing Journal, 6(1), 63-86

Pettigrew, A.M., 1990, Longitudinal field research on change: theory and practice, Organization Science, 1(3), 267-271

Remenyi, D., Williams, B., Money, A. & Swartz, E., 1998, Doing research in business and management, an introduction to process and method, London: Sage Publications

Robson, C., 2004, Real World Research, 2nd ed., Oxford: Blackwell Publishing

Stake, R.E., 1995, *The art of case study Research: Perspectives and Practice*, London: Sage

Sutton, R. & Callahan, A., 1987, "The stigma of bankruptcy: spoiled organizational image and its management", *Academy of Management Review*, 14(4), 532-50

Trauth, E.M., 1997, Achieving the research goal with qualitative methods: lessons learned along the way, in Information Systems and Qualitative Research, A.S.

Lee, J. Liebenau and JI DeGross (Eds) London: Capman and Hall, 1997, p225-245.

Trauth, E.M., 2001, *Qualitative research in IS: Issues and Trends*, London: Idea Group Publishing.

Van Maanen, J., 1988, *Tales of the Field: on Writing Ethnography*, Chicago: University of Chicago Press.

Vaughan, D., 1992, "Theory elaboration: the heuristics of case analysis", In C.C. Ragin & H.S. Becker (eds), *What is a Case? Exploring the Foundations of Social Inquiry* (pp.173-292), Cambridge: Cambridge University Press.

Walsham, G., 2002, "Interpretive case studies in IS research: nature and method", in *Qualitative Research in Information Systems*, Myers, M.D. and Avison, D.E. (eds.), 2002, London: Sage Publications.

Yin, R.K., 1984, *Case Study Research*, CA: Sage Publications.

Yin, R.K., 1994, *Case study Research – Design and Methods*, applied social research methods series, 5, 2nd Ed., CA: Sage Publications

Yin, R.K., 2003, *Case Study Research Design and Methods*, 3rd Ed., UK: Sage Publications

Zuboff, S., 1988, In the age of the smart machine, New York: Basic Books

Applying a Behavioural Simulation for the Collection of Data

Kristina Risom Jespersen
Aarhus University, Department of Economics, Denmark
Originally published in EJBRM (2005) Volume 3: Issue 2.

Editorial Commentary

The development of the internet and WWW has had significant impact on the possibilities for researchers. In many regards these are to be welcomed, but only after careful consideration of what they actually entail. In too many cases the ability to contact and elicit responses from large numbers of people using email, web pages, social networks and the like can become a substitute for a well-designed research project; but this should not be taken to imply that all web-based research suffers from such faults.

Kristina Risom Jespersen's paper exemplifies a thoughtful approach to research design centring on web-based data collection; specifically what she refers to as 'interactive data collecting methods' and 'collection of real-time data'. Using such real-time methods can bring to light issues around the ways in which respondents actually learn as they participate in the research; hence the focus on 'behavioural simulation'.

The paper also raises the issue of some of the caveats and pitfalls that confront researchers aiming to use web-based research techniques. Using the web offers rich possibilities for data gathering and usable sources, but it also exacerbates existing issues such as survey fatigue, poor analysis, data glut, validation and so on.

Leading Issues in Business Research Methods

Abstract: To collect real-time data as opposed to retrospective data requires new methodological traits. One possibility is the use of behavioural simulations that synthesize the self-administered questionnaire, experimental designs, role-playing and scenarios. Supported by Web technology this new data collection methodology proves itself valid and with high appeal to respondents.

Keywords: Real-time data collection, simulation, Web technology

1 Introduction

As the complexity of problems and the speed of changes increase for companies, the accuracy of research relies on the measurement of behaviour close to the real world of the respondents. Recent reviews in various research fields of the social sciences have pointed at the need for more interactive data collecting methods (Zaltman 1997; Englis and Solomon 2000). The collection of real-time data as opposed to retrospective data requires new methodological traits.

Another aspect stressing the development of new data collection methodologies is the prediction that response rates of e-mail surveys will follow that of paper surveys (Shenan 2001). To obtain data, to make people invest time in research projects, research has to follow the information 'rules' of society. Here the increased number of media, the habitually use of the Internet and mobile phones as well as a TV set on multiple channels, makes heavy calls on research to be an interesting experience for researchers to be able to collect the important and necessary data. Not because people do not find science important but because time is a scarce resource in heavy demand. Hence, investing time in research projects has to give the respondents something more than being polite and helpful towards the researcher.

The purpose of this paper is to discuss and demonstrate the benefits and challenges of behavioural simulations supported by Web technology as a new methodological trait. Specifically how behavioural simulations as data collecting vehicles also act as learning tools for the respondents thereby giving immediate return in the time invested.

The concerns of this paper are the methodological contribution of simulations, the benefits of Web technology followed by a discussion of the validity of data collected with simulations. Finally, a designed behavioural simulation is presented as an example, before stating implications and future trends.

2 The contribution of a behavioural simulation

To understand the methodological contribution of a simulation it is beneficial to look at the research area of agent-based simulations. The first agent-based computational economic models were influenced by experimental economics, which at the time mainly focused on markets and games composed of real human agents (Chen 2004). A criticism of experimental economics on information utility states that the problem lies with the utility functions and whether these resemble the true utilities of information, because human agents are subject to biases, errors, and misconceptions (Einhorn and Hogarth 1981; Feldman and March 1981; Chaturvedi, Mehta et al. 2004). Parallel to this, behavioural economic research proved that the biases creating inference in experimental economics are similar to those in real life. Humans optimize their behaviour as assumed in experimental economics, but from a satisfying criterion because humans are bounded rational (Newell and Simon 1972; Bettman, Payne et al. 1993; March and Simon 1994).

For the understanding of the effect of bounded rationality in economic models, the research area of agent-based simulations emerged (Chen 2004) as a way to observe actual behaviour as opposed to behaviour deduced from a set of axioms. It is this objective to observe actual behaviour that makes simulations a useful platform for the need to collect real-time data in social sciences. The spin-off from behavioural simulations is that participants are able to learn from them; thereby the models exhibit intelligence (Potgieter and Bishop 2002; Wahle, Bazzan et al. 2002; Boer, Ebben et al. 2003; Chaturvedi, Mehta et al. 2004; Hare and Deadman 2004).

Hence, a behavioural simulation makes it possible to collect data on how decision-makers apply and learn from information in the decision-making processes in companies.

Adapting the knowledge on agent-based modelling (Chaturvedi, Mehta et al. 2004; Chen 2004), a behavioural simulation synergizes the benefits of self-administered questionnaires and the experimental design, and furthermore introduces role-playing (Dabholkar 1994; Armstrong 2000) and scenario (Frederickson 1984; Frederickson 1985; Eroglu 1987; Sanderson and Sanderson 2000; White, Varadarajan et al. 2002) strategies as very effective methods to ensure high interaction with the respondents.

The aim of the questionnaire is two-fold in ensuring that information about the decision behaviour in companies is retained and in validating the observed behaviour of respondents in the simulation as to whether it resembles behaviour in companies. Hence, with the questionnaire the specification of the decision parameters is ensured.

Where a questionnaire represents the scope, an experiment focuses on depth by offering the opportunity to give a standardized and controlled presentation of the surroundings (the environment) of the decision situation (Perkins and Rao 1990).

Hence, contrary to the questionnaire the experiment introduces activity and dynamics though the setting is more simplified than the 'real world'; for example, the technological development, the competitive environment, or the uncertainty of demand. As such exogenous factors to the decision-making process can be specified and controlled in the simulation through experimental design. Using the questionnaire for measurement and the experiment for variation, these two methodologies provide the environment for the simulation. To make the simulation interactive role-playing and scenarios are essential methods.

Traditionally, role-playing has been used to forecast decisions in conflict situations among interacting groups, but it can also be used to predict decisions by an individual not interacting directly with others (Armstrong 2000). More importantly the similarity between laboratory research and role-playing is well documented (Dabholkar 1994). The advantage of role-playing is that roles influence a person's perception of a situation. Participants are asked to engage in the role description and then either to imagine their actions or to act them out - in both cases as they would in fact do, i.e. managers should not play customers or vice-versa. The key is to make the role realistic (Eroglu 1987; Armstrong 2000). Therefore, with role-play the decision-maker in the simulation can be specified. Table 1 provides some basic design principles.

Table 1: Basic design principles for role-playing* (Jespersen 2004; Armstrong 2000)

The role-players should be similar to those being represented, meaning that a role-player should act as him/herself
Role-players should read instructions for their roles before reading about the situation
The administrator provides a short yet comprehensive description and creates realistic surroundings in order to provide a realistic enactment of the situation

The scenario is the situation in which the role-play is acted out by the participants and is therefore the heart of the simulation. The strength of using scenarios as frames for the decision-making process is that it makes the respondents relate more directly to the posed subjects, and to a high degree this results in more accurate responses (Eroglu 1987). The ability of a scenario is threefold in that it (i) increases interest in participation, (ii) makes it possible to create a realistic context, and (iii) provides all respondents with a standard stimulus (Frederickson 1984; Frederickson 1985; White, Varadarajan et al. 2002). Also when respondents are presented with a scenario before decision-making, their attention is guided to the relevant problem area. From this viewpoint, the scenario can successfully complement the experimental design by providing control of the decision-making process investigated. Thus, the scenario defines the behaviour of the artificial reality in the model.

The methodological contribution of simulations is a symbiosis of four acknowledged research methods. At the same time, these methods make the simulation very complex. Thus the key to make a simulation suitable for data collection purposes is Web technology, because Web technology can carry out the large database structure upholding the simulation and making the simulation active and dynamic. Therefore, the possibilities with a simulation as a platform for a data collection methodology are closely linked to the use of Web technology when collecting data.

3 The benefits of Web technology

Another important data collection issue is item The use of computers for the collection of data through various methods is well known. As early as in the 1970s the first computerized experiment was launched. Especially within the field of decision-making, experiments have been computer-interactive from early on (Connolly and Thorn 1987). In a study comparing Web-versions with laboratory studies, Krantz and Dalal (2000) found a surprising match for surveys, scales and experimental variables thereby stressing the power of the Web as both a research medium and as experimental medium. For research purposes the computational intelligence available with the Web is still by and large an unexplored territory in social sciences (Stanton 1998; Birnbaum 2000; Englis and Solomon 2000; Reips 2000; Klassen and Jacobs 2001; Jespersen 2004).

Declining response rates – often termed 'survey fatigues' – is of major concern to research. The use of emails has made it easier to target respondents but also easier for respondents to opt-out of research studies (Stanton 1998; Reips 2000; Sheehan 2001). Collecting data with simulations by use of Web technology places the data collection methodology in a known medium for playing games and being active. Hence the appeal of behavioural simulations can be expected to be higher due to Web technology (Stanton 1998; Birnbaum 2000; Englis and Solomon 2000; Reips 2000; Klassen and Jacobs 2001; Jespersen 2004) visualizing the virtual decision-making process. Additionally, as games give players satisfaction from playing, so simulations will provide respondents with satisfaction of a problem-solving experience close to the real worlds of the respondents. Other possible reasons why the response rate may increase with Web technology are (i) the minimization of the response time for participants, (ii) the ease and flexibility of participation since the Internet is available twenty-four hours, seven days a week, and (iii) the lower cost for participants (Birnbaum 2000; Coderre and Mathieu 2004). Still, the experience from email surveys that response rates declines just as for postal surveys may indicate to researchers that they should be very careful about the design of the data collection on the Web. Hence, the design of a Web-based methodology has to be very user-oriented. If the design becomes too heavy or too boring, then participants will drop out as they do on regular web pages.

Another important data collection issue is item completion. Here the Web technology is powerful. Item completion can be simplified through the use of pull-down menus, check boxes, radio button scales, and drop-down scales. These options really make the web-based approach user-friendly. Furthermore, the pages can be programmed to check whether all items have been completed before giving access to the next page, thereby eliminating missing values. Additional four advantages of the web technology can be listed: (i) it is easy to modify the research instrument or to create multiple experimental versions, (ii) the automated data collection eliminates coding errors, (iii) reduction of experimenter effects, and (iv) the ability to reach a larger and more diverse subject pool. But also, the following disadvantages have appeared: (i) the potential for systematic bias and measurement error and (ii) the unwillingness of respondents to provide sensitive information over what they view as insecure lines (Birnbaum 2000), as well as iii) the issue of technical variance among respondents and iv) the issue of a self-selected sample (Reips 2000). Thus, as with any data collection methodology care and consideration should be demonstrated in order to maintain data validity.

4 Ensuring the validity of data

For Web technology supported simulations to become a new methodological trait, the data collected by means of this new research strategy are to be proved valid. Applying Web technology to the data collection vehicle raises the issue of convergent validity compared to a laboratory based study. Comparing laboratory and Web versions of surveys, scales and experimental variables, Krantz and Dalal (2000) find a remarkably consistent correspondence between the two, thereby proving the validity of Web technology as part of research strategies. A notion supported by Coderre and Mathieu (2004) finding that the predictive power of information gathered by email survey outperformed that observed with postal or telephone collected information.

Another issue of internal validity is construct validity by which the results of the data collected with simulations follow theoretically predicted trends. Paying attention to the details when creating the virtual world of the simulation will ensure construct validity. Research using agent-based computational modelling proves that this is not a critical issue for simulations though much lies with the thoroughness of the researcher (Wahle, Bazzan et al. 2002; Boer, Ebben et al. 2003; Chaturvedi, Mehta et al. 2004).

The external validity of data collected with simulations is very critical for the generalization of the research results. Despite the many benefits of a simulation it is a constructed reality that the respondents enter. This constrains the analysis results and introduces the possibility of explaining nothing but the behaviour within the simulation. To counter this criticism several validation questions should be designed into the simulation to observe whether the simulated managerial decision-making process resembles the actual decision-making processes in the participating companies. Still, it must be expected that some results can be explained by the behaviour of the respondents being influenced by the simulation as are decision-makers in specific decision-making situations in companies. Furthermore to validate data, knowledge of various decision-making characteristics should be obtained from the respondents using a questionnaire mapping relevant environmental and company moderators of the behaviour of the respondents.

Combining simulations and Web technology introduces a new type of validity known in agent-based modelling as solution validity (Chaturvedi, Mehta et al. 2004; Jespersen 2004). Solution validity ensures the compatibility between the empirical data collection methods and the model solution in order to secure reliable and valid data. This means restraining the technological possibilities. Though a model of a real decision-process, some constraints have to be imposed on Web technology. A simple example is the habitually used back and forward buttons on the Internet. If these are not locked, the respondents would be able to go back and alter decisions without the researcher's knowledge. Such a simple design consideration would jeopardize the data validity.

The data validity issue is always critical when collecting data but the dimensions to consider are increased when Web technology is applied and several methodologies are combined into one. Still, behavioural simulations will not jeopardize the validity of data collected, if designed properly.

5 Info@performance.NPD

The behavioural simulation as the data collection instrument example was developed for a study of new product development decision-making (Jespersen 2004). The aim was to gain greater insights concerning the value of information when new products are screened in the various phases of the new product development process. The analysis of the information value was two-dimensional, including both the value-for-money and the decision-value of information. Hence, the behavioural simulation focused on the information processing cycle of decision-makers, i.e. whether information was acquired, and whether the acquired information was used for the screening decisions.

5.1. The model: A virtual New Product Development (NPD) process

A virtual NPD process was created in which the participants were asked to acquire information for the evaluation of a new product idea as the product idea moved through the NPD process from idea to market planning. Hence, the simulation ended with the decision whether to launch or not. Because the game scenario used the Internet as medium, it was named Info@performance.NPD. Figure 1 depicts the structure of the simulation.

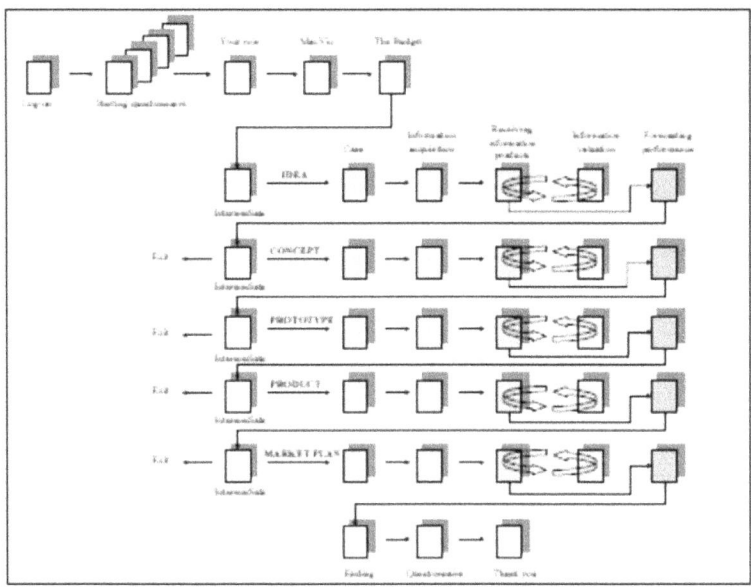

Figure 1: The simulation structure

The starting questionnaire contained questions on new product development in the companies related to market orientation, strategy, budget, new product evaluation and information use. Then, the participants were asked to play the role of the new product development manager in the company MacVic1 and were given a job description. Hereafter followed a brief account of the new product development situation in MacVic followed together with an introduction of the virtual company MacVic.

The description of MacVic focused on the external environmental conditions under which MacVic conducts business. As part of the simulation, the participants were given a monetary budget as they would have in their companies. The budget ensured that the participants had to decide among the different information products, since it was only large enough to cover two-thirds of all the information products in the simulation. The size and use of the budget were validated with a cross analysis of questions from the starting questionnaire.

The simulated NPD process in the game scenario contained a thorough description of the status of the product idea in the five phases of the development process (idea, concept, prototype, product, and market planning) along with a total of thirty-six information products available at different points in the product development process. The available information products that the participants could acquire were designed in accordance with the 'best practices' guidelines developed by research on NPD success and failure (Booz, Allen et al. 1968; Cooper and Kleinsmidt 1987; Souder 1989; Montoya-Weiss and Calantone 1994; Brown and Eisenhardt 1995; Cooper and Kleinsmidt 1995; Crawford 1997; Benedetto 1999; Cooper 1999; Henard and Szymanski 2001). Hence the information products were different in each phase of the NPD process, but always represented the four information types - secondary market information, primary market information, secondary technical information, primary technical information. Furthermore, the information products were ensured a realistic touch through discussions of content, format and costs with professional market research companies. Additionally, the level of competitive stress facing MacVic and as such the participants was designed experimentally and regulated at three levels – low, medium, and high. The participants would encounter competitive stress in the concept and the prototype phases. To measure whether the acquired information was useful to the decision-making each phase ended with the participants evaluating the potential of the new product idea in the simulation on a scale of 0 to 100.

To illustrate the game scenario - Info@performance.NPD, figure 2 shows the concept phase of the NPD process in the simulation. From these webpages it should be possible to get an idea of how the simulation worked. The first Web-page is a description of the product development in the concept phase (picture 1) - what had happened to the product idea since the idea phase. Then the participant can choose from a list of information products (picture 2). The participant rates each information product on an importance scale. The participant then receives the ordered product (pictures 3-4), and rates the value of the individual information product (picture 5). Finally, the participant is asked to evaluate the product idea (picture 6).

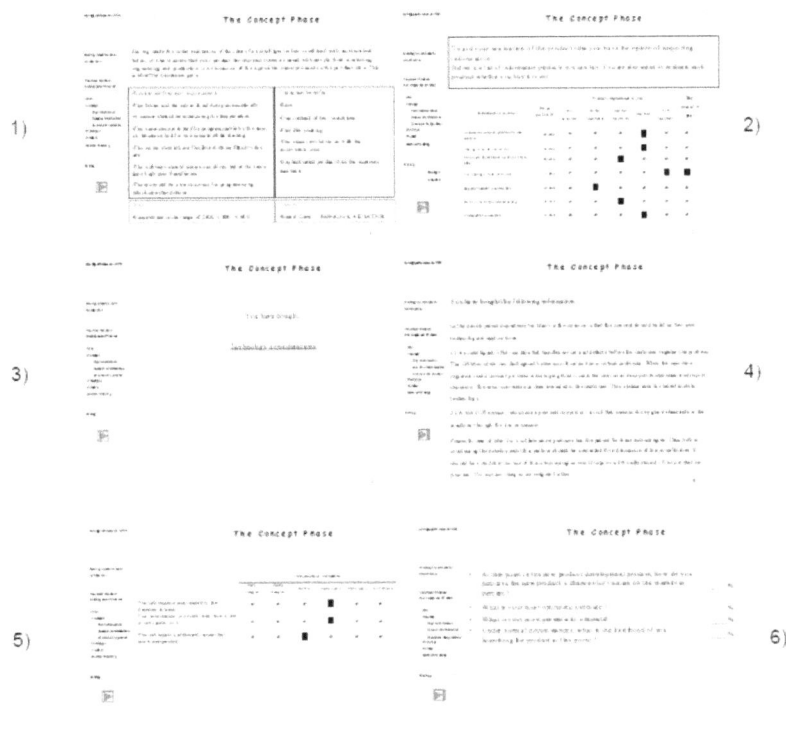

Figure 2: The concept phase simulation in Info@performance.NPD

5.2. Sampling

The sample constitutes larger International companies having their R&D unit placed in Denmark. The targeted companies develop either high or low technology products for the consumer market. Low technology products were represented by the food industry whereas high technology products were represented more diversely by industries such as telecommunication, personal computers, kitchen hardware, speakers, washing machines, tumblers, and headphones. The selection criterion was that the company did product development of consumer products in Denmark. This reduced the population of high technology companies tremendously, and introduced another constraint on the low technology companies: The food companies had to be of a reasonable size because primarily large high technology companies are performing new product development in Denmark. The participants were found either on basis of their job title as R&D manager/director or through organograms from which it was possible to determine whether it would be relevant to contact the marketing, engineering or project manager. A total of 42 companies used the simulation.

5.3. Data validity

Two important aspects of the simulation as a data collection methodology are data validity and the judgment by the participating companies. Data validity was found through analyses of i) the budget, which showed that the participants used the same amount of money in the simulation as they would have in their companies, ii) the price of the different information products, where the relation between importance and the acquisition of an information product demonstrated a reasonable pricing in the simulation, and iii) the information utility of the individual information products. With high average ratings for all information products on the dimensions – relevance, quality and novelty – the information products did not obscure the decision-making process. The participants evaluated the simulation on four dimensions – coherent and easily comprehended new product development process, realistic content, exiting participation, and time consumption (see figure 3).

In general the simulation was found fun to do and very realistic. The only negative aspect was as expected the time used for participation. Though the measured time for participation was sixty minutes with the possibility to break this time down in minor intervals, the reaction to time from the participants was expected as time is always critical. Despite of this several participants expressed their positive experience of science going new ways. All of which seems promising for behavioural simulations as a new methodological trait.

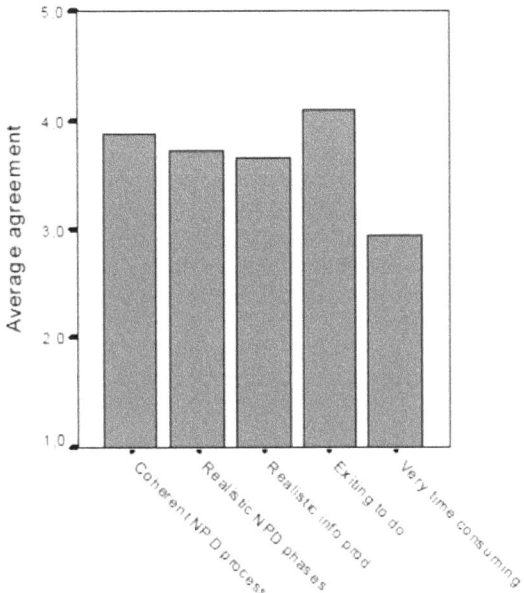

Figure 3: Appeal of the behavioural simulation

6 Implications and future trends

A behavioural simulation is a suitable methodology for the collection of real-time data in all fields as it provides high interaction with respondents and immediate pay-back through learning for the time invested in participation. Furthermore simulations appeal to respondents by applying Web technology. Also, the combination of several methodological traditions is found beneficial for future methodological developments as this will also encourage new collaborations among research fields thereby enhancing the research contribution of future research.

Of course behavioural simulations are to be used with extreme care to both design and sampling in order to ensure validity as well as generalisability. Also the speedy technological development imposes a great challenge on researchers and as such the behavioural simulation can only be expected to be a continuous development to preserve its high appeal.

References

Armstrong, J. S. (2000). Role playing: A method to forecast decisions. *Principles of forecasting: A handbook for Researchers and Practitioners*. J. S. Armstrong, Norwell, MA: Kluwer Academic Publishers, 2000.

Benedetto, C. A. D. (1999). "Identifying the key success factors in new product launch." *Journal of Product Innovation*

Coderre, F. and A. Mathieu (2004). "Comparison of the quality of qualitative data obtained through telephone, postal and email surveys." *International Journal of Market Research* 46(3): 347-357.

Connolly, T. and B. K. Thorn (1987). "Predecisional Information Acquisition: Effects of task variables on suboptimal search strategies." *Organizational Behaviour and Human Decision Processes* 39: 397-416.

Cooper, R. G. (1999). "From Experience: The Invisible Success Factors in Product Development." *Journal of Product Innovation Management* 16: 115-133.

Cooper, R. G. and E. J. Kleinsmidt (1987). "Success factors in product innovation." *Industrial marketing management* 16: 215-223.

Cooper, R. G. and E. J. Kleinsmidt (1995). "New Product Performance: Keys to Success, Profitability & Cycle Time Reduction." *Journal of Marketing Management* 11: 315-337.

Crawford, C. M. (1997). *New products management*, IRWIN.

Dabholkar, P. A. (1994). "Incorporating Choice into an Attitudinal Framework: Analyzing Models of Mental Comparison Processes." *Journal of Consumer Research* 21(June): 100-118.

Einhorn, H. and R. Hogarth (1981). "Behavioural Decision Theory: Processes of Judgement and Choice." *Annual review of Psychology* 32: 53-88.

Bettman, J. R., J. Payne, et al. (1993). *The Adaptive decision maker*, Cambridge University Press.

Birnbaum, M. H. (2000). *Psychological Experiments on the Internet*, Academic Press.

Boer, L. d., M. Ebben, et al. (2003). "Studying purchasing specialization in organizations: a multi-agent simulation approach." *Journal of purchasing and supply management* 9: 199-206.

Booz, Allen, et al. (1968). *Management of new products*, Booz, Allen and Hamilton.

Brown and Eisenhardt (1995). "Product development: past research, resent finding and future directions." *The Academy of management review* 20(2): 343-78.

Chaturvedi, A., S. Mehta, et al. (2004). "Agent-based simulation for computational experimentation: Developing an artificial labour market." *European Journal of Operational Research* (In press).

Chen, S.-H. (2004). "Computational intelligence in economics and finance: Carrying on the legacy of Herbert Simon." *Information Sciences* (In press).

Englis, B. G. and M. R. Solomon (2000). "LIFE/STYLE ONLINE: A web-based methodology for visually-oriented consumer research." *Journal of Interactive Marketing* 14(1): 2-14.

Eroglu, S. (1987). *The Scenario Method: A theoretical, not theatrical, approach.*

AMAEducators Proceedings.
Feldman, M. S. and J. G. March (1981). "Information in Organizations as signal and Symbol." *Administrative Science Quarterly* 26: 171-186.
Frederickson, J. W. (1984). "The comprehensiveness of strategic decision processes: Extension, Observation, future directions." *Academy of Management Journal* 27(3): 445-466.
Frederickson, J. W. (1985). "Effects of decision motive and organizational performance level on strategic decision processes." *Academy of Management Journal* 28(4): 821-843.
Hare, M. and P. Deadman (2004). "Further towards a taxonomy of agent-based simulation models in environmental management." *Mathematics and Computers in Simulation* 64: 25-40.
Henard, D. H. and D. M. Szymanski (2001). "Why some new products are more successful than others." *Journal of marketing research* 38(August): 362-375.
Jespersen, K. R. (2004). Information and New Product Development Decision-making. *Department of Marketing, Informatics and Statistics*. Denmark, The Aarhus School of Business.
Klassen, R. D. and J. Jacobs (2001). "Experimental comparison of Web, electronic and mail survey technologies in operations management." *Journal of Operations Management* 19: 713-728.
March, J. and H. Simon (1994). *Organizations*, Blackwell Publishers, USA.
Montoya-Weiss and Calantone (1994). "Determinants of New Product Performance: A review and meta-analysis." *Journal of Product Innovation Management* 11(11): 397-417.
Newell, A. and H. A. Simon (1972). *Human Problem Solving*, Prentice-Hall, INC.
Perkins and Rao (1990). "The role of experience in information use and decision making by marketing managers." *Journal of marketing research* Feb: 1-10.
Potgieter, A. and J. Bishop (2002). Bayesian agencies in control. *Computational Intelligence in Control*. M. Mohammadian. Hersey, PA, USA, IDea Group Inc.: 168.
Reips, U.D. (2000). *The Web Experiment Method: Advantages, Disadvantages, and Solutions. Psychological Experiments on the Internet*. M. H. Birnbaum, Academic Press: Chapter 4.
Sanderson, A. and S. Sanderson (2000). *Design and Manufacturing Learning Environment: Innovation and product family management.*
Sheehan, K. (2001). "E-mail Survey Response Rates: A review." *Journal of Computer Mediated Communication* 6(2).
Souder, W E (1989) *Managing new product innovations*, Mass., Lexington Books.
Stanton, J. M. (1998). "An Empirical Assessment of Data Collection using the Internet." *Personnel Psychology* 51(3): 709-725.
Wahle, J., A. L. C. Bazzan, et al. (2002). "The impact of real-time information in a two-route scenario using agent-based simulation." *Transportation Research Part C* 10: 399-417.
White, J. C., P. R. Varadarajan, et al. (2002). "The effect of Cognitive Style and Per-

ceived Organizational Culture on Managers Interpretation of and Response to Marketing information." *Journal of Marketing*.

Zaltman (1997). "Rethinking market research: Putting People Back in." *Journal of Marketing Research* 34(November): 424-437.

Individualised Rating-Scale Procedure: A Means of Reducing Response Style Contamination in Survey Data?

Elisa Chami-Castaldi, Nina Reynolds and James Wallace
School of Management, University of Bradford, UK
Originally published in EJBRM (2008) Volume 6: Issue 1.

Editorial Commentary

Most research involves actions which necessarily have an impact on the research domain itself: Positioning oneself as a 'neutral observer' is rarely possible, and interviewing people or simply asking them question has an effect on the participants themselves as well as the research context in general. There are various ways in which such characteristics might be taken into account and allowed for in developing research findings.

In undertaking survey research there are a whole host of issues involved even before respondents get a chance to complete the survey itself – e.g. question design, pilot studies, and sampling. Thereafter there are further key issues such as response bias and differences in various respondents' understanding of the questions themselves. The authors here refer to a generic concern with 'response style contamination'.

Following an overview of various topics on this theme, they outline their specific proposal which is aimed at 'rating-scale length': Using an approach that allowed respondents to select their own rating scales – IRSP (individualised rating-scale procedure). At first glance this seems to be a recipe for disaster, leading to misaligned results and at best only the weakest of bases for coherent and comparable results. In fact the outcome is far more promising than this, although it is notable that the in-depth findings actually come from face-to-face debriefings rather than the survey itself.

Abstract: Response style bias has been shown to seriously contaminate the substantive results drawn from survey data; particularly those conducted using cross-cultural samples. As a consequence, identification of response formats that suffer least from response style bias has been called for. Previous studies show that respondents' personal characteristics, such as age, education level and culture, are connected with response style manifestation. Differences in the way respondents interpret and utilise researcher-defined fixed rating-scales (e.g. Likert formats), poses a problem for survey researchers. Techniques that are currently used to remove response bias from survey data are inadequate as they cannot accurately determine the level of contamination present and frequently blur true score variance. Inappropriate rating-scales can impact on the level of response style bias manifested, insofar as they may not represent respondents' cognitions. Rating-scale lengths that are too long present respondents with some response categories that are not 'meaningful', whereas rating-scales that are too short force respondents into compressing their cognitive rating-scales into the number of response categories provided (this can cause ERS contamination – extreme responding). We are therefore not able to guard against two respondents, who share the same cognitive position on a continuum, reporting their stance using different numbers on the rating-scale provided. This is especially problematic where a standard fixed rating-scale is used in cross-cultural surveys. This paper details the development of the Individualised Rating-Scale Procedure (IRSP), a means of extracting a respondent's 'ideal' rating-scale length, and as such 'designing out' response bias, for use as the measurement instrument in a survey. Whilst the fundamental ideas for self-anchoring rating-scales have been posited in the literature, the IRSP was developed using a series of qualitative interviews with participants. Finally, we discuss how the IRSP's reliability and validity can be quantitatively assessed and compared to typical fixed researcher-defined rating-scales, such as the Likert format.

Keywords and Key phrases: scale length, response styles, response bias, survey research, cross-cultural surveys, individualised rating-scale procedure

1 Introduction

Responses to survey questions include both attitudinal information and response bias. The latter can cause measurement error (Greenleaf 1992a), however, it is the former that is of interest. As such, response bias, that is a tendency to respond systematically to questionnaire items on some basis other than the content of those items, needs to be removed from the data before research results will reflect the construct of interest (Paulhus 1991). Response bias can occur due to the presentation of the construct or measurement instrument; or to respondents trying to portray themselves in a certain way. The former is known as response style, the latter as response set (Rorer 1965). Both types of response bias reduce the validity of research findings (Broughton and Wasel 1990). This paper shows how research instrument design might be used to address response style bias.

Response style bias can result in spurious findings, construct design can affect its manifestation, and it varies along with individual characteristics and across cultures (Berg and Collier 1953; Couch and Keniston 1960; Hamilton 1968; Lorr and Wunderlich 1980; Crandall 1982; Bachman and O'Malley 1984; Cheung and Rensvold 2000). Response style bias is of particular concern in cross-cultural research (Douglas and Craig 1983; Bachman and O'Malley 1984; Ross and Mirowsky 1984; Farh and Dobbins 1991; Chen, Lee et al. 1995; Javeline 1999; Stening and Everett 2001; van Herk, Poortinga et al. 2004).

This paper briefly reviews the types of response style bias; their measurement, current techniques for reducing their contamination of survey data; and their connection to rating-scale length. Subsequently, the paper details the development of the Individualised Rating-Scale Procedure (IRSP), which seeks to address the problem of response styles by means of a dynamic respondent-centred method of attitude measurement. The paper concludes by outlining how the technique's reliability and validity can be tested.

2 Background

2.1. Response bias, data analysis and rating-scale length

Response styles can be divided into three main groups: those related to the use of particular scale points (e.g. extreme responding and mid-point responding), the spread of responses (e.g. index of dispersion), and the respondent's reaction to item direction (e.g. acquiescence) (Diamantopoulos, Reynolds et al. 2006). Response style bias can affect both level and structural comparability in cross-cultural research (van de Vijver and Leung 1997), and can result in the appearance of differences between groups when no differences actually exist and/or can hide real differences between groups (Heide and Gronhaug 1992; Baumgartner and Steenkamp

2001). They can increase the association between variables so that significant relationships appear, yet response style bias can also decrease associations resulting in no apparent relationships in the data (Chun, Campbell et al. 1974; Lorr and Wunderlich 1980; Bardo and Yeager 1982b; Heide and Gronhaug 1992). Various techniques can be used to reduce response style bias (e.g., partial correlations, ANCOVA, etc), however, these generally require the researcher to estimate the extent to which response style bias is present.

Three main methods exist to estimate response style bias; using uncorrelated items to estimate response styles (Greenleaf 1992b); collecting both attitudinal and behavioural information as response style bias can then be estimated due to its lesser impact on more concrete (behavioural) information (Greenleaf 1992a); and estimating response styles from existing questionnaire items (Baumgartner and Steenkamp 2001). However, all have flaws: The first requires a large bank of uncorrelated items from which to draw (and assumes the items are uncorrelated across cultures), the last assumes that existing items on a single questionnaire would not share common variation. The problems with the second method of measuring response styles is that it is sometimes difficult to develop behavioural measures that directly relate to attitudinal constructs, and that doing so could greatly increase the length of any questionnaire (Chami-Castaldi, Reynolds et al. 2006).

Researchers aim to choose a scale length such that it is long enough to maximise the amount of information that can be collected, yet short enough to get accurate responses (Cox III 1980). One of the concerns when deciding on rating-scale length is its effect on response style bias. While a longer rating-scale is likely to lower extreme responding (Hui and Triandis 1989), it is also likely to increase scale attenuation (Wyer 1969). As such a balance is needed and six or seven response categories have long been considered appropriate (Miller, 1956). Nevertheless, if an 'ideal' rating-scale length could be used (for each respondent), then response styles would be less likely to manifest. Theoretical antecedents of response styles are either dispositional (characteristics of the individual) or situational (context or stimulus related) (Snyder and Ickes 1985; Baumgartner and Steenkamp 2001). The effects of these are considered below.

2.2. Response bias - dispositional and situational effects

Dispositional effects, of personality (Cronbach 1946; Cronbach 1950; Berg and Collier 1953; Lewis and Taylor 1955; Zax, Gardiner et al. 1964; Iwawaki and Zax 1969; Norman 1969; Merrens 1971; Crandall 1982); age (Osgood, Suci et al. 1957); education (Light, Zax et al. 1965); gender (Berg and Collier 1953; Lewis and Taylor 1955); culture (Smith 2004); and occupation and social class (see Hamilton (1968) for a summary of these studies) have been studied in relation to response style. The findings are varied and can appear contradictory. However, what can be said is that there appears to be a link between personal characteristics and response styles, and thus it can be hypothesised that:

H1: A respondent's 'optimum' number of response categories will be related to the respondent's characteristics.

Situational factors can discourage or encourage response style manifestation (Snyder and Ickes 1985; Baumgartner and Steenkamp 2001). As such the researcher's measurement choices can directly impact on the data collected from respondents, they should be considered carefully (Rossiter 2002). Factors such as rating-scale length and rating-scale format have been shown to have significant effects on response style bias (Bardo and Yeager 1982b). As such, it is hypothesised that:

H2: Rating-scales with the number of response categories closest to the respondent's 'optimum' number, will be least affected by response style bias.

Traditionally designed measurement instruments usually decide on a standardised rating-scale length for all respondents. Advances in scale development, however, indicate that this may not be necessary.

2.3. Respondent-defined rating-scales

There have been several researchers, in the past, that have argued the benefits of involving the respondent in the generation of more meaningful rating-scales (Kilpatrick and Cantril 1960; Battle, Imber et al. 1966; Donnelly and Carswell 2002; Nugent 2004).

Leading Issues in Business Research Methods

Theoretically, it could be argued that there are three key ways in which a respondent could self-anchor a rating-scale:

- Verbally anchor the scale endpoints,
- Numerically anchor the rating-scale endpoints (i.e. defining the number of response categories they would like to use),
- Conceptually anchor the scale endpoints.

Previous studies have experimented with allowing respondents to conceptually anchor the scale endpoints, in that fixed numerical endpoints are shown to the respondent, before they are asked to anchor the two extreme endpoints with a meaningful scenario (specified by the researcher).

Kilpatrick and Cantril (1960) describe their self-anchoring scale approach as one in which each respondent is asked to describe, in terms of his/her own perceptions, the top and bottom of the dimension on which scale measurement is desired, and then to employ this self-defined continuum as a measuring device. Nugent (2004, p. 171) asked respondents "to imagine a thermometer-type instrument that measures the magnitude of ... depression, with higher scores indicating a greater intensity problem with depression and lower scores indicative of a lower magnitude problem." Respondents conceptualised their maximum and minimum depression intensities by imagining what, for them, would be the most/least depressing scenario they could picture. Bloom et al. (1999) defined this as an individualised rating scale. Measures from these conceptually-anchored rating-scales were found to be reliable (Battle, Imber et al. 1966; Morrison, Libow et al. 1978) and valid (Battle, Imber et al. 1966; Bond, Bloch et al. 1979; Mintz, Luborsky et al. 1979).

These studies demonstrate that respondents can self-anchor a rating-scale, conceptually. Should respondents also be capable of verbally-anchoring and numerically-anchoring their own rating-scales, this would maximise the meaningfulness of the rating-scale. Allowing each respondent to individualise their own rating-scale should, theoretically, account for both dispositional and situational antecedents of response style, and as such result in measures that more accurately reflect respondents' actual opinion (Viswanathan, Sudman et al. 2004). As such, it is hypothesised that:

H3: Measuring constructs using respondent-defined rating-scales will produce more valid measures.

The theoretical issues surrounding the use of individualised rating-scales to minimise measurement error has been considered above. However, before these hypotheses could be tested, it was necessary to determine the feasibility of such a technique and develop a working version.

3 Methodology – Development of the individualised rating-scale procedure (IRSP)

Existing methods of self-anchoring rating-scales do not use the three theoretically possible methods – conceptually, verbally and numerically anchoring – simultaneously. The proposed method, would have respondents independently anchor the numerical as well as verbal endpoints. As such it was necessary to determine the method's feasibility and develop suitable instructions so that respondents could successfully generate personally meaningful response categories.

When examining the feasibility of individualised rating-scales, the concept of agreement/disagreement was chosen to be the focus of measurement. This concept is frequently used in surveys; when measuring respondents' opinions towards products/services (i.e. to what extent they agree/disagree with items), when measuring respondents' psychological characteristics (i.e. Likert-type rating-scales measuring the extent of agreement with a statement representing the 'self'). If an individualised rating-scale procedure (IRSP) were feasible, it would be necessary to compare its performance against a typically-used measurement tool. Given Likert formats are frequently used to measure agreement/disagreement, it was deemed practical and useful that the substantive focus for the IRSP would be on its ability to measure respondents' agreement/disagreement with items.

3.1. Phase one – Qualitative exploration & development

To assess the feasibility of the technique and aid its development, fifteen semi-structured in-depth interviews using different verbal and numerical anchoring methods, were conducted. These provided a rich qualitative ground for exploring the order of instructions, phrase structure, semantics and pictorial aids that yielded the most meaningful rating-scales for respondents.

3.1.1. Main findings

In brief, the results of the interviews indicated that the technique was feasible by:

- Including a visual aid (horizontal line with neutral marked at its centre) to help respondents define their 'ideal' rating-scale.
- Giving respondents a conceptual definition of the agreement and disagreement endpoints.
- Having respondents verbally anchor their endpoints, resulting in them having personally-meaningful representations of the extreme positions.
- Having respondents decide on the number of response categories they want to use.
- Having respondents practice using their individualised rating-scale (IRS) by rating a small batch of uncorrelated items (Greenleaf's (1992b) 16 uncorrelated items were used, given their particular suitability), with the option to revise their numerical endpoints. This task allowed respondents to assess the meaningfulness and distinctness of their response categories before proceeding to the main survey.

3.1.2. The question of comparable data analysis

Prior to this preliminary testing, the issue of comparable data analysis was considered. Given that, even if it were theoretically possible for respondents to numerically (and verbally) anchor their own rating-scales, we considered an important question: 'How can researchers analyse responses obtained from a group of respondents that each have their own uniquely defined number of response categories?' This problem was deemed to be solvable if certain controls were implemented:

- That the concept of agreement/disagreement would be measured on a bipolar rating-scale with a neutral point at its centre,
- That the neutral point be numerically anchored at '0', with its conceptual definition defined to the respondent. This is to ensure that each respondent is given the same conceptual definition of the neutral point (i.e. the same point of origin).
- That the endpoints of the scale represent the respondent's conceptual agreement/disagreement extremes (i.e. that the endpoints to the right/left of neutral represent 'the most they (the respondent) could possibly agree/disagree with a statement'. This is necessary in order

to capture a respondent's entire continuum of cognitive agreement/disagreement.
- That it is assumed that the distance between adjacent intervals on the rating-scale is equal.

The implementation of these controls would allow scores from rating-scales of different lengths, to be converted into a common scores-index, enabling comparable data analysis. This is analogous to a researcher converting data recorded in different units of measurement into a common unit of measurement, such as imperial units (feet, inches) into metric units (metres, centimetres). Figure 1 illustrates this point.

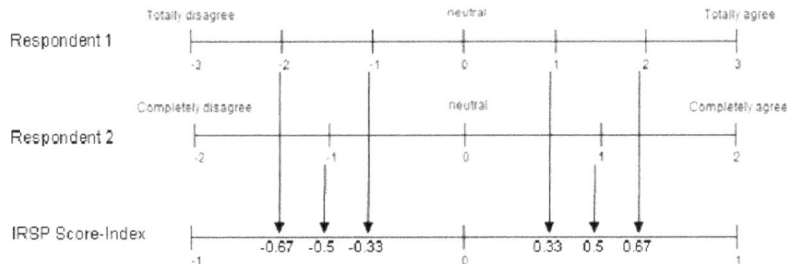

Figure 1: Translation of individualised rating-scale ratings into the IRSP score-index

Notice that in this example, Respondent 1 has chosen verbal anchors that, for him/her, represent his/her conceptual extreme points on the agreement/disagreement continuum. Whilst Respondent 2 has chosen different verbal anchors, conceptually, they represent the same extreme positions. This is an important control in order for differing rating-scales to produce data that is comparable. Here, if Respondent 1 rated their particular agreement with a statement (using their IRS) as '3', this score would be converted into the IRSP score-index of '1'. Should they report a score of '-2', this would be converted to a '-0.67' in the IRSP score-index.

When considering data comparability in this context, it is useful to reflect upon an observation made by Kilpatrick and Cantril (1960: 4),

"One may question the method by asking, are the data comparable from person to person, or group to group, when one allows each individual to anchor the scale on his own terms? Our position is that they are psycho-

logically directly comparable, that is, the scale level selected by one person or group (average of selections) can be specifically and meaningfully said to be higher, lower, or equal to the scale level of some other individual or group, because the frames of reference of the replies are in fact similar psychologically [...] Meaningful numerical comparisons are then possible."

Given this method of measurement is dynamic and respondent-specific, it was clear that a computer program was required, to further develop the technique. This would provide respondents with the facility to use interactive visual aids, with their individualised rating-scales being presented to them on screen, to be used to rate survey statements. There was enough data from phase one, to inform the creation of the IRSP software.

3.2. Phase two – Creation of the IRSP software & further development

Using bespoke online survey software, phase two aimed to (a) determine whether more meaningful response categories could be developed using IRSPversion1 or IRSPversion2, (b) ensure that respondents found the resultant survey user-friendly, and (c) ensure data capture was accurate. Sixteen in-depth interviews were conducted using verbal protocols followed by retrospective debriefings (Taylor and Dionne 2000). Respondents were asked to use an online survey to create an individualised rating-scale (using either IRSPv1 or IRSPv2) and rate items using their individualised rating-scale (IRS) whilst 'thinking aloud' (verbal protocol), and were subsequently interviewed about their experiences with the exercise (retrospective debrief). Given that response styles have been linked with dispositional characteristics, these surveys used several psychological scales, and provided the opportunity to test the suitability of these scales for future IRSP development.

3.2.1. Main findings
Listed are some of the findings that were particularly pertinent or interesting:
- The IRSP survey was viable.
- Respondents carrying out IRSPv2 seemed to produce more personally-meaningful rating-scales, than respondents carrying out IRSPv1. For example, the mysterious attraction to '±10' numerical endpoints (mentioned in Chami-Castaldi, Reynolds et al. 2006), only occurred with respondents that carried out IRSPv1.

- Insights were gained, where respondents chose different verbal anchors for the endpoints of agreement and disagreement.
- Insights were gained, with respondents who chose not to use an equal number of response categories for the positive (agree) and negative (disagree) sides of the neutral point.
- Allowing respondents to practice using their IRS on Greenleaf's 16 uncorrelated items, proved a valuable part of the process for several reasons;
- Respondents could ascertain the ease-of-use of their IRS.
- Respondents could reflect on their responses to the items, and give second thought as to whether their response categories are distinctly meaningful to them, before proceeding to the rest of the survey. This stage allowed respondents to 'reduce' or 'increase' their rating-scale lengths.
- The verbal protocols showed that respondents who had a tendency to acquiesce, for example, became conscious of it when reflecting on their use of their IRS on Greenleaf's items. In some of the retrospective debriefs, these respondents said that after realising this, they subsequently tried to be more honest and accurate about their opinions when rating items in the main survey.
- Qualitative insights gained after each protocol-debrief interview, frequently led to immediate improvements/modifications for both IRSPv1 and IRSPv2. This meant that IRSP development and data collection was done concurrently.

Due to word limit constraints, only some of these findings will be discussed in more detail.

The quantitative data collected from this small sample of 16 respondents, together with the protocol-debrief qualitative insights, appeared to suggest that the IRSPv2 was more effective than the IRSPv1 (in having respondents produce more meaningful response categories). The mean number of response categories for those that used the IRSPv1 was 11.38, with a standard deviation of 7.05. Whereas the mean for those that used the IRSPv2 was 8.88, with a standard deviation of 5.35. Figure 2 helps to illustrate this point.

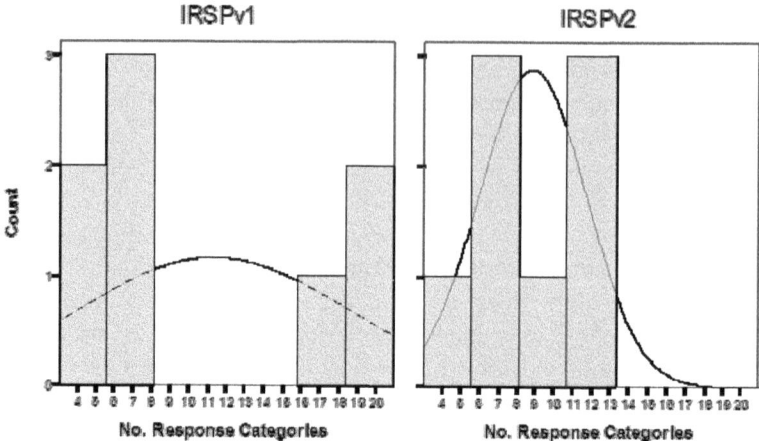

Figure 2: Respondents' chosen no. categories on versions 1 and 2 of the IRSP.

On the whole, respondents were able to easily anchor their own verbal endpoints on the agree/disagree continuum in both versions of the IRSP. There were only three respondents who chose peculiar verbal endpoints, shown in the table below (respondents 13, 5 and 11).

Table 1: Verbal endpoints inputted by respondents (phase two)

*Please note that the Verbal Endpoints reflect respondents' actual spelling.						IRSPv1	
Respondent	Age	M/F	First Language	Ethnicity	National Identity	Verbal Endpoint* (agree)	Verbal Endpoint* (disagree)
1	22	M	French	Other	French	totally	totally
4	24	M	English	White	English	definatley	completley
6	22	F	English	White	English	absolutely	Absolutely
8	21	M	English	White	English	strongly	Strongly
9	25	M	English	White	English	Fully	Fully
13 a	20	F	Polish	White	Polish	minimaly	slightly
15	21	F	Guajarati	Asian/ Indian	British	totally	highly
16	19	F	English	Black African	English	totally	completely

Leading Issues in Business Research Methods

*Please note that the Verbal Endpoints reflect respondents' actual spelling.						IRSPv1	
Respondent	Age	M/F	First Language	Ethnicity	National Identity	Verbal Endpoint* (agree)	Verbal Endpoint* (disagree)
2	21	M	Punjabi	Asian/ Pakistani	British	totally	fully
3	24	M	English	White	British	totally	totally
5 b	26	M	Chinese	Asian/ Chinese	British	ok	not ok
7	18	F	English	White	English	totaly	totaly
10	22	M	German	White	English German	Fully	fully
11 c	22	M	English	White	English	Agree	Strongly
12	29	F	Swedish	White	Swedish	defenetly	totally
14	20	F	English	White	English	definitely	completely

a   This respondent indicated that she misunderstood the verbal anchoring instructions, perhaps due to the language barrier.

b   This respondent indicated that he misunderstood the verbal anchoring instructions, perhaps due to the language barrier.

c   This respondent indicated that he had misunderstood the first verbal anchoring instruction, partly as a result of trying to rush through the exercise, and not reading all the instructions. This explains why his verbal endpoint for 'agree' did not appear to meet the conditions set.

In their retrospective debriefs, respondents 13 and 5 felt that they had misunderstood the verbal anchoring instructions as a result reading the instructions improperly and possibly the language barrier (given that their first languages are Polish and Chinese, respectively). Respondent 11 apologised for his seemingly unusual "agree" verbal endpoint, explaining that he had rushed through the exercise and had not read through all the instructions. Nonetheless, these three respondents (together with all the other respondents) indicated that when rating statements, they treated the endpoints on each side of the continuum as 'the most they could possibly agree/disagree with a statement'.

Insights into how some of the respondents conceptually anchored their endpoints before choosing their verbal anchors, proved interesting. Our prompts were worded carefully, so as to encourage respondents to choose personally meaningful verbal labels (i.e. that they would most naturally use). Several respondents talked about the specific scenarios they had pictured when choosing their verbal anchors. For example, Respondent 6 was asked what she was picturing when she chose the word 'absolutely', and whether she pictured herself talking to somebody. She said "Talking to my mum! [Laughs]." She confirmed that she pictured herself saying "I absolutely agree" to something her mum might say. She felt she would equally use the word 'absolutely' when expressing her extreme disagreement in a conversation with her mother.

Where respondents chose to use different verbal anchors to represent their agreement/disagreement extremes (respondents 4, 15, 16, 2, 12, 14 in Table 1), their reasons for doing so were explored in the retrospective debriefs. It was clear that the verbal anchors they generated were personally meaningful to them, when you consider some of the reasons they gave;

Respondent 16
""I completely agree" doesn't sound like something I would say, whereas, "I completely disagree" is something I would say." She indicated that both her chosen verbal endpoints represented the most she could possibly agree/disagree with something, however, she felt that she would naturally place different adverbs before 'agree' and 'disagree'.

Respondent 4
"When I saw 'agree', - I just - 'definitely' sprung to mind. I think it's the way I talk...maybe I associate 'definitely' with more positive things. And then, um, when I saw the 'disagree' side of things – I just – thought of another word really. I suppose 'completely' just sprung to mind, I don't know if I associate that with being more firm and disagreeing...it was just my opposite."

It is worth noting that all respondents who chose different verbal endpoints indicated that both of their endpoints (although different) represented, for them, their extremes on the agreement/disagreement cognitive continuum. This echoed some of the findings from phase one of our research study (Chami-Castaldi, Reynolds et al. 2006).

This is a particularly interesting finding, given that respondents have been shown to interpret standardised verbal anchors in different ways; inten-

Leading Issues in Business Research Methods

sity, quality (Rohrmann 2003). Rohrmann (2003) highlighted the disadvantages of using standardised (i.e. for all respondents) verbal anchors; inferior measurement quality and proneness to cultural biases. He emphasised the need to create rating-scales using verbal anchors which reflect the cognitions of respondents.

In phase one, it was discovered that some respondents desired numerically-imbalanced rating-scales, in that either the positive (agree) or negative (disagree) side of the continuum had more intervals than on the other side. We ensured that the IRSP software, allowed such respondents to individualise their own rating-scales in this manner. See respondents 4, 16 and 14 in Table 2.

Table 2: Numerical endpoints inputted by respondents (phase two)

Resp	Verbal Endpoint (agree)	Verbal Endpoint (disagree)	Numerical Endpoint (agree)	Numerical Endpoint (disagree)	Modified Numerical Endpoint (agree)	Modified Numerical Endpoint (disagree)
IRSPv1						
1	totally	totally	8	-8		
4c	definatley	completley	3	-3	3	-2
6	absolutely	Absolutely	2	-2		
8	strongly	Strongly	2	-2		
9	Fully	Fully	10	-10		
13	minimally*	slightly*	3	-3		
15	totally	highly	10	-10		
16a	totally	completely	3	-4		
IRSPv2						
2	totally	fully	3	-3	2	-2
3	totally	totally	3	-3		
5	ok*	not ok*	6	-6		
7	totaly	totaly	5	-5		
10	Fully	fully	3	-3		
11	Agree*	Strongly	2	-2		
12	defenetly	totally	4	-4		
14b	definitely	completely	6	-5	5	-4

a *This respondent opted for a numerically-imbalanced scale, in that they desired more response intervals for disagreeing then for agreeing.*

[b] *This respondent opted for a numerically-imbalanced scale, in that they desired more response intervals for agreeing then for disagreeing.*
[c] *This respondent initially defined their IRS as [-3←0→3], which is numerically balanced. He subsequently modified it, after rating Greenleaf's items, to a numerically-imbalanced scale [-2←0→3].*
* *The reason for these peculiar verbal anchors was explained in Table 1.*

Interestingly, respondents 14 and 16 defined a numerically-imbalanced IRS right from the start, whereas respondent 4 initially defined his extreme disagree at '-3' and his extreme agree at '3', providing him with a numerically-balanced IRS with seven categories (a typical length with Likert formats). Respondent 4, after completing Greenleaf's items, realised that whilst he was using all of his varying levels of agreement, he didn't think any 'finer' than two stages when it came to rating his level of disagreement with something. Respondent 14 also chose to modify her IRS (from [-5←0→6] to [-4←0→5]), before proceeding to the main survey. The process of practicing the use of her IRS on Greenleaf's items, led her to evaluate that whilst she did not need quite so many response categories, she still desired more "shades of grey" when 'agreeing' than when 'disagreeing'. This highlights another potential problem with having respondents use researcher-defined fixed rating-scales to rate statements. It is clear that some respondents gradate their levels of agreement to a greater/lesser extent than with disagreement.

This has implications for the instrument validity of researcher-defined fixed rating-scales, and lends further support to the argument for individualised rating-scales

Some respondents became aware of their tendency to adopt a particular response style, after using their IRS to rate Greenleaf's 16 uncorrelated items, and being prompted to reflect upon their responses (a pictorial aid with instructions assisted them with this reflection). One particularly interesting case was respondent 4. When prompted to reflect on the meaningfulness of his [-3←0→3] IRS (after using it to rate Greenleaf's statements), not only did he modify his numerical endpoints (feeling "more comfortable" with a numerically-imbalanced [-2←0→3] IRS), he stated that prior to this point (in his retrospective debrief) that "I didn't realise I was such an agreeing person." When asked whether his realisation of this affected the way he completed the rest of the survey, he responded "I looked at the statements [psychological items] like I did with the first set [referring to

Leading Issues in Business Research Methods

Greenleaf's items] and just thought, "do I completely agree with this?" Um, I didn't want it to be as neutral as before. I wanted to be a bit more assertive with my answers."

When comparing the spread of responses on Greenleaf's uncorrelated items using his [-3←0→3] IRS (Figure 3), to the spread of responses on the subsequent items using his modified [-2←0→3] IRS (Figure 4), it would seem that his tendency to acquiesce was reduced.

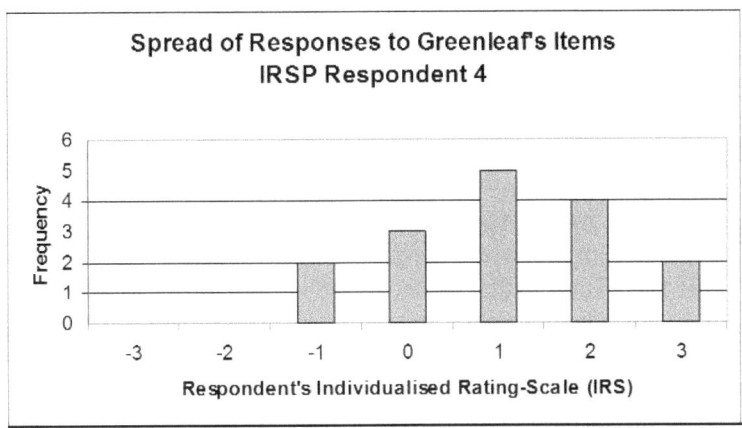

Figure 3: Spread of responses to Greenleaf's uncorrelated items.

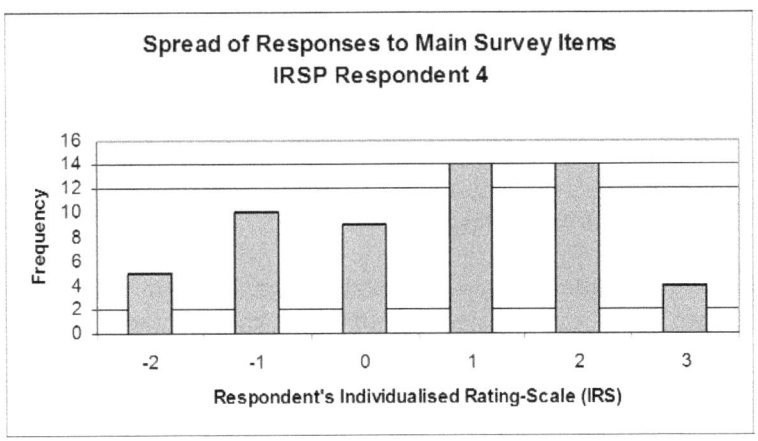

Figure 4: Spread of responses to Greenleaf's subsequent items

3.3. Phase three – IRSP software development & pilot test
A pilot survey with 51 respondents, 24 using IRSPv1 and 27 using IRSPv2, was conducted. This phase was necessary in order to;
- provide a live test for the robustness of the IRSP survey software (i.e. respondents simultaneously completing the survey).
- provide additional data to decide whether IRSPv1 or IRSPv2 would be chosen for the reliability and validity assessment.
- examine how effectively respondents were able to independently carry out the online survey.

Unfortunately, these findings cannot be discussed within the scope of this paper.

4   Future development
In response to Baumgartner and Steenkamp's (2001) call for forms of measurement that are resistant to response style bias, this paper has considered the impact of rating-scale length on response styles. The literature affirms that there is no single 'optimum' rating-scale length for all situations, as it is dependent on the respondent in question (Bonarius 1971; Hui and Triandis 1989; Si and Cullen 1998). This work has established the feasibility of respondents defining their own individualised rating-scales. However, while it may be possible to have individualised rating-scales, the reliability and validity of this measurement method has not yet been established.

Further quantitative research is necessary in order to test the hypotheses presented earlier in this paper (H1 to H3). The use of a multi-group experimental design is planned, together with the inclusion of previously validated psychological constructs in the online survey. This would help determine test-retest reliability, internal consistency, discriminant, convergent and nomological validity (Bagozzi 1994).

To conclude, if individualised rating-scales can be shown to reduce response style bias, then it would be possible to greatly improve research instrument design. Proving this method is legitimate, would be particularly advantageous for cross-cultural researchers where response style bias is especially problematic.

Acknowledgements

We would like to thank Patrick Oladimeji for building the IRSP Survey Software without which we could not have developed the IRSP technique further. His impressive programming skills and hard work have provided us with the tools necessary to continue developing the IRSP and to test it in a forthcoming online survey.

References

Bachman, J. G. and O'Malley, P. M. (1984), "Yea-Saying, Nay-Saying, and Going to Extremes: Black- White Differences in Response styles." *Public Opinion Quarterly*, Vol. 48, No. 2, pp 491-509.

Bagozzi, R. P. (1994). 'Measurement in Marketing Research: Basic principles of questionnaire design', in R. P. Bagozzi (ed.) *Principles of Marketing Research*, Massachusetts, USA: Basil Blackwell Ltd.

Bardo, J. W. and Yeager, S. J. (1982b), "Consistency of response styles across types of response formats." *Perceptual and Motor Skills*, Vol. 55, No. 1, pp 307-310.

Battle, C., Imber, S., Hoehn-Sario, A., Nash, E. and Frank, J. (1966), "Target complaints as criteria of improvement." *American Journal of Psychotherapy*, Vol. 20, No. pp 184-192.

Baumgartner, H. and Steenkamp, J.-B. E. M. (2001), "Response Styles in Marketing Research: A Cross-National Investigation." *Journal of Marketing Research*, Vol. 38, No. 2, pp 143-156.

Berg, I. A. and Collier, J. S. (1953), "Personality and group differences in extreme response sets." *Educational & Psychological Measurement*, Vol. 13, No. pp 164-169.

Bloom, M., Fischer, J. and Orme, J. (1999). *Evaluating practice: Guidelines for the accountable professional*, 2nd, Boston: Allyn & Bacon.

Bonarius, J. C. J. (1971). *Personal Construct Psychology and Extreme Response Style: An interaction model of meaningfulness, maladjustment and communication* Amsterdam: Swets & Zeitlinger, N.V.

Bond, G., Bloch, S. and Yalom, I. (1979), "The evaluation of a "target problem" approach to outcome measurement." *Psychotherapy: Theory, Research, and Practice*, Vol. 11, No. pp 48-54.

Broughton, R. and Wasel, N. (1990), "A text-stimuli presentation manager for the IBM PC with ipsatization correction for response sets and reaction times." *Behaviour Research Methods, Instruments and Computers*, Vol. 22, No. 4, pp 421-423.

Chami-Castaldi, E., Reynolds, N. L. and Cockrill, A. (2006). Respondent-Defined Scale Length: A means of Overcoming Response Style Contamination? ANZMAC Conference 2006: Advancing Theory, Maintaining Relevance., Queensland University of Technology, Gardens Point Campus, Brisbane, Australian and New Zealand Marketing Academy (ANZMAC).

Chen, C., Lee, S.-y. and Stevenson, H. W. (1995), "Response style and cross-cultural comparisons of rating scales among East Asian and North American students." *Psychological Science,* Vol. 6, No. 3, pp 170-175.

Cheung, G. W. and Rensvold, R. B. (2000), "Assessing Extreme and Acquiescence Response Sets in Cross-Cultural Research Using Structural Equations Modelling." *Journal of Cross-Cultural Psychology,* Vol. 31, No. 2, pp 187-212.

Chun, K.-T., Campbell, J. B. and Yoo, J. H. (1974), "Extreme response styles in cross-cultural research. A reminder." *Journal of Cross-Cultural Psychology,* Vol. 5, No. 4, pp 465-480.

Couch, A. and Keniston, K. (1960), "Yeasayers and naysayers: Agreeing response set as a personality variable." *Journal of abnormal and social psychology,* Vol. 60, No. 2, pp 151-174.

Crandall, J. E. (1982), "Social interest, Extreme response style, and implications for Adjustment." *Journal of Research in Personality,* Vol. 16, No. 1, pp 82-89.

Cronbach, L. J. (1946), "Response sets and test validity." *Educational and Psychological Measurement,* Vol. 6, No. pp 475-494.

Cronbach, L. J. (1950), "Further evidence on response sets and test design." *Educational & Psychological Measurement,* Vol. 10, No. pp 3-31.

Diamantopoulos, A., Reynolds, N. L. and Simintiras, A. C. (2006), "The impact of response styles on the stability of cross-national comparisons." *Journal of Business Research,* Vol. 59, No. 8, pp 925-935.

Donnelly, C. and Carswell, A. (2002), "Individualized outcome measures: A review of the literature." *Canadian Journal of Occupational Therapy,* Vol. 69, No. 2, pp 84-94.

Douglas, S. P. and Craig, C. S. (1983). *International Marketing Research* Englewood Cliffs: N. J.: Prentice Hall.

Farh, J.-L. and Dobbins, G. H. (1991), "Cultural relativity in action: A comparison of self-ratings made by Chinese and U.S. workers." *Personnel Psychology,* Vol. 44, No. 1, pp 129-147.

Greenleaf, E. A. (1992a), "Improving rating scale measures by detecting and correcting bias components in some response styles." *Journal of Marketing Research,* Vol. 29, No. 2, pp 176-188.

Greenleaf, E. A. (1992b), "Measuring extreme response style." *Public Opinion Quarterly,* Vol. 56, No. 3, pp 328-351.

Hamilton, D. L. (1968), "Personality attributes associated with extreme response style." *Psychological Bulletin,* Vol. 69, No. pp 192-203.

Heide, M. and Gronhaug, K. (1992), "The impact of response styles in surveys: A simulation study." *Journal of the Market Research Society,* Vol. 34, No. 3, pp 215-230.

Hui, C. H. and Triandis, H. C. (1989), "Effects of culture and response format on extreme response style." *Journal of Cross-Cultural Psychology,* Vol. 20, No. 3, pp 296-309.

Iwawaki, S. and Zax, M. (1969), "Personality dimensions and extreme response tendency." *Psychological Reports,* Vol. 25, No. pp 31-34.

Javeline, D. (1999), "Response effects in polite cultures: A test of acquiescence in Kazakhstan." *Public Opinion Quarterly,* Vol. 63, No. 1, pp 1-28.

Kilpatrick, F. P. and Cantril, H. (1960). *Self-Anchoring Scaling: A Measure of Individuals' Unique Reality Worlds* Washington DC: The Brookings Institution.

Lewis, N. A. and Taylor, J. A. (1955), "Anxiety and extreme response preferences." *Educational and Psychological Measurement,* Vol. 15, No. pp 111-116.

Light, C. S., Zax, M. and Gardiner, D. H. (1965), "Relationship of age, sex, and intelligence level to extreme response style." *Journal of Personality and Social Psychology,* Vol. 2, No. 6, pp 907-909.

Lorr, M. and Wunderlich, R. A. (1980), "Mood states and acquiescence." *Psychological Reports,* Vol. 46, No. 1, pp 191-195.

Merrens, M. R. (1971), "Personality correlates of extreme response style: A function of method of assessment." *Journal of Social Psychology,* Vol. 85, No. 2, pp 313-314.

Mintz, J., Luborsky, L. and Christoph, P. (1979), "Measuring the outcomes of psychotherapy: Findings of the Penn psychotherapy project." *Journal of Clinical and Consulting Psychology,* Vol. 47, No. pp 319-334.

Morrison, J., Libow, J., Smith, F. and Becker, R. (1978), "Comparative effectiveness of directive vs. nondirective group therapist style on client problem resolution " *Journal of Clinical Psychology,* Vol. 34, No. pp 186-187.

Norman, R. P. (1969), "Extreme response tendency as a function of emotional adjustment and stimulus ambiguity." *Journal of Consulting and Clinical Psychology,* Vol. 33, No. pp 406-410.

Nugent, W. R. (2004), "A validity study of scores from self-anchored-type scales for measuring depression and self-esteem." *Research on Social work practice,* Vol. 14, No. 3, pp 171-179.

Osgood, C. E., Suci, G. J. and Tannenbaum, P. H. (1957). *The measurement of meaning* Urbana: University of Illinois Press.

Paulhus, D. L. (1991). 'Measurement and control of response bias', (ed.) *Measures of personality and social psychological attitudes*: Academic Press, Inc.

Rohrmann, B. (2003). *Verbal qualifiers for rating scales: Sociolinguistic considerations and psychometric data.* Australia University of Melbourne: 1-29.

Rorer, L. G. (1965), "The great response-style myth." *Psychological Bulletin,* Vol. 63, No. 3, pp 129-156.

Ross, C. E. and Mirowsky, J. (1984), "Socially-Desirable Response and Acquiescence in a Cross-Cultural Survey of Mental Health." *Journal of Health and Social Behaviour,* Vol. 25, No. 2, pp 189-197.

Si, S. X. and Cullen, J. B. (1998), "Response categories and potential cultural bias: Effects of an explicit middle point in cross-cultural surveys." *International Journal of Organizational Analysis,* Vol. 6, No. 3, pp 218-230.

Smith, P. B. (2004), "Acquiescent Response Bias as an Aspect of Cultural Communication Style." *Journal of Cross-Cultural Psychology,* Vol. 35, No. 1, pp 50-61.

Snyder, M. and Ickes, W. (1985). *Personality and social behavior,3rd,* New York: Random House.

Stening, B. W. and Everett, J. E. (2001), "Response Styles in a Cross-cultural Managerial Study." *The Journal of Social Psychology,* Vol., No. 122, pp 152-156.

Taylor, K. L. and Dionne, J.-P. (2000), "Accessing Problem-Solving Strategy Knowledge: The Complementary Use of Concurrent Verbal Protocols and Retrospective Debriefing." *Journal of Educational Psychology,* Vol. 92, No. 3, pp 413-425.

van de Vijver, F. J. R. and Leung, K. (1997). *Methods and data analysis for cross-cultural research* Thousand Oaks: Sage Publications Inc.

van Herk, H., Poortinga, Y. H. Y. H. and Verhallen, T. M. M. (2004), "Response Styles in Rating Scales: Evidence of Method Bias in Data From Six EU Countries." *Journal of Cross-Cultural Psychology,* Vol. 35, No. 3, pp 346-360.

Viswanathan, M., Sudman, S. and Johnson, M. (2004), "Maximum versus meaningful discrimination in scale response: Implications for validity of measurement of consumer perceptions about products." *Journal of Business Research,* Vol. 57, No. 2, pp 108-124.

Zax, M., Gardiner, D. H. and Lowy, D. G. (1964), "Extreme response tendency as a function of emotional adjustment." *Journal of Abnormal and Social Psychology,* Vol. 69, No. 6, pp 654-657.

Pragmatic Research Design: an Illustration of the Use of the Delphi Technique

Trevor Amos and Noel Pearse
Rhodes University, Grahamstown, South Africa
Originally published in EJBRM (2008) Volume 6: Issue 2.

Editorial Commentary

In their account of the use of the Delphi technique, Trevor Amos and Noel Pearse report on a project that aimed to use the knowledge of domain experts as a primary resource. The paper focuses on research into the way in which higher education institutions might prepare students so that they are 'still able to be entrepreneurial 25 to 40 years after graduating'. This seems a somewhat bizarre question: It assumes that students are initially entrepreneurial when they first graduate; also that they can learn such skills in the first place. But as a basis for use of the Delphi technique it is highly illustrative. The paper refers to a variety of different sources on use of the technique, and the nature of its expected outcomes: In particular the issue of 'consensus'.

Abstract: The creation of wealth is an important issue in any society, and entrepreneurship is regarded as an important catalyst in the creation of new wealth. This presents a challenge to develop entrepreneurship successfully. An important site for the development of entrepreneurship is higher education. The challenge however, is that there is a lack of a general understanding on how to educate students for entrepreneurship. In addition, current thought and practice on entrepreneurship education is historically biased, implying that graduates are essentially prepared for the past instead of for the future. From the perspective of higher education, the problem is how to develop current students to be entrepreneurial in the future. What is needed is to project into the future and then to develop an understanding of what should be taught as well as how it should be taught today. A versatile research technique that can assist in achieving this objective is the Delphi technique, as it is used to conduct futures research or research into areas where knowledge is incomplete. The Delphi method is a type of group interview, using the collective opinion of knowledgeable experts. The technique makes use of several rounds of data collection and feedback to create a consensus of opinion. Making use of the Delphi technique, research is being designed that will formulate expert-based strategic guidelines on entrepreneurial education within the South African higher education sector. The aim of this paper is to illustrate the research design considerations that arise in the use of the Delphi technique for this purpose and how they are addressed. The main characteristics of the Delphi are presented and arguments for the use of the Delphi within a constructivist paradigm are discussed. Practical issues related to the design of the Delphi, panel-member selection, and the formulation of panel questions, are examined. In illustrating these design considerations, the paper demonstrates a pragmatic approach to research design as well as the importance of creating coherence between the research question, the research paradigm, the research method and its use, encouraging research practitioners to adopt a more systematic, deliberate and philosophically-based approach to research design.

Keywords: entrepreneurship, Delphi technique, higher education, entrepreneurial education, innovation, research design.

1 Introduction

This paper presents a research practitioner's perspective of the design and application of a futures research technique, namely the Delphi. The aim of the paper is to identify the design considerations that arise in the use of the Delphi technique and illustrate how they are addressed. The paper applies this illustration in the use of the Delphi, to research being conducted into identifying an appropriate and effective teaching and learning process for entrepreneurial education in South African universities. The paper begins by introducing the origins of the Delphi technique and its main characteristics and types, before providing the context of the relevant research question. In the light of the research question, the appropriateness of the Delphi is considered and justified, followed by a discussion of the philosophical considerations and practical issues in planning the use of the Delphi, and how they are addressed. This example of the use of the Delphi, serves to highlight the interface and tension between the design requirements posed by the research problem versus those requirements imposed by the typical conventions of a research method, and illustrates how a researcher needs to grapple with both philosophical and practical requirements to develop a coherent design that is customised to the particular study's needs.

2 The Delphi technique

The Delphi technique has its origins in Defence research in the United States in the 1950's. "Project Delphi" was the name given to a study of expert opinion originally conducted in the United States of America (USA) at the Rand Corporation during the 1950's for defense research (Dalkey and Helmer, 1963). The method brings a broad range of perspectives and ideas to bear on problem solving from a comprehensive panel of experts responding to feedback (Gibson and Miller, 1990). The method was used by the Rand Corporation to "... obtain the most reliable consensus of opinion of a group of experts ... by a series of intensive questionnaires interspersed with controlled opinion feedback" (Dalkey and Helmer, 1963:458). The purpose of the original study was "... to apply expert opinion to the selection, from the viewpoint of a Soviet strategic planner, of an optimal U.S industrial target system and the estimation of the number of A-bombs required to reduce the munitions output by a prescribed amount" (Dalkey and Helmer, 1963:459).

The Delphi technique is typified by five main characteristics which are discussed in more detail below, namely (1) its focus on researching the future or things about which little is known, (2) reliance on the use of expert opinion, (3) utilising remote group processes, (4) the adoption of an iterative research process, and (5) the creation of a consensus of opinion.

Firstly, Delphi is a futures technique used for "developing forecasts of future events" (Stewart and Shamdasani, 1990:23), for conceptualizing and inventing the future, recognizing that quantitative forecasting tools alone cannot solve forecasting problems, as the historical data on which these techniques depend are unavailable or because the available data provide little or no insight into the probability of events of interest (Stewart and Shamdasani, 1990). It is also useful where there is a "lack of agreement or incomplete state of knowledge concerning either the nature of the problem or the components which must be included in a successful solution" (Delbecq, *et al*, 1975:5), or when modelling is difficult (Gibson and Miller, 1990). In such cases a satisfactory course of action needs to be invented or discovered (Delbecq, Van de Ven and Gustafson, 1975). As a method of data collection and analysis, Beech (1999) argues that the Delphi method produces data that would otherwise be impossible or difficult to obtain.

Secondly, the technique is characterized by the use of a group format (Stewart and Shamdasani, 1990; Denzin and Lincoln, 1994) in the form of panels of knowledgeable experts. The collective opinion of these experts is used as the source of information. Clayton (1997) defines an expert as someone who has the required knowledge and experience to participate in a Delphi. The membership of a panel may be national or international and may come from the same discipline or from different social/professional stratifications.

Thirdly, the Delphi is a form of remote group communication (Jeffery, *et al* 2000) in that it typically does not require face-to-face contact and is particularly useful for involving experts, users, resource controllers or administrators who cannot come together physically (Delbecq, *et al*, 1975). Communication with the individual panel members is typically via mail or faxed but there is also evidence of e-mail being used to distribute the questionnaires (Saint-Germain *et al*, 2000). Saint-Germain *et al,* (2000:163) argue that "the e-mail version of the Delphi method preserves much of the traditional method ... can also improve upon the traditional method ... and provide a quicker response and cut the drop-out rate among participants".

Fourthly, the Delphi uses an iterative research process. The typical Delphi requires a group of relevant experts to respond to an iterative series of written questionnaires (called rounds) interspersed with summarized information and feedback of opinions derived from earlier responses to stimulate thinking mailed or faxed to each respondent individually with the objective of the group reaching consensus.

A fifth characteristic of the Delphi is the development of consensus. Consensus is typically observed through the convergence of variances or the decrease of standard deviations in subsequent iterations (Linstone and Turoff, 1975) and defined as an agreement in opinion of all concerned or as a majority view (Williams and Webb, 1994).

3 Researching entrepreneurial education in South Africa

In South Africa, the changing social and economic needs of a global world as well as South African legislation is emphasising the need for higher education in the country to become more responsive to the nation's needs. Current economic and social indicators in South Africa as well as future projections point to a desperate need for wealth creation in the face of a critical skills shortage.

An important catalyst in wealth creation is entrepreneurship (Timmons, 1999). But, an "entrepreneurial culture" is still missing in South Africa, as well as the broader presence of entrepreneurs as initiators and innovators (Louw, Du Plessis, Bosch and Venter,1997; Van Aard, Van Aard and Bezuidenhout, 2000). Intervention in facilitating the permeation of entrepreneurship in any economy is clearly sensible (Binks and Vale, 1990). In particular, Binks and Vale (1990:173) call for "… investment in educational and attitudinal policies which encourage freedom of thought, creativity, and imagination". According to Davidson (2002:19), "entrepreneurs are made, not born", and there seems to be general agreement in the literature and growing evidence that entrepreneurship can be developed through education (Brockhaus, 1991; McMullan and Vesper, 2000; Kent. Cited in Cronje, Du Toit & Motlatla, 2000; Ronstadt, 1987).

The most obvious and ideal place for entrepreneurship education is the university (Hull, Bosley and Udell, 1980; McMullan and Long, 1987). In fact, Chia (1996) argues that the cultivation of the entrepreneurial imagination is the single most important contribution of universities to their national economies. Congruence between the output of higher education and the needs of an economy is of vital importance (Department of Education, 1997) as is the appropriateness and effectiveness of the teaching and learning process (Scott, 1994). A critical issue is not whether entrepreneurship can be taught but rather how it can best be taught (in addition to the content, educators are challenged with designing effective teaching and learning processes and opportunities), for pedagogies to reflect the changing times and for the field of entrepreneurship education to stay on the "cutting edge" (Solomon, Duffy and Tarabishy, 2002).

Timmons (1999) argues that it is the result of entrepreneurship that counts. Ideally what is needed then is Schumpeterian or N-entrepreneurship (entrepreneurial activity that relies upon a completely new combination of resources) as compared to routine entrepreneurship (entrepreneurial activity that refines existing combinations) (Leibenstein, 1968). Marginal micro-enterprises providing what Bhidê (2000:360) calls " ... routine services in mature fields such as lawn care and beauty salons" are not required, as their high rate of appearance and disappearance has limited economic significance (Bhidê, 2000). Schumpeter (1934) identified innovation as the single factor that specifically distinguishes entrepreneurial from other activities and the driving force for creating new demand and therefore wealth. For Schumpeter an entrepreneur is "the person who destroys the existing economic order by introducing new products and services, by creating new forms or organisation, or by exploiting new raw materials" (Bygrave. In Bygrave, 1997:1).

While literature highlights the function of the entrepreneur in an economy as that of innovation, there is a lack of understanding of the "psychology" or qualities of an individual who can be innovative. Also, Coberly (1996) argues that educators need to help people prepare for a continuously changing workplace and for the future. However, it is difficult doing this when there is a lack of knowledge and understanding of what that future will be like. What is needed is to develop an understanding of the future economy as the context wherein graduates will need to see and realise innovative opportunities. In addition, there is a need to determine the qualities of an innovative individual in light of the context in which the person will apply their ability to innovate. Having developed an understanding of the qualities of innovative individuals for the future economy, the next question concerns what Higher Education needs to do to develop entrepreneurs.

In the light of this discussion, the research question being posed in this study is "What should Higher Education be doing to ensure that students are still able to be entrepreneurial 25 to 40 years after graduating?"

Addressing this question involves addressing three subsidiary questions, which also provide the basis of a three-phase research procedure. These questions are:

1. What sector of the South African economy will most likely offer the greatest potential for entrepreneurial opportunities in the next 25 to 40 years?
2. What qualities are needed by graduates to equip them to be innovative entrepreneurs in the future?
3. What should Higher Education in South Africa do to prepare/develop students to constructively participate in the future economy as innovative entrepreneurs?

4 The relevance of the Delphi technique for the research problem

In examining the key characteristics of the Delphi technique, its relevance to addressing the above research question becomes clear. Firstly, the research focuses on future requirements rather than current practice. Secondly, relatively little is known about these requirements. While the Delphi technique is able to address these requirements, most other research methods are not, as they tend to focus on historical or current realities. Even survey designs which may ask respondents for their opinions of the future, are restrictive in that they present a preconceived construction, usually derived from the literature, which itself has a historical bias.

Thirdly, the research questions lend themselves to making use of a wide range of experts. However, these groups of experts are geographically dispersed both within South Africa, and internationally. Fourthly, the research is an iterative process, requiring an answer to one question before proceeding to the next. With regard to data collection, most other research designs are restricted in time and place and do not engage with the research participants in setting the direction of the research and collaboratively and progressively constructing an answer to the research question. While longitudinal research designs are less restrictive with respect to their time dimension, they do not have the same flexibility as the Delphi in allowing the emergence of the research problem, and focus on the unfolding of events in current reality, rather than on future projections. Similarly, while case studies may document the unfolding of events and processes over time, they are also historically focused. Furthermore, the Delphi explicitly facilitates the interaction of experts in this construction process rather than assuming that the researcher holds the monopoly on knowledge construction. This implies that not any and every opinion is accepted at face value, but through the iterative process, needs to stand up to the scrutiny of experts.

However, the question of meeting the Delphi characteristic of consensus requires a more detailed discussion, as the use of a technique that traditionally produces quantified results within a recognizably positivist approach does not seem to serve the requirements of this research. Given the research question, the entrepreneurship education research process required here is essentially qualitative in nature with exploration, identification and description of multiple realities as the main intention, rather than the determination of a single consensus.

While consensus was originally thought of in a statistical sense, different understandings of the idea of consensus are reflected in different versions of the Delphi technique that have emerged. There are three main variations, namely the numeric, the policy and the historic versions (Strauss and Ziegler, 1975; Reid. In Ellis, 1988). The numeric Delphi represents its original design, which aims to specify a single or minimum range of numeric estimates through the use of summary statistics. On the other hand, the policy Delphi and historic Delphi tend to produce more qualitative responses (Reid. In Ellis, 1988). The policy Delphi does not focus on establishing a single consensus relative to a specific reality but on the exploration, generation and definition of several alternatives and the arguments for and against each of these alternatives (Strauss and Ziegler, 1975; Mitchell, 1991) along with their underlying assumptions and views (Turoff. In Linstone and Turoff, 1975). The historic Delphi is retrospective and aims to "... explain the range of issues that fostered a specific decision or the identification of the range of possible alternatives that could have been poised against a certain past decision" (Strauss and Ziegler, 1975:253). Reid (in Ellis, 1988) states that with the policy and historic versions of Delphi "the collation of these responses will require some subjective judgments, but the normal practice is to feed back the full range of opinions or statements produced with some indication of the strength of support for each, and to invite the panel to reconsider on the basis of this information".

Considering the different approaches to the achievement of consensus should be reflected in debates about the research paradigm underlying the use of the Delphi technique, but explicitly debating and identifying the appropriate paradigm is often neglected.

The Delphi however does have a hybrid epistemological status as it straddles the qualitative and quantitative divides (Critcher and Gladstone, 1998), and evident in the literature is use of modified Delphi methods (Jeffery, Hache and Lehr, 1995; Cox and Hooper, 1998; Stewart and O'Halloran, 1999). Selecting from the range of paradigms identified by Guba (1990), when considering the ontology and epistemology appropriate to this research design, a constructivist paradigm is adopted.

Firstly, the research adopts a relativist ontology. This implies that "realities exist in the form of multiple mental constructions, socially and experientially based, local and specific in nature" (Guba, 1990; Guba and Lincoln. In Denzin and Lincoln, 1998:200). Also, the three-phase approach to the Delphi which is proposed here not only attempts to bring together multiple realities and perspectives at each phase, but in progressing from one phase to the next also entails the combination of different worlds, as the research moves from the realm of South African economic futures, to psychological requirements, to questions of educational policy, curriculum, teaching and learning within higher education.

Secondly, the research adopts a subjectivist, transactional epistemology. Subjective interaction is used to access the realities that exist only in the minds of respondents (Guba, 1990). The investigator and the object of investigation are assumed to be interactively linked with the "findings" being the creation of the process of interaction between the two, literally being created as the investigation proceeds (Guba and Lincoln. In Denzin and Lincoln, 1998; Guba, 1990). The conventional distinction between ontology and epistemology consequently disappears (Guba and Lincoln. In Denzin and Lincoln, 1998). A hermeneutic/dialectic methodology is used to identify the variety of constructions that exist and bring them into as much consensus as possible (Guba, 1990). The constructions are elicited and refined through interaction between and among investigator and respondents and interpreted using conventional hermeneutical techniques (Guba and Lincoln. In Denzin and Lincoln, 1998; Guba, 1990).

In the entrepreneurship education Delphi, the researcher essentially adopts a role of what Miller and Crabtree (1992) call the constructivist inquirer. Here the researcher performs "... an ongoing iterative dance of discovery and interpretation" (Miller and Crabtree, 1992:11). The final aim is

"... to distill a consensus construction that is more informed and sophisticated than any of the predecessor constructions" (Guba and Lincoln. In Denzin and Lincoln, 1998:207).

5 Practical issues in the Delphi research design and procedure

While it has been argued that the Delphi technique is both relevant and flexible enough to be useful in addressing the entrepreneurial education research question posed above, there are still a number of practical considerations that need to be addressed, namely designing the Delphi, member selection and panel questions. These considerations need to be addressed in the context of the paradigm relevant to the research question and in light of the fact that the research consists of three phases to systematically address the three subsidiary questions.

5.1. Delphi design

Delphi typically uses one panel with a number of rounds. However, the range of expertise and layering of the questions for this research requires a phased approach of three Delphi studies each with its own number of rounds. Each Delphi has its own objective yet is relevant to the next Delphi.

In phase one the focus is on clarification of the nature of the future economy. From the perspective of entrepreneurship education, where entrepreneurial opportunities are most likely to be found in the future economy need to be identified, in order to help clarify educational priorities. The objective of the phase is to identify a sector/area in the economy that will most likely make a significant contribution to economic growth and hence offer entrepreneurial opportunities. Another objective is to determine the technical skills domain of graduates entering the economic sector identified. A tension that emerges in this phase concerns the role of published literature versus the role of expert opinion, whether a Delphi is required, and if so, for what purpose. Published reports are available on the future growth areas and skill requirements of the South African economy, but these reports tend to have a shorter time horizon than 25-40 years from now. The suitability of a numeric version of the Delphi in this phase consequently arises from the need to establish consensus around economic and educational priorities 25-40 years from now.

Phase two of the research moves onto the qualities that will be required of the innovative entrepreneur participating in the economy in the next 25 to 40 years. This phase requires a policy-type Delphi. The objective of this phase is to formulate a profile of the person who will be able to participate successfully as an innovative entrepreneur in the identified sector of the economy.

Having an idea of the profile of the innovative entrepreneur in mind, the focus shifts in the third phase to the preparation and education of these individuals within the Higher Education context of South Africa. The objective of the phase is to identify what Higher Education in South Africa needs to do to prepare and develop students to participate in the economy in 25-40 years as innovative entrepreneurs. Here the policy variation of Delphi is appropriate in that the focus is more on the exploration of alternatives regarding what can be done to prepare and develop innovative entrepreneurs. Three separate Delphi panels can be used with alumni of entrepreneurship education programmes first judging the teaching and learning practices and processes that were used in their education, current academics teaching entrepreneurship in South Africa judging the adequacy of what is currently being done in the light of the requirements identified, and lastly educationalists and academics teaching entrepreneurship in South Africa creating insight into what higher education can do to develop the innovative entrepreneur.

5.2. Member selection

An important practical consideration here concerns who is most qualified as an expert to serve on a particular Delphi panel. Again this decision is influenced by the objective of the particular Delphi.

Phase One requires panel members to be experts on the South African economy. Criteria for membership to the panel will be based on their representation on bodies such as the South African Department of Trade and Industry (DTI), or the Human Sciences Research Council (HSRC), since they are involved in futures research relevant to the South African economy and the future skills requirements.

Given the objective of phase two, experts can include those knowledgeable in the area of entrepreneurship. Criteria to be used to identify experts include individuals occupying an endowed Chair in the area of entrepreneurship. The task of this panel of experts will initially be that of creating insight into the qualities of an innovative entrepreneur and to judge the appropriateness and importance of the qualities.

Given the objective of phase three, individuals who can assist in this phase include alumni who will be selected on the basis of having graduated from a university programme designed specifically to develop entrepreneurs, educationalists selected on the basis of their role in the South African Higher Education Quality Committee (HEQC) and academics responsible for designing entrepreneurship programmes and teaching entrepreneurship in South Africa universities.

5.3. Panel questions

The future focus of the research is a particular challenge for researchers. The challenge is to get individuals to see into the future, which in itself is difficult. Questions arise as to the appropriate time period in the future, how to get panel members to project themselves into the relevant time period, and how to get them to provide valid and reliable information. Much depends on the formulation of the question for panel members. The question for panel members would be "What do you envisage the economic growth areas to be in 25 to 40 years from now, and what academic disciplines would primarily be required to realise this growth?"

With the results of phase one in mind, the panel members in phase two need to generate a profile of an innovative entrepreneur who is a graduate from one of the specified academic disciplines, and is able to participate in an innovative way in the specified sector of the economy. A question for panel members might be "What knowledge, understanding, skills, behaviour, attitudes and thinking are required of the innovative entrepreneur?"

The third phase, involving Delphi panels would pose different questions to each panel. Alumni would need to initially describe the teaching and learning activities and processes used in their education and would then be asked to judge these activities and processes. Academics involved in teaching entrepreneurship will describe the teaching and learning activities and processes used to develop entrepreneurs and would be asked to judge the activities and processes in the light of the results generated in the previous phases. Academics teaching entrepreneurship as well as educationalists would be asked "What do Universities in South Africa need to do to prepare and develop students as innovative entrepreneurs?"

6 Conclusion

This paper illustrates a pragmatic approach to research design. In illustrating the use of the Delphi in this paper, it is apparent that the research problem at hand drove research design considerations. Therefore, the research design needs to adapt to the research problem's requirements, rather than being imposed upon and reformulating the problem. The Delphi technique is a versatile research method used for futures research, or for research into areas where knowledge is incomplete. As illustrated above, no other research design seems to offer the same degree of versatility. However, when using the technique, this versatility may lead to superficial consideration being given to its appropriate use, from the perspective of the philosophy of the research, and the overall coherence of the research design. The researcher needs to systematically think through and construct the relationship between the research problem, the appropriate research paradigm and the design of the research. By engaging in debate about the philosophy of the research design, the researcher is able to not only determine the relevance of the Delphi but also to plan the appropriate use of the technique. In considering entrepreneurial education research, these considerations were evident in the formulation of the research paradigm and in the design of a three-phase approach.

In planning the use of the Delphi careful attention needs to be paid to practical issues in the design and use of the Delphi. In particular, the researcher needs to carefully consider the specific purpose for which the Delphi is to be used in the research which in turn assists in determining the type of Delphi. In considering the purpose, it is useful to formulate clear objectives for the Delphi in line with the research question. It is also useful to clarify the task of the panel in terms of either judging information and/or creating an understanding, or new knowledge. Attention also needs to be paid to who will be selected and on what basis, to participate as members of the panel. Finally, attention needs to be paid to the questions to be posed to the panel to elicit information relevant to the research question. The objectives for the Delphi assists in the formulation of questions, but the biggest challenge here is to understand the concept of the future in relation to the research question, and to formulate questions for the panel which will elicit information relevant to the research.

References

Beech, B. (1999) Go the Extra Mile: use the Delphi Technique. *Journal of Nursing Management*, Vol. 7, No. 5, pp 281-288.

Bhidè, A.V. (2000) *The Origin and Evolution of New Businesses*, Oxford University Press, New York.

Binks, M. and Vale, P. (1990) *Entrepreneurship and Economic Change*, McGraw-Hill Book Company, London.

Brockhaus, R.H. (1991) Entrepreneurship Education and Research Outside North America, *Entrepreneurship Theory and Practice*, Vol. 15, No. 3, pp 77-84.

Bygrave, W.D. (1997) *The Portable MBA in Entrepreneurship*. 2nd edition. John Wiley & Sons, Inc, New York.

Chia, R. (1996) Teaching Paradigm Shifting in Management Education: University Business Schools and the Entrepreneurial Imagination, *Journal of Management Studies*, Vol. 33, No. 4, pp 409-428.

Clayton M (1997) Delphi: a Technique to Harness Expert Opinion for Critical Decision-Making Tasks in Education *Educational Psychology*, Vol. 17, Iss 4, pp 373-386.

Cronje, G.J. de J., Du Toit, G.S. & Motlatla, M.D.C. (2000) *Introduction to Business Management*, 5th Edition, Oxford University Press, Cape Town.

Dalkey, N and Helmer, O. (1963) An Experimental Application of the Delphi Method to the use of Experts, *Management Science*, Vol. 9, pp 458-467.

Davidson, P. (2002) What Entrepreneurship Research can do for Business and Policy Practice. *International Journal of Entrepreneurship Education*, Vol. 1, No. 1, pp 2-24.

Delbecq, A.L., Van de Ven, A.H. and Gustafson, D.H. (1975) *Group Techniques for Program Planning: a Guide to Nominal Group and Delphi Processes*, Scott, Foresman and Company, Glenview, Illinois.

Denzin, N.K. and Lincoln, Y.S. (1994) *Handbook of Qualitative Research*, SAGE Publications, London.

Department of Education. (1997) *White Paper on Higher Education 3, a Programme for the Transformation of Higher Education*, Pretoria: Department of Education. http://www.polity.org.za/govdocs/white_papers/highed.html.

Ellis, R. (1988) Editor. *Professional Competence and Quality Assurance in the Caring Professions*, Chapman and Hall, London.

Gibson, L.J. and Miller, M.M. (1990) A Delphi Model for Panning "Preemptive" Regional Economic Diversification, *Economic Development Review*, Vol. 8, No. 2, pp 34-41.

Hull, D.L., Bosley, J.J. and Udell, G.G. (1980) Renewing the Hunt for the Heffalump: Identifying Potential Entrepreneurs by Personality Characteristics. *Journal of Small Business Management*, Vol. 18, No. 1, pp 11-18.

Jeffery, D., Ley, A., Bennun, I. And McLaren, S. (2000) Delphi Survey of Opinion on Interventions, Service Principles and Service Organization for Severe Mental Illness and Substance Misuse Problems, *Journal of Mental Health*, Vol. 9, Issue 4, pp 371-384.

Leibenstein, H. (1968) Entrepreneurship and Development. *The American Economic Review*, Vol. LVIII, No. 2, pp 72-83.

Linstone, H.A. and Turoff, M. (1975) Introduction. In Linstone, H.A. and Turoff, M. (eds) *The Delphi Method: Techniques and Applications*, Addison-Wesley Publishing Company, London.

Louw, L., Du Plessis, A.P., Bosch, J.K. & Venter, D.J.L. (1997) Empirical Perspectives on the Entrepreneurial Traits of Undergraduate Students at the University of Port Elizabeth: an Exploratory Study, *Management Dynamics: Contemporary Research*, Vol. 6, No. 4, pp73-90.

McMullan, W. and Vesper, K.H. (2000) Becoming an Entrepreneur: a Participant' Perspective. *Entrepreneurship and Innovation*, February, pp 33-43.

McMullen, W.E. & Long, W.A. (1987) Entrepreneurship Education in the Nineties, *Journal of Business Venturing*, Vol. 2, No. 3. pp 261-275.

Mitchell. V.W. (1991) The Delphi Technique: an Exposition and Application. *Technology Analysis and Strategic Management*, Vol. 3. No. 4, pp 333-357.

Ronstadt, R. (1985) The Educated Entrepreneurs: a new era of Entrepreneurial Education is Beginning. *American Journal of Small Business*, Vol. 10, No. 1. pp 37-53.

Saint-Germain, M.A., Ostrowski, J.W. and Dede, M.J. (2000) Oracles in the Ether: Using an e-mail Delphi to Rvise an MPA Curriculum, *Journal of Public Affairs Education*, Vol. 6, No. 3, pp 161-172.

Schumpeter, J.A. (1934) *The Theory of Economic Development: an Inquiry into Profits, Capital, Credit, Interest and the Business Cycle*, translated by Opie, R. (1949), Harvard Business Press, Cambridge, Massachusetts.

Scott, I. (1994) *The Role of Academic Development Programmes in the Reconstruction and Development of Higher Education*, A draft position paper produced for the IDT-sponsored investigation into future funding mechanisms for Academic Development programmes.

Stewart, D.W. and Shamdasani, P.N. (1990) *Focus Groups: Theory and Practice*, SAGE publications, London.

Strauss, H.J. and Zeigler, L.H. (1975) The Delphi and its Uses in Social Science Research, *The Journal of Creative Behaviour*, Vol. 9, No. 4, pp 253-259.

Timmons, J.A. (1999) *New Venture Creation: Entrepreneurship for the 21st Century*, 5th edition, Irwin McGraw-Hill, Boston.

Van Aardt, I., Van Aardt, C. and Bezuidenhout, S. (2000) *Entrepreneurship and New Venture Management*, 2nd Edition, Oxford University Press, Cape Town.

Williams, P.L. and Webb, C. (1994) The Delphi Technique: a Methodological Discussion. *Journal of Advanced Nursing*, No. 19, pp 180-186.

Googling Companies - A Webometric Approach to Business Studies

Esteban Romero-Frías
University of Granada, Spain
Originally published in EJBRM (2008) Volume 7: Issue 1

Editorial Commentary
This is another example of a paper that takes account of the opportunities afforded by the development of the internet and WWW to offer new ways of thinking about research. The paper uses an existing research approach – bibliometrics – and applies it to the WWW, in the context of business research. The research itself makes imaginative use of the data, developing insights that the number and nature of weblinks might be indications of business similarities, potential competitors, and overall performance. The author provides some general pointers to sources on the new approach of Webometrics, and then offers brief accounts of some case studies from the literature.

Abstract: So far Internet studies have focused mainly on using website content for gathering business information, however web hyperlinks have not been exploited enough for business purposes yet. Webometric techniques are based on the exploitation of information contained in the hyperlinks that connect the different documents contained on the Web. Webometrics could be considered as a new discipline that applies bibliometric techniques to the quantitative study of the Web, but also a discipline that progressively develops its own concepts and methodology. So far studies in this field have focused on academic and scholarly web spaces; however this methodology is equally applicable to commercial sites which are more predominant on the Web. This paper is intended to show how webometric techniques could be applied to business and management studies. Therefore, it describes a number of basic concepts and techniques and the way in which they have been applied to these fields so far. Firstly, some studies found that the number of links pointing to companies' websites correlates significantly with the business performance measures of the entity. This finding suggests that links to a website could be used as a timely indicator of business performance. Secondly, the examination of co-links, which refers to web pages that links two business sites simultaneously, have been used for competitive intelligence purposes. These studies are based on the idea that the number of co-links to the websites of a pair of companies is a measure of the similarity between them. For instance, this similarity measure between companies in the same industry can provide information about their competitive positions. Finally, motivations for the creation of hyperlinks to business sites could be analysed through a content analysis approach in order to get confirmation about the business relevance and nature of links. This view complements the quantitative perspective to link and co-link research, providing a brand new approach to business studies.

Keywords: web mining, webometrics, business intelligence, business management, internet studies

1 Researching the Web: why hyperlinks do matter

Since its creation in 1989, the World Wide Web (the Web) has revolutionised the Internet, facilitating the access to information to many potential users. Two decades later, the Web has become part of the daily lives of many people all over the world, causing deep social transformations that social scientists struggle to understand. Moreover, for the past five years, the Web has undergone significant changes by the popularisation of the so-called Web 2.0 (O'Reilly, 2005). This has provoked a democratisation of the information creation tools in such a way that millions of people have started to participate in a global conversation based on the use of no cost, user friendly, multimedia and Web-based software (Jenkins, 2006). The blossoming of publishing on the Web has made the media more difficult to understand, always in a process of constant change, described by many as chaotic, uncontrolled and of poor quality (Keen, 2007). However, the Web and the Internet as a whole are the largest repositories of information ever known in history.

In 2008, the official Google blog (2008) reported that the number of pages indexed had grown to more than one trillion (as in 1,000,000,000,000) unique URLs (Uniform Resource Locators). Technorati (2009), the main blog search engine, reported to be tracking on the order of 133 million blogs by the end of 2008. Most, if not all, of the human activities, whether they are political, social, educational or economical are reflected on the

Internet, and some have developed native online phenomena that would not exist in the offline world.

The available collection of information makes it possible to define the Web as an enormous unstructured and heterogeneous database that, despite its appearance, is not randomly built. This implies that this could be exploited from different perspectives (based on content, structure and user behaviour) in order to study unique online phenomena or offline phenomena reflected in the Web. A basic component of the array of information available is the hyperlink.

A hyperlink is a reference or navigational element in a document to another section of the same document or to another document that may be on or part of a different domain. Hyperlinks represent the hidden structure of the Web connecting different sites and we pages that would stay isolated unless the specific URL is known (Berners-Lee, 1999). They can be regarded as an endorsement of a target page, especially if the creator has placed that link because it points to a useful or relevant resource. The creation and exploitation of hyperlinks are not an irrelevant phenomena, but imply significant social repercussions (Turow and Lokman, 2008). It is not meaningless that currently most of the search engines use link analysis as part of their algorithms to crawl websites and to rank the pages (Batelle, 2005).

Google's market dominance derives originally from the technological lead established by the Pagerank system introduced in 1998 (Brin and Page, 1998). This Pagerank is based on hundreds of factors that have changed over time in order to avoid manipulation, but basically follows two principles:
- Web pages that have more links pointing to them are considered to be more relevant.
- Not all the hyperlinks have the same value. Those links established by relevant web pages are more valuable than others from less well known web pages.

However, hyperlinks are not a perfect source of evidence because many of them have not been created by a thoughtful process in order to endorse or discredit a webpage. Many links are created for navigational purposes within a site; others are just automatically created by content management systems or, in the worse case, they are just spam or lists of URLs created to perform better in the search engines rankings.

Hyperlinks constitute the raw basic material of quantitative research in the Web, as performed by Webometrics.

2 An introduction to Webometrics

The idea of the Web as a distributed database that is exponentially growing over time has been appealing for Data Mining research. There is a great potential for analysis by mining the website content, document structure, site relations, and user behaviour (Benoît, 2002). In this context, Webometrics has developed into a new discipline that studies Web-phenomena from a quantitative point of view.

2.1. Definition

The origin of Webometrics can be found in the field of Information Science. Thelwall, Vaughan and Björneborn (2005: 81) point out that the discipline "emerged from the realization that methods originally designed for bibliometric analysis of scientific journal article citation patterns could be applied to the Web, with commercial search engines providing the raw data". In fact, the idea that a link pointing to a webpage means a 'vote' to that webpage or document is based on bibliometric methods to rank scientific production (Garfield, 1979). The term Webometrics was first coined by Tomas Almind and Peter Ingwersen in 1997 and seems to be widely accepted by the research community together with the term Cybermetrics. Björneborn (2004) defined both terms by limiting their research areas. Webometrics is "the study of the quantitative aspects of the construction and use of information resources, structures and technologies on the Web drawing on bibliometric and infometric approaches" (in Björneborn and Ingwersen, 2004: 1217), while Cybermetrics does the same but on the whole Internet. Hence, Cybermetrics is more focused on the study of non web-based Internet phenomena, e.g. emails, chat, newsgroup studies, etc. Figure 1 shows the location and overlapping of these disciplines in the general context of Information Science.

Recent developments within the field suggest a move in the scope of the definition into a more general social science research approach instead of an approach that is mainly based on an informetric and bibliometric perspective. Thelwall (2009: 6) defines Webometrics as "the study of web-based content with primarily quantitative methods for social science research goals using techniques that are not specific to one field of study". Interdisciplinary research is getting more significant by enlarging the types of subjects of study and the techniques used. This evolution aligns with the definition of Internet research given by Hine (2008: 537): "Internet research itself is not a discipline but an interdiscipline, a field or a research network populated by heterogeneous perspectives."

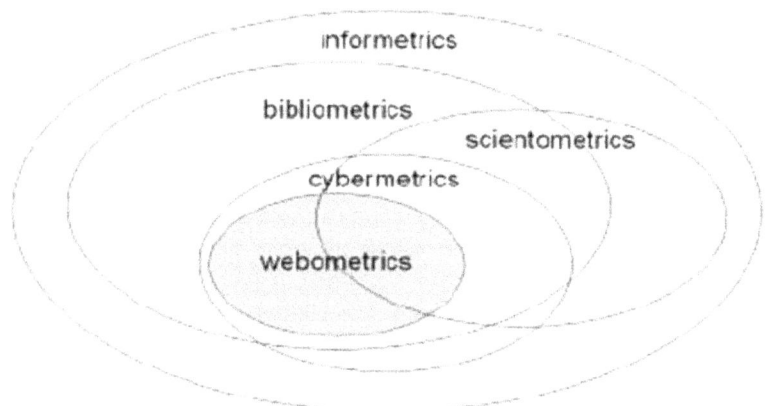

Figure 1: Webometrics and Cybermetrics in the context of Information Science (Björneborn and Ingwersen 2004: 1217)

2.2. Basic concepts

Björneborn and Ingwersen (2004) carried out the first attempt to develop a consistent terminology on the webometric field. Some years later, Thelwall and Wilkinson (2008) proposed a generic lexical framework that, based on the previous work, intended to unify and extend existing methods through abstract notions of link lists and URL lists.

Figure 2 shows a diagram of the Web where the circles represent different types of nodes (websites, web pages, etc.) and the arrows connections between them. The squares within the dashed line rectangle are nodes that are considered for analysis in a given research. They are especially useful to illustrate a specific type of analysis, the so called, co-link analysis.

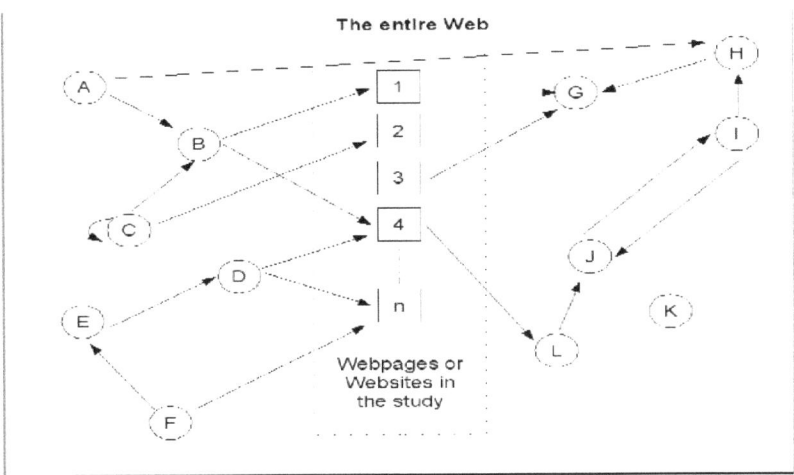

Figure 2: Diagram with different types of links existing in the Web.

Letters in the diagram represent any type of document in the Web, whether it is a webpage or a website, for instance. The following basic webometric terms (Björneborn and Ingwersen, 2004) can be explained by reference to Figure 2:

- **Inlink**: B has an inlink from A.
- **Outlink**: A has an outlink to B.
- **Self-link**: C has a self-link.
- **Page or site isolated**: K is isolated as it does not have any inlinks or outlinks.
- **Reciprocal links**: I and J have reciprocal links.
- **Transversal link**: A has a transversal outlink to H. This type refers to a link that joins to different areas of the Web that are not well interconnected.
- **Co-inlinks**: 1 and 4 have a co-inlink, as B links both of them simultaneously.
- **Co-outlinks**: G has a co-outlink, as 1 and 3 are linking to it.

This paper basically focused on inlink and co-inlink analysis, as most of the webometric research on business is based on these two concepts. Co-inlink analysis is referred simply as co-link analysis later in this paper.

2.3. Methodology

Before reviewing the application of webometric techniques to business research, this paper offers a general overview of the methodology. The application of bibliometric techniques to the Web had derived from the similarities between hyperlinks and academic citations, considering that both point from a source document to a target document. Nevertheless, important differences exist.

In this paper, we briefly describe three main types of techniques based in the use of commercial search engines to gather raw data. For a more systematic approach, a complete and didactic reference is Thelwall (2004; 2009).

2.3.1. Web impact analysis

Web impact analysis provides evidence for the impact or the spread of ideas, brands, organisations, etc. on the Web by measuring and analysing the URLs retrieved by commercial search engines in response to a specific query. This approach is especially useful as an exploratory approach for further research, although it has some significant drawbacks. For instance, one such problem is the extent to which the keyword used matches or does not the subject under research. This technique is the only one in this paper that is not based on the analysis of hyperlinks, however as it is the most intuitive one is appropriate to introduce the subject.

The main problems come from keywords that are too common or have different meanings, resulting in a wide variety of results that do not necessarily match the issue under study. In this case, it is necessary to filter out false matches. However, this is not always possible due to search engines limitations (see section 2.4).

Practical example: To carry out a basic impact analysis of two commercial banks in the UK, queries ["Royal Bank of Scotland"] and [Barclays] could be searched on Google, Yahoo! or Bing (MSN). Nevertheless, the number of matches is so high that the researcher might need to refine the search in order to focus on a specific issue concerning the companies. For instance, to explore the effects of the financial crisis on the banks, queries could be formulated such as ["Royal Bank of Scotland" AND "financial crisis"] and [Barclays AND "financial crisis"].

2.3.2. Link impact analysis

Link impact analysis is based on the comparison of the number of web pages or websites that link to a set of web pages or websites under research. The purpose of this type of research is, according to Thelwall (2009: 28), "to evaluate whether a given website has a high link-based web impact compared to its peers". Also inlink counts can be an indirect gauge of other attributes of the organization represented by the website. For instance, this has been traditionally used, within the academic field, as a potential estimator of research performance (Smith and Thelwall, 2002). This method is more accurate than the previous one because false matches are surely avoided. However, other problems need to be taken into account, e.g. the search engines set restrictions on search of inlinks (see section 2.4), or the company is using more than one corporate URL.

Practical example: Following up the aforementioned example, to carry out a link impact evaluation of the two companies, the queries that should be used on Yahoo! (the search engine with the best array of functions for this purpose) would be as follows: [linkdomain:rbs.com -site:rbs.com] and [linkdomain:barclays.com -site:barclays.com]. The results would be the estimated total number of links that point to the specific domain except the links that come from the same domain or self-links.

2.3.3. Co-link analysis

Co-link analysis could be classified as a type of link relationship mapping techniques (Thelwall, 2009). These are based on the link data that interconnect a set of websites in different ways in order to draw a diagram that illustrates the relationships between them. In particular, co-link analysis is based upon the number of web pages that link at the same time two web pages or sites belonging to the group of entities under study. This description fits the concept of co-inlink previously explained. As we mentioned before, co-link is often used as equivalent to the co-inlink concept. It is the case in this paper.

Co-links are analogous to the bibliometric concept of co-citation (Small, 1973). Co-link analysis has also been demonstrated to be a useful tool to reveal the cognitive or intellectual structure of a particular field of study (Zuccala, 2006). This method is particularly useful when websites interlink each other very rarely. It is the case of commercial websites that scarcely link the website of a competing company, especially when they are in the same industry (Vaughan *et al*, 2006). The explanation to this could be that companies seem to avoid diverting web traffic to competitors (Shaw, 2001). Moreover, as Vaughan (2006) points out, co-link data are more robust than inlink data as the former are less easily manipulated. Multidimensional scaling and network diagrams are often used to show the data gathered and to interpret results.

Practical example: The query [linkdomain:rbs.com -site:rbs.com linkdomain:barclays.com -site:barclays.com] would retrieve the estimated total number of links that point simultaneously to both domains except the links that come from the same domain or self-links.

To conclude this section, some final considerations need to be done. Due to the origins of the discipline, so far the majority of webometric research has been carried out in the academic field. Thelwall, Vaughan and Björneborn (2005: 113) acknowledge this situation and point out that "This is ironic given that the Web is dominated by commercial sites". Webometrics is progressively enlarging its scope, focusing upon political websites (Foot and Schneider, 2006; Park and Thelwall, 2008), social networking (Thelwall, 2008b; 2008c; 2008e) and commercial websites (see section 3).

2.4. Collecting data using commercial search engines

Search engines are crucial for webometric research, because their databases are the source of information that covers most of the Web. Despite the fact that personal web crawlers can be used to automatically download pages and extract their links, commercial search engines have been used extensively for research especially when large areas or potentially the whole Web are the object of the study.

In order to perform a better research using commercial search engine data, it is fundamental to get a good understanding of the industry context, the advanced functions offered and the limitations.

A feature of the search-engine market is the oligopoly of three search-engine operators Google, Yahoo! and Live Search (Microsoft) which, from a global perspective, share the majority of the generalist search-engine market. In specific areas of the Web the are other players such as Technorati for searching blogs. Search engine industry is under a constant process of change and innovation. This issue has been treated by many papers in recent years (Bar-Ilan, 2004; Vaughan and Thelwall, 2004; Lewandowski, Wahlig and Meyer-Bautor, 2006; Evans, 2007; Thelwall, 2008d).

As already mentioned, commercial search engines are the only source of data that covers the entire Web. However there are some significant limitations derived from the use of commercial search engines:
- Search engines do not index the entire Web (Sherman and Price, 2001; Bar-Ilan, 2004; Thelwall, Vaughan and Björneborn, 2005).
- Ranking systems eliminate similar or identical pages in their results, in order to avoid providing useless information (Gomes and Smith, 2003; Thelwall, 2008a).
- Crawling and reporting algorithms are commercial secrets and, therefore the exact criteria used to rank the information is unknown (Thelwall, Vaughan and Björneborn, 2005).
- The total number of results offered by search engines are estimates as they use algorithms that prioritise response time rather than exhaustiveness (Björneborn and Ingwersen, 2001).
- Results can be subject to national or language biases (Vaughan and Thelwall, 2004).
- The results can fluctuate and change over the time. In addition, only a few number of pages are accessible (usually just a maximum of 1000).

Commercial search engines are the best and unique source of information we have for certain types of webometric research, however they are not designed with this academic purpose and the results are not as exhaustive as we would desire. At this moment, Yahoo! is the search engine that is more useful for webometric research (Thelwall, 2008d). Yahoo! inlink data can be gathered in two different ways, through the general Yahoo! search engine and through Yahoo! Site Explorer. Despite the latter specializing in web structure information, complex queries can only be submitted through the general Yahoo! search engine interface.

Nevertheless, collecting data can be a very time consuming process if using the web interface. This problem could be overcome by specialized software based on the application programming interfaces (API) developed by search engines and other services on the Web.

3 A webometric approach to business studies

Internet research applied to companies can provide new insights on Competitive Intelligence (CI) in order to help companies generate and maintain a competitive advantage (Porter, 1980). CI consists of a systematic plan to obtain and analyse information about competitors and general trends in the industry (Kahaner, 1996). The abundance of information available in the Internet generates new opportunities and challenges for businesses that need to monitor changes around them in order to compete in better conditions.

In the last decade, a few Web hyperlink analysis have been conducted for CI purposes with promising results (Reid, 2003; Tan et al., 2002). For example, Reid (2003) proposed a link analysis method which analysed a particular website, but not the global context of the Web. Over the last 5 years, Vaughan and colleagues have investigated the relationships between inlink counts and business performance measures as well as the application of co-link research to companies' websites.

3.1. Do inlinks and financial variables correlate?

Vaughan and colleagues' research on commercial websites has explored quantitative relationships between inlink counts and business performance variables. Vaughan and Wu (2004) made the first attempt to prove the hypothesis that the number of inlinks to commercial sites correlates with financial variables. This study tests the hypothesis in two groups of Chinese companies. Group 1 is made up of China's top 100 Information Technology (IT) companies and group 2 is comprised of top 100 privately owned companies.

The IT industry was selected because companies in this industry, by the nature of their activity, are likely to be leaders in utilizing the Web for commercial purposes. Experience has shown that different industries, have distinct patterns in the use of web technologies and therefore only homogeneous companies are likely to be comparable. Group 1 constitutes a homogeneous group of companies in terms of business activity, whereas group 2 is not homogeneous.

The financial variables available were: gross revenue, profit, export revenue and research and development expenses (for group 1); and, gross revenue (for group 2). Inlink data to each company website were collected using major commercial search engines at that time: Google, AltaVista, AllTheWeb and MSN Search. Also, the variable website age was used based on previous evidence (Vaughan and Thelwall, 2003) showing that inlinks to a website correlated with the age of the site, this is, older sites receives more inlinks. This data were retrieved from the Wayback machine in the Internet Archive (www.archive.org).

Spearman correlations in Table 1 show significant relationships between inlink counts and the three accounting variables. Results suggest that inlinks could be considered as a complementary performance indicator of a company.

Table 1: Spearman's correlations between business performance measures and inlinks (Vaughan and Wu, 2004)

	Gross revenue	Profit	Research and development expenses
Inlink count	.51	.30	.64
Inlink count / Website age	.50	.30	.63

All correlation coefficients in the table are statistically significant at .01 level.

Vaughan and Wu (2004: 494) suggest that the strong correlation found with research and development expense "could mean that companies that invest more in research and development have a better Web presence and that their sites are more visible and attract more links to them". No significant correlation was found between inlink count and export revenue. However, export revenue only represents a small fraction (around 8%) of the gross revenue and therefore it seems not to be of relevance as a global performance indicator.

In relation to group 2 consisting of heterogeneous companies, there is no significant relationship between inlink count and gross revenue. As previously mentioned, this group is made up of companies belonging to different industries. Vaughan and Wu (2004: 494) conclude that "link count can be an indicator of business performance only when homogeneous group of companies are being compared".

In a second paper, Vaughan (2004b) studied the same relationships for the top 100 IT companies in China and the top 51 IT companies in the United States (US). Spearman's test in Table 2 shows significant correlations, lending support to the conclusion raised in the previous study. It is worth noting that the two sets of correlation coefficients are very similar in spite of the remarkable differences between both countries.

Table 2: Spearman's correlations between business performance measures and inlinks (Vaughan, 2004b)

	Inlink count & Gross revenue	Inlink count & Profit	Inlink count / Website age & Gross revenue	Inlink count / Website age & Profit
China	.51	.30	.50	.30
United States	.51	.35	.58	.37

All correlation coefficients in the table are statistically significant at .01 level.

In a third study (Vaughan, 2004a), all Canadian and United States IT companies were examined. This time, in order to raise more general conclusions, the whole population of the companies in the industry was analysed. Also a new variable, the number of employees, is used to measure the size of the company. This variable is intended to oversee the effect that a larger company will tend to have larger revenue if the rest of the variables remain constant. Apart from confirming previous evidence, the results in Table 3 demonstrate that there is still a significant correlation, even after considering the company size.

Table 3: Correlation between business performance measures and inlinks (Vaughan, 2004a)

	Inlink count & Number of employees	Inlink count & Revenue	Inlink count & Revenue per employee	Inlink count / Website age & Revenue	Inlink count / Website age & Revenue per employee
Canada	.57	.55	.35	.55	.36
United States	.68	.71	.53	.67	.51

All correlation coefficients in the table are statistically significant at .01 level.

Romero-Frías and Vaughan (2009a) analysed the top 50 international banks by using two different webometric techniques, inlink analysis and co-link analysis. The banking industry was selected due to its economic significance in the financial crisis context and its high level of internationalization.

More recently, new research has sought to confirm this evidence by exploring different types of industries.

Two sets of inlink counts (December 2008 and June 2009) and a set of financial variables for the year 2007 (including total assets, total liabilities, total revenue, net income, earnings before tax and return on assets) were taken into account in the study. Spearman's test showed that a majority of the correlation coefficients were significant at the .01 level. Only return on assets was found not significant.

Findings show that inlink counts could be used as a gauge of the banks' financial position and financial performance measures in absolute terms. However, there is no evidence when we refer to relative financial measures, such as return on assets. This could be explained by the absolute nature of the figure "inlink counts", as it accumulates all links pointing to a webpage since its creation. This is similar to the nature of financial position variables and, somehow, to the financial performance measures as revenue or total income tend to increase over time based on previous performance.

These results are also consistent with the results reported by Romero Frías, Vaughan and Rodríguez Ariza (2009). This study extended previous research by finding evidence of significant correlations between inlink counts and financial variables in several industries in the United States. The study analysed five different industries (commercial banks, construction of buildings, general merchandise store, utilities and mining), as well as the companies in the Dow Jones Industrials. The following economic variables for the years 2005-2007 were collected: number of employees, total assets, net income, total revenue, EBITDA, return on assets (ROA) and return on equity (ROE). Inlink data were retrieved from Yahoo! in January and May 2009. Due to the non normality of the inlink variables and other financial variables, Spearman's test was used. Correlations for the Dow Jones set of companies were not significant, confirming the evidence that only homogeneous companies in terms of activity are comparable (Vaughan and Wu, 2004). Significant correlations were found, to different extents, for all the industries, except for the Construction one. The Store industry had the positive and highest correlation coefficients with all the financial variables, including ROA and ROE. Utilities was the second industry regarding the level of correlation and the number of variables that were correlated, followed by the Banking and Mining industries.

In comparison to the results of Romero-Frías and Vaughan (2009a), correlation coefficients for the US banking industry are higher than for the global banking industry. This could be explained by the homogeneous competitive conditions that exist in the US market versus the heterogeneous markets where the top international banks operate. For instance, the extent to which the Internet is used for commercial purposes in the different countries could also be an explanatory variable.

It is worth remarking that correlation does not mean causation. The large number of inlinks that a company's website attracts does not cause the better financial performance. Although it is clear that a positive web image may constitute an intangible asset for a company and therefore can generate future incoming resources, it is more feasible that a bank that is doing well financially is able to maintain a high profile on the Web, maybe through the development of e-commerce practices. As the economy becomes more and more digital and information-based, companies are prompted to monitor if their web presence is in accordance to their financial importance. Web presence measured by inlink count could be an appropriate gauge to evaluate intangible assets related to the Internet.

3.2. Co-link analysis

Web co-link analysis for business information started by focusing on a single industry (Vaughan and You, 2006) or on a specific sector within an industry (Vaughan and You, 2008; Vaughan and You, 2009).

Based on the results of past studies, Vaughan and You (2006) applied co-link analysis to map business competitive positions of 32 telecommunication companies. The hypothesis under examination is that the number of co-links to the websites of each pair of companies is a measure of the similarity between the two companies. This means that the more co-links the two companies have, the more related they are from the point of view of the sites that link to them. 32 companies were selected according to the following criteria: companies from different parts of the world, from different sectors within the telecommunications industry and top companies in terms of revenue. Co-link data was collected in order to reflect the business relationships in two markets, the global market and the Chinese market. For this purpose, global Yahoo! and Yahoo! China, the top search engine in China at the time of the research, were used respectively to collect the data. The symmetrical co-link matrix obtained was analysed using multidimensional scaling (MDS), which generated a map showing the relative positions of the companies in the industry. An MDS map depicting the relative positions of companies in the global market is shown in Figure 3.

The companies are clearly clustered into the sectors of the telecommunications industry as labelled in Figure 2. The companies that are not grouped into clusters present specific features which explain their positions. The authors concluded that the maps obtained are consistent with the competition landscape of the industry. Findings suggest that co-link data do contain information about the relationship among companies. Vaughan and You (2006: 618) assert that:

"Highly co-linked companies are highly related in their products and the market. Since related companies are competitors (they serve the same market needs), it follows that co-link data can be used to map the competitive position of companies."

A more recent paper (Vaughan and You, 2008) proposed a method that combines page content mining (keyword) and Web structure mining (co-link data) to achieve a more detailed picture of a particular sector within an industry. The WiMAX sector of the telecommunication industry was chosen specially because this acronym is used only to refer to this particular technology and therefore it avoids the problem of false matches. 39 companies were included in the study and two sets of co-link data were collected (with and without keyword) using the MSN search engine. By adding the keyword WiMAX to the search, only web pages that mention that word are retrieved. This implies removing pages that co-link the two companies for reasons other than the companies' activities in this particular sector. The maps obtained by applying Multidimensional Scaling are shown in Figure 4.

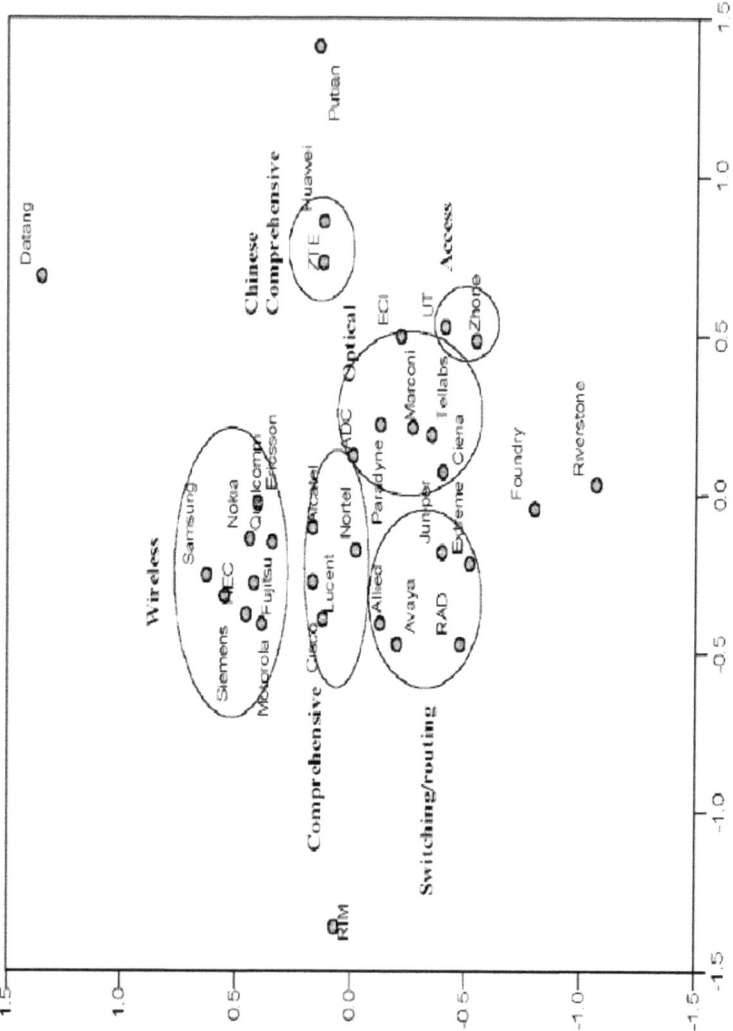

Figure 3: MDS mapping result based on global Yahoo! data (Vaughan and You, 2006: 619)

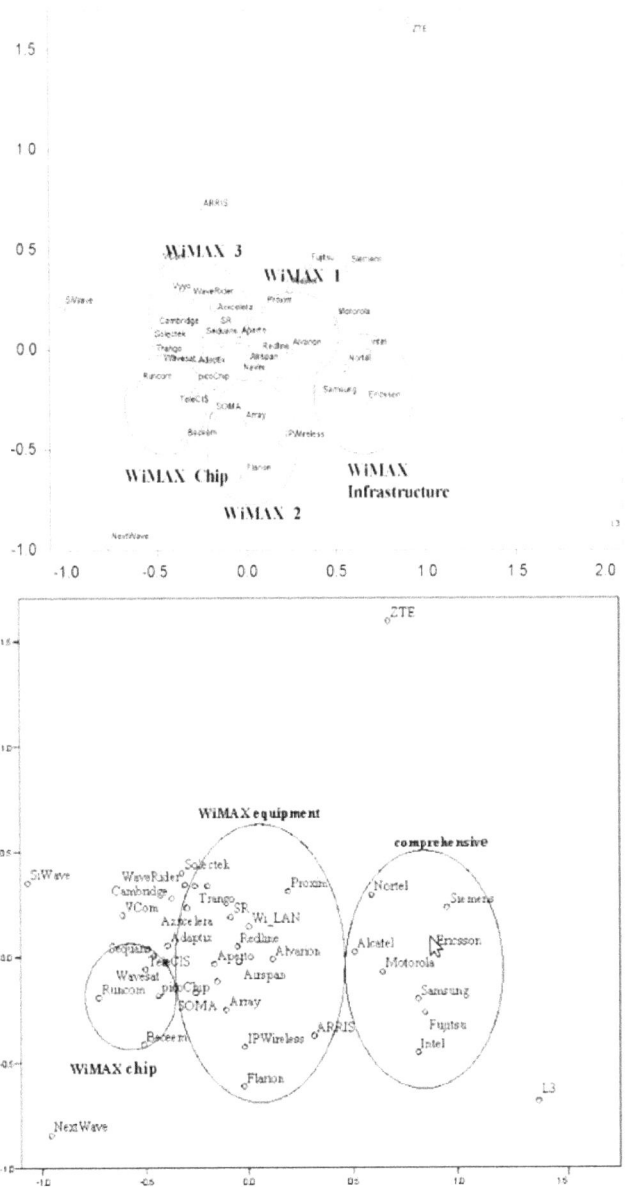

Figure 4: MDS map without the keyword (left) and MDS map with the keyword WiMAX (right) (Vaughan and You, 2008: 438 and 439).

The first map, without the keyword (left), shows clusters of companies in terms of their overall competitive positions in the telecommunication industry. Three main groups are identified: "WiMAX chip", "WiMAX equipment" and "comprehensive" companies that offer a wide variety of products and services. The second map, with the keyword (right), is able to present companies in five main groups that reflect their competitive positions within the WiMAX sector.

This map shows a more detailed analysis on the relationships between telecommunication companies but only from the point of view of the WiMAX services they provide. The authors compared their analysis of the sector with results obtained by independent market research, finding their conclusions a great match. This study proves that by adding a keyword to the query in the search engine, the information obtained about the relative positions of the companies in the sector is more accurate and meaningful.

The methodology developed in these papers has also been tested and verified in other countries and other industries. Romero-Frías and Vaughan (2009a) analysed the evolution of the top 50 international banks through co-link analysis, finding the existence of 3 main clusters of banks: Asian, European and the so called English-speaking banks that include banks from United States, United Kingdom, Australia and Canada. Vaughan, Tang and Du (2009) studied China's chemical industry and electronics industry. Finally, Romero-Frías and Vaughan (2009b) extended the use of co-link analysis into the banking industry in the US in order to test the feasibility of combining page content with co-link data to monitor financial crisis.

Parallel to these studies on homogeneous sets of commercial websites, research on heterogeneous websites has been carried out to test the triple helix theory on the Web (Stuart and Thelwall, 2006; García-Santiago and de Moya-Anegón, 2009). In this line, Romero-Frías and Vaughan (2010) extended co-link analysis to websites of heterogeneous companies belonging to five stock exchange indexes. The companies selected are the biggest in their respective economies and therefore have a significant web presence. In addition, they are also likely to receive more attention from users, competitors, government and other economic agents. When applying co-link analysis to companies belonging to different industries, the interpretation of co-link as a similarity measure does not stand only for competitive relationships, but for a wide variety of interactions, such as alliances and other linkages between distinct industries. The main conclusion of the study indicates that the degree in which the industrial activity is information centred determines the position of the companies in the MDS maps of the different indexes. The so called information centred industries include mainly IT, media, and financial companies, among others. Co-link analysis could reveal the extent to which certain industries are involved in an ongoing process of business model transformation.

3.3. Content analysis

Qualitative research is a necessary complement to quantitative research because it provides confirming evidence about the relevant nature of the links being analysed. First study on commercial websites was carried out by Vaughan *et al* (2006). This study examined three items from a set of web pages: country location of linking web pages, types of sites that created the links and motivations for linking. They analysed 418 links to US companies and 390 links to Canadian companies randomly taken from inlinks to companies studied in Vaughan (2004a). The results conclude that the vast majority of links to business sites are business related, supporting the relevance of link impact analysis for data mining purposes on commercial sites. Regarding motivations for linking, findings show that most types of links came from online directories (22,5%), list of companies (19,6%) and news articles (12,4%). The predominance of inlinks described as directories and list of companies, besides the fact that only 2 out of the 808 links studied pointed to competitors, indicate that co-link could be a fruitful direction to study business competition, as already explained in the previous section.

Content analysis has also been carried out to study the motivations for co-link creation. Vaughan *et al* (2007) used content analysis of co-link pages to examine whether co-links had business purposes and why co-links were created. 495 co-link pages to 32 telecommunication companies (the same as used in Vaughan and You, 2006) were classified. 68.5% of co-links were created by commercial sites and 57.6% of co-links pointed to related products or companies. Also, these authors (2007: 447) conclude that "co-links to homepages are more likely to connect highly related businesses and to show a true business relationship between co-link companies."

4 Concluding ideas and future research

This paper has offered an overview of the webometric methodology to perform quantitative research of the web phenomena. The increasing importance of a hyperlinked society highlights the relevance of this approach to business studies. So far, most of the research on commercial websites has been carried out from an information science perspective, but there is a promising and wide field to explore different types of business issues by using information extracted from the Web. Additional work still needs to be done in analysing different industries and regions and in developing business applications to benefit from the findings up-to-date. It would be useful to monitor the Web periodically to analyse how web variables and economic variables correlate over time. Moreover, explanatory models based on multivariate regression need to be explored.

To conclude, the use of alternative sources to collect web data represent a new horizon for researching in social sciences. In this line, an improvement in the possibilities offered by search engines is to be expected, in particular based on a semantic analysis of internet contents and in the development of more powerful APIs.

References

Almind, T. C. and Ingwersen, P. (1997) 'Infometric analyses on the World Wide Web Methodological approaches to 'webometrics'', *Journal of Documentation*, 53(4), pp 404-426.

Bar-Ilan, J. (2004) 'The use of Web search engines in information science research', in Cronin, B. (Ed.), *Annual review of information science and technology*, pp. 231–288, Medford, NJ: Information Today.

Battelle, J. (2005) *The Search: How Google and Its Rivals Rewrote the Rules of Business and Transformed Our Culture*, London: Portfolio.

Benoît, G. (2002) 'Data mining', in Cronin B. (ed.), *Annual Review of Information Science and Technology*, Vol. 36 (1), pp 265-310, Medford, NJ: Information Today.

Berners-Lee, T. (1999) *Weaving the Web*, San Francisco: Harper.

Björneborn, L. (2004) *Small-world link structures across an academic Web space: A library and information science approach*, Doctoral dissertation, Royal School of Library and Information Science, Copenhagen, Denmark, [online], Available: http://vip.db.dk/lb/phd/phd-thesis.pdf, [consulted 21 Jul 2008].

Björneborn, L., and Ingwersen, P. (2001) 'Perspectives of webometrics', Scientometrics, 50(1), 65–82.

Björneborn, L., and Ingwersen, P. (2004) 'Toward a basic framework for webometrics', *Journal of the American Society for Information Science and Technology*, 55(14), pp 1216–1227.

Brin, S. and Page, L. (1998) 'The anatomy of a large-scale hypertextual Web search engine', *Computer Networks and ISDN Systems*, 30, pp 1-7.

Evans, M. P. (2007) 'Analysing Google rankings through search engine optimization data', *Internet Research*, 17(1), pp 21-37.

Foot, K & Schneider, S (2006) *Web campaigning*, Cambridge, MA: MIT Press.

García-Santiago, L. and de Moya-Anegón, F. (2009) 'Using co-outlinks to mine heterogeneous networks', *Scientometrics*, 79(3), pp. 681-702.

Garfield, E. (1979) *Citation indexing: Its theory and applications in science, technology and the humanities*, New York: Wiley.

Gomes, B. and Smith, B.T. (2003) Detecting query-specific duplicate documents. U.S. Patent 6,615,209, [online], Available: http://www.patents.com/Detecting-query-specific-duplicate-documents/US6615209/en-US/, [consulted 15 Nov 2009].

Google blog (2008) 'We knew the web was big...', [online], Available: http://googleblog.blogspot.com/2008/07/we-knew-web-was-big.html, [consulted 14 Jan 2009].

Hine, C. (2008) 'Internet Research as an Emergent Practice', in Hesse-Biber, S. N. and Leavy, P. (2008) *Handbook of Emergent Methods*, pp 525-541, New York: The Guilford Press.

Jenkins, H. (2006) *Convergence Culture: Where Old and New Media Collide*, Cambridge, MA: MIT Press.

Kahaner, L. (1996) *Competitive Intelligence – How to Gather, Analyze, and Use Information to Move Your Business to the Top*, 7th ed., New York, NY: Touchstone.

Keen, A. (2007) *The Cult of the Amateur: How the Democratization of the Digital World is Assaulting Our Economy, Our Culture, and Our Values*, New York: Doubleday Currency.

Lewandowski, D Wahlig, H and Meyer-Bautor, G (2006) 'The freshness of web search engine databases' *Journal of Information Science*, 32(2), pp 131–148.

O'Reilly, T. (2005) 'What is Web 2.0. Design Patterns and Business Models for the Next Generation of Software', [online], Available: http://www.oreillynet.com/pub/a/oreilly/tim/news/2005/09/30/what-is-web-20.html [consulted 17 Jan 2009].

Park, H W & Thelwall, M (2008) 'Web linkage pattern and social structure using politicians' websites in South Korea', *Quality & Quantity*, 42(6), pp 687-697.

Porter, M. E. (1980). *Competitive Strategy: Techniques for Analyzing Industries and Competitors*, New York, NY: Free Press.

Reid, E. (2003) 'Using Web link analysis to detect and analyze hidden Web communities', in Vriens, D (Ed.). *Information and Communications Technology for Competitive Intelligence*, pp57-84, Hilliard, Ohio: Ideal Group Inc.

Romero Frías, E., Vaughan, L. and Rodríguez Ariza, L. (2009) 'El recuento de enlaces a sitios Web comerciales como indicador de las variables de desempeño y posición financiera de la empresa: estudio empírico de diversos sectores empresariales en Estados Unidos', XV Congreso de la Asociación Española de Contabilidad y Administración de Empresas, Valladolid, Spain, September 23-25, 2009.

Romero-Frías, E. and Vaughan, L. (2009a) 'A Webometric analysis of the global banking industry', 35th EIBA Annual Conference, Valencia, Spain, December 13-15, 2009.

Romero-Frías, E. and Vaughan, L. (2009b) 'Financial Distress of U.S. Banking Industry Viewed through Web Data', 12th International Conference on Scientometrics and Informetrics ISSI 2009, Rio de Janeiro, Brazil, July 14-17, 2009.

Romero-Frías, E. and Vaughan, L. (2010) 'Patterns of Web Linking to Heterogeneous Groups of Companies: The Case of Stock Exchange Indexes', to appear in Aslib Proceedings.

Shaw, D. (2001) 'Playing the links: interactivity and stickiness in .com and 'not.com' websites', *First Monday*, 6(3), [online], Available at: http://firstmonday.org/htbin/cgiwrap/bin/ojs/index.php/fm/article/view/837/746 [consulted 10 May 2009].

Sherman, C., and Price, G. (2001) *The invisible Web*, Medford, NJ: Information Today, Inc.

Small, H. (1973) 'Co-citation in the scientific literature: A new measure of the relationship between two documents', *Journal of the American Society for Information Science*, July-August: pp 265–269.

Smith, A. and Thelwall, M. (2002) 'Web Impact Factors for Australasian universities', *Scientometrics*, 54, pp 363-380.

Stuart, D. and Thelwall, M. (2006) 'Investigating triple helix relationships using URL citations: a case study of the UK West Midlands automobile industry', *Research Evaluation*, 15(2), pp 97–106.

Tan, B., Foo, S. and Hui, S. C. (2002) 'Web information monitoring for competitive intelligence', *Cybernetics and Systems*, 33(3), pp 225-251.

Technorati (2009) 'State of Blogosphere', [online], Available at: http://technorati.com/blogging/article/state-of-the-blogosphere-introduction/ [consulted 15 Nov 2009].

Thelwall, M. (2004) *Link Analysis: An Information Science Approach*, San Diego: Academic Press.

Thelwall, M. (2008a) 'Extracting accurate and complete results from search engines: Case study Windows Live', *Journal of the American Society for Information Science and Technology*, 59(1), pp 38-50.

Thelwall, M. (2008b) 'How are social network sites embedded in the web? An exploratory link analysis', *Cybermetrics*, 12(1), paper 1.

Thelwall, M. (2008c) 'No place for news in social networking web sites?', *Online Information Review*, 32(6), pp 726-744.

Thelwall, M. (2008d) 'Quantitative comparisons of search engine results', *Journal of the American Society for Information Science and Technology*, 59(11), pp 1702-1710.
Thelwall, M. (2008e) 'Text in social network web sites: A word frequency analysis of Live Spaces', *First Monday*, 13(2).
Thelwall, M. (2009) *Introduction to Webometrics. Quantitative Web Research for the Social Sciences*, Morgan & Claypool.
Thelwall, M., Vaughan, L. and Björneborn, L. (2005) 'Webometrics', in Cronin B. (ed.), *Annual review of information science and technology*, 39, pp 81-135, Medford, NJ: Information today.
Thelwall, M. and Wilkinson, D. (2008) 'A generic lexical URL segmentation framework for counting links, colinks or URLs', *Library & Information Science Research*, 30, pp. 515–526.
Turow, J. and Tsui, L. (eds.) (2008) *The Hyperlinked Society: Questioning Connections in the Digital Age*, Ann Arbor: University of Michigan Press.
Vaughan, L. (2006) 'Visualizing Linguistic and Cultural Differences Using Web Co-Link Data', *Journal of the American Society for Information Science and Technology*, 57(9), pp 1178-1193.
Vaughan, L. (2004a) 'Exploring website features for business information', *Scientometrics*, 61(3), pp 467-477.
Vaughan, L. (2004b) 'Web hyperlinks reflect business performance—A study of US and Chinese IT companies', *Canadian Journal of Information and Library Science*, 28(1), pp 17–31.
Vaughan, L. and Thelwall, M. (2003) 'Scholarly use of the Web: What are the key inducers of links to journal web sites?', *Journal of the American Society for Information Science and Technology*, 54, pp 29-38.
Vaughan, L. and Thelwall, M. (2004) 'Search engine coverage bias—Evidence and possible causes', *Information Processing and Management*, 40(4), pp 693–707.
Vaughan, L. and You, J. (2006) 'Comparing business competition positions based on Web co-link data—The global market vs. the Chinese market', *Scientometrics*, 68(3), pp 611–628.
Vaughan, L. and You, J. (2008) 'Content assisted web co-link analysis for competitive intelligence', *Scientometrics*, 77(3), pp 433-444.
Vaughan, L., and Wu, G. Z. (2004) 'Links to commercial websites as a source of business information', *Scientometrics*, 60(3), pp 487–496.
Vaughan, L., and You, J. (2009), 'Keyword enhanced Web structure mining for business intelligence', *Lecture Notes in Computer Science*, Vol. 4879, pp. 161–168.
Vaughan, L, Gao, Y and Kipp, M. (2006) 'Why are hyperlinks to business Websites created? A content analysis', *Scientometrics*, 67(2), pp291–30
Vaughan, L., Kipp, M. and Gao, Y. (2007) 'Are co-linked business web sites really related? A link classification study', *Online Information Review*, 31(4), pp 440–450.

Vaughan, L., Tang, J. and Du, J. (2009) 'Examining the robustness of Web co-link analysis', *Online Information Review*, 33(5), pp. 956-972.

Zuccala, A. (2006) 'Author Cocitation Analysis Is to Intellectual Structure A Web Colink Analysis is to...?', *Journal of the American Society for Information Science and Technology*, 57(11), pp 1487-1502.

The Factors that Influence Adoption and Usage Decision in SMEs: Evaluating Interpretive Case Study Research in Information Systems

Japhet Lawrence
University of Kurdistan-Hawler, Erbil, Kurdistan Region of Iraq
Originally published in EJBRM (2010) Volume 8: Issue 1.

Editorial Commentary

Although this seems to be yet another grounded theory study, the main issue dealt with in this paper is that of evaluation. Moreover the case study under consideration concerns SMEs, and draws upon a range of sources that are widely covered in the literature; including the technology acceptance model [TAM] which many would argue is far too widely covered!

Japhet Lawrence provides a useful example of how research can provide incremental insights and draw ideas together from a wide spectrum of areas including data analysis, interpretive methods, Klein and Myers' principles for conducting fieldwork, and discussions around evaluation.

Abstract: The conventions for evaluating information systems case studies conducted according to the natural science model of social science are now widely accepted, as a valid research strategy within the Information System research community. While these criteria are useful in evaluating case study research conducted according to the natural science model of social science, however, they are inappropriate for interpretive research. The nature and purpose of interpretive research differs from positivist research. Although, there are no agreed criteria for evaluating research of this kind, nonetheless, there must be some criteria by which the quality of interpretive research can be evaluated. This paper evaluates a case study research conducted under the interpretive philosophy. The paper discusses the criteria proposed by Myers (1997) for evaluating interpretive research in information systems.

Keywords: Interpretive research, case study, IS evaluation, internet, SME

1 Introduction

This paper presents an evaluation of an interpretive in-depth case study. It uses Myers (1997) for the evaluation. The conventions for evaluating information systems case studies conducted according to the natural science model of social science are now widely accepted. Benbasat et al (1987), Lee (1989) and Yin (1994) formulated a set of methodological principles for case studies that were consistent with the conventions of positivism. As a result, case study research is now accepted as a valid research strategy within the Information System research community. The principles proposed in their work have become the de-facto standard against which most case study research in information systems is evaluated. However, while their criteria are useful in evaluating case study research conducted according to the natural science model of social science, the positivist criteria they suggest are inappropriate for interpretive research.

The use of interpretive approach is relatively new to information systems field, the approach has emerged as a valid and important strand in information systems research and most mainstream IS journals now welcome interpretive research and significant groups of authors are working within the interpretive tradition (Walsham, 1995). One of the main aims of interpretive research is seeking meaning in context. The use of interpretive perspective can help researchers to understand human thought and action in social and organisational contexts. It has the potential to produce deep insights into information systems phenomena including the use and the management of information systems. The interpretive research does not subscribe to the idea that a pre-determined set of criteria can be applied in a mechanistic way, it does not follow that there are no standards at all by which interpretive research can be judged.

Striving and ensuring rigor in interpretive study requires different criteria through which one views and judges the quality and completeness of the research process. Many researchers (Orlikowski et al, 1991; Walsham, 1993, 1995; Klein and Myers, 1999) have addressed qualitative research and they have shown how the nature and purpose of interpretive research differs from positivist research. At present, there are no agreed criteria for evaluating research of this kind. Nonetheless, there must be some criteria by which the quality of interpretive research can be evaluated. Myers (1997) and Klein and Myers (1999) have proposed a set of criteria for the conduct and evaluation of interpretive research in information systems.

This study is not concerned with adhering to the scientific tenets of precision and replication, instead the study is concerned in seeking a theory that is compatible with evidence that is both rigorous and relevant and generally useful to other areas. The remainder of the paper is structured as follows. It begins with an overview of case study method and a discourse on the use of case study in Information Systems. This will be followed by a description of the procedures involved in collecting and analyzing data in grounded theory method. Then the criteria proposed by Myers (1997) for evaluating interpretive research will be discussed in relation to this particular study. Myers suggests that interpretive research can be evaluated in terms of theory and in terms of data. Finally, the paper presents further research and some conclusions

2 Methodology

2.1. Case study

The purpose of using case study was to provide an understanding of the factors that influence Small to Medium-sized Enterprises (SMEs) decision to adopt and use Internet in business. The aims of using case study are: (1) to elicit qualitative information (2) to produce an in-depth and holistic study (Yin, 1994), that gives the reader sufficient contextual and environmental descriptions to allow them to transfer the case studies based on conceptual applicability. The case studies are reported with sufficient detail and precision to allow judgements about transferability. (3) And to generate theory which is fully grounded in the data (Dey, 1993). The case study involved extensive interviewing of key participants (e.g. company owner or manager in each of the SMEs), coupled with the use of documentary evidence such as company reports.

Case study has a long tradition in IS research as a method of providing rich and contextual data, and it is the most widely used qualitative research method in information systems research (Benbasat et, 1987; Orlikowski and Baroudi, 1991; Galliers, 1992; Myers, 1997; Yin, 1994; Gable, 1994; Walsham, 1993, 1995; Cavaye, 1996). Orlikowski and Baroudi (1991), Benbasat et al (1987) and Myers (1997) argue that case study method is particularly appropriate for the study of information systems development, implementation and use within organizations. It is particularly appropriate when theoretical knowledge on the phenomenon under investigation is limited and an understanding is not well developed (Benbasat et al, 1987), these include areas where a phenomenon is dynamic and not yet mature or settled, such as Internet adoption and usage where there are few existing theories to explain the phenomenon.

The benefits of multi-case study have been discussed by other information systems researchers (Yin, 1994; Benbasat et al, 1987). According to Yin, case study can involve single or multiple cases and numerous levels of analysis. Yin suggests that multiple case designs are desirable when the intent of the research is descriptive, theory building or theory testing. Benbasat et al. (1987) argue that multiple case studies enable the researcher to relate differences in context to constants in process and outcome and also multiple cases allow for cross case analysis and the extension of theory. Miles and Huberman (1984) add that multiple cases enable the researcher to verify that findings are not merely the result of idiosyncrasies of the research setting.

Earlier studies (Baker et al, 1997; Poon and Swatman, 1999) on SMEs and the Internet have made use of multi-case studies to gather data. The multi-case study was designed as a series of interviews and site visits. Most authors are vague when it comes to suggesting how many actual cases to study, but Eisenhardt (1989) suggests that multiple case designs require the study of at least four, but not more than ten cases. For pragmatic reasons of time, the number of cases in this study was planned in advance; the study involved seven SME cases that were purposefully selected.

2.2. Case participants

The criteria for inclusion were based on a need for each participating SME to conform to the definition of SMEs and a willingness on the part of the SME owners/mangers to disclose details of their business. Several potential SMEs were rejected on the grounds that they did not satisfy the criteria. A total of seven SMEs that satisfied the criteria were chosen to participate in this study. These SMEs were chosen across business sectors so that the study could investigate the existence of sector-independent issues. This was important to avoid observations specific to a particular sector. The first SME was selected at random from the seven SMEs to provide the first body of data. Then subsequent data collection was guided by the theoretical sampling principle of grounded theory as defined by Strauss and Corbin (1990); i.e. sampling on the basis of concepts that have proven theoretical relevance to the evolving theory. The primary details of the SMEs that participated in the case study are shown in table 1 in no significant order.

Table 1: Details of SMEs that participated in the case study

SMEs	Type of business	Size (employees)	Turnover (£m)	Est'd
BIL	Peugeot cars franchise holder	20	7.5	1932
BPC	Publishing	25	N/A	1973
SAH	Health care	200	6	1969
MGL	Manufacturer of contract carpets	9	1.7	1972
AL	Manufacturer and seller of educational engineering equipment	40	5-7	1960
FP	Specialist flooring manufacturer	110	N/A	1984
CLR	Cigarette paper manufacturer	180	N/A	N/A

Source: (case study data, 2006)

3 Data analysis

Grounded theory is chosen for analysing the case study data, with the aim of generating a descriptive and explanatory theory of the adoption of the Internet rooted in the experiences of the SMEs. It is a general style of doing analysis that does not depend on any particular disciplinary perspectives (Strauss 1987). A grounded theory is one that is discovered, developed, and provisionally verified through systematic data collection and analysis of data pertaining to a particular phenomenon (Strauss and Corbin, 1990).

Strauss (1987) emphasises the usefulness of the case study approach when used with grounded theory. It is an inductive, theory discovery methodology that allows the researcher to develop a theoretical account of the general features of a topic while simultaneously grounding the account in empirical data (Martin and Turner, 1986; Glaser and Strauss, 1967). This generative approach seemed particularly useful here given that the objective of the case study was the discovery of theory that explains the factors that influence adoption of the Internet in SMEs.

Grounded theory is iterative, requiring a steady movement between concept and data, as well as comparative, requiring a constant comparison across types of evidence to control the conceptual level and scope of the emerging theory. It offers a way of attending in details to qualitative material in order to develop systematically theories about the phenomena being studied. Turner (1981) suggests that grounded theory is particularly well suited to dealing with qualitative data of the kind gathered from participant observation, from the observation of face-to-face interaction, from semi- structured or unstructured interviews, from case-study material or documentary sources. Typically, these particular kinds of inquiry generate large amounts of data, which accumulate in non-standard and unpredictable formats. The grounded theory approach offers the researcher a strategy for sifting and analysing material of this kind. A particular strength of utilising grounded theory is that a documented record of the progress of the analysis is generated. Hence, it is always possible to trace the derivation of any concept or model by checking back through the data and memos.

The focus here is on developing a context-based description and explanation of the phenomenon, rather than an objective, static description expressed strictly in terms of causality (Boland, 1979, 1985; Chua, 1986; Orlikowski and Baroudi, 1991). The research developed theory which described and explained the adoption and usage of the Internet in terms of an interaction of contextual conditions, actions, and consequences, rather than explaining variance using independent and dependent variables (Orlikowski, 1993).

3.1. Grounded theory analysis of case data

The data analysis process involved identifying patterns in the case study data. These patterns included issues raised repeatedly across interviews, commonly found in Internet commerce activities or opinions, which kept re-appearing. The data were analysed within each case as well as across the cases to detect similarities and compare differences. The initial concepts that emerged in one case context were then contrasted, elaborated, and qualified in the other. Within the first case, the iterative approach of data collection, coding, and analysis was more open-ended, and generative, focusing on the development of concepts, properties, and relations, and following the descriptions of how to generate grounded theory set out by Glaser and Strauss (1967) and Eisenhardt (1989). The detailed write-up of the cases and all the data generated by interviews, and documentation were examined and coded by focusing on the factors that influence adoption and use of the Internet in business.

The case data was read and categorised into concepts that were suggested by the data rather than imposed from outside. This is known as open coding (Strauss and Corbin, 1990, 1998) and it relies on an analytic technique of identifying possible categories and their properties and dimensions. Once all the data were examined, the concepts were organised by recurring theme. These themes became prime candidates for a set of stable and common categories, which linked a number of associated concepts. This is known as axial coding (Strauss and Corbin, 1990) and it relies on a synthetic technique of making connections between subcategories to construct a more comprehensive scheme.

The case data were then re-examined and re-coded using this proposed scheme, the goal being to determine sets of categories and concepts that covered as much of the data as possible. This iterative examination yielded a set of broad categories and associated concepts that described the salient conditions, events and experiences associated with adoption and use of the Internet in this first SME case. These initial concepts guided the remaining case study, allowing the process of data collection, coding, and analysis to be more targeted. Following the constant comparative analysis method (Glaser and Strauss, 1967), the initial SME case's experiences were systematically compared and contrasted with the second SME case. This analysis also used Miles and Huberman's (1984, 1994) technique for across-site pattern comparison and clustering that involves matrix displays to compare key events, triggers, and outcomes.

Data from the second SME case was first sorted into the initial concepts generated by the first SME data. It soon became clear however, that the initial concepts generated by the first SME case did not accommodate some of the findings emerging from the second SME case. Accommodating the second SME case's experiences, led to some important elaborations and clarifications in the emerging theoretical framework, and forced a reconsideration of some of the first SME case's experiences. For example, the category environmental factor did not include a concept of external pressure from trading partners, as this was not salient in the first SME case. The second SME case's experiences, however, indicated that they started using the Internet because they were pressurised into doing so by their trading partners, which was indeed very relevant in shaping the interpretations and use of the Internet, and substantially influenced their decision to adopt the Internet.

The process of comparing and contrasting the SME case data was repeated for the remaining SME cases. Redefining the initial concepts to incorporate considerations of the second SME case's experiences required returning to the first SME case data, and re-sorting and re-analysing them to take account of the richer concepts and more complex relations now constituting the framework. This ability to incorporate unique insights during the course of the study is one of the benefits of a grounded theory technique, an example of what Eisenhardt (1989) labels "controlled opportunism," where "researchers take advantage of the uniqueness of a specific case and the emergence of new themes to improve resultant theory".

The iteration between data and concepts ended when enough categories and associated concepts had been defined to explain what had been observed at all the SME cases, and no additional data was found, to develop or add to the set of concepts and categories, a situation Glaser and Strauss (1967) refer to as "theoretical saturation". The resultant framework is empirically valid as it can account for the unique data of each SME case, as well as generalise patterns across all the SME cases (Eisenhardt, 1989). The core categories and subcategories that emerged from the analysis are shown in table 2.

Table 2: Core categories and subcategories that emerged from the data analysis

Core categories	Subcategories
Technological factors	Compatibility
	Complexity
	Cost effectiveness
	Benefits of using the Internet *The Internet generates new business opportunities* *Communication medium to improve organisational efficiency* *Better customer service* *Easy entry into new markets* *Promotional and adverting* *Global markets reach* *Easy access to global information*
	Perceived usefulness of the Internet
	Perceived richness of the Internet
	Perceived Ease of use of the Internet
Organisational factors	Management Support
	Organisational resources
	Organisational size
Environmental factors	Competitive pressure
	External pressure
Barriers to Internet adop-	Security
	Lack of knowledge
	Cost of Investment
	Limitation of infrastructure
	Uncertainty about the Internet
	Limitation of personal contact
	Lack of universal electronic payment systems

Source: fieldwork 2006

4 Evaluation of interpretive research in terms of theory

With regard to theory, Myers (1997) suggested that interpretive research could be evaluated in terms of its contribution to the field and whether the author has developed or applied new concepts or theories? The theoretical focus of this study was the factors influencing adoption and use of Internet in small to medium-sized enterprises (SMEs). The result of the case study analysis was used to develop a theoretical model that explains the factors that influence SMEs decision to adopt and use the Internet in business. The results of the case study were discussed in terms of the categories that emerged from the grounded theory analysis process (see Table 2 for the categories that emerged from the case study analysis) and integrated insights from the existing body of literature. The theoretical model was then revisited and reconsidered in light of the literature review and the empirical findings. Existing literature has also been integrated into the reporting and discussion of this research study.

Another key issue considered by Myers (1997) is whether the author offers rich insights into the human, social and organisational aspects of information systems development and application. The analysis of the data from the field study provided rich insight into how SMEs currently use the Internet to carry out tasks, and it offers a far richer understanding of the factors that influence their decision to adopt the Internet. The rich varieties of SMEs' viewpoints were captured through the use of different data collection techniques, such as questionnaire and interview. Each of these techniques offered a different avenue for the SMEs to express their perception of Internet usage in business and the materials provided consistency in the same procedures being used for each case (Yin, 1994). The use of multiple techniques to elicit SMEs' viewpoints acted as a means of testing one source of information against other sources and this helped in improving the quality of data and provided a richer, contextual basis for interpreting and validating results (Kaplan and Duchon, 1988).

The final key issue Myers (1997) considered is whether or not the study contradicts conventional wisdom and thus provides richer understanding. The study developed a theoretical model that provided a far richer understanding of the factors that influence SMEs decision to adopt and use the Internet in business. The categories of technological, organisational and environmental factors were shown to be relevant in influencing adoption and use of the Internet while barriers to Internet adoption hinder adoption of the Internet. The theoretical model proposed in the study (see figure 1) is different from the existing frameworks of Rogers (1983) diffusion of innovation theory and the technology acceptance model of Davis (1989), because the proposed model added new constructs to these theories.

The technology acceptance model (Davis, 1989) with its two constructs of perceived usefulness and perceived ease of use and the diffusion theory

(Rogers, 1983) with its innovation attributes are limited in explaining the adoption and use of the Internet in SMEs. These models considered only the technological aspect of adoption of innovation; they are based on the deterministic assumptions of technological imperative, and hence discount the importance of human intentions and action in shaping the adoption and use of technology. They are variance models, and hence do not adequately capture the contextual issues that are fundamental in explaining adoption of Internet in SMEs.

The theoretical model developed in this study redressed the limitations of these models by accounting for organisational and environmental factors relevant to adoption and usage of IS in organisations. The result has shown that other factors such as organisational characteristics (e.g. resources) and environmental characteristics (external pressure) are necessary in explaining the adoption and use of the Internet in SMEs. The study extended the diffusion of innovation theory and the technology acceptance model by adding these new constructs of organisational and environmental factors to better explain the adoption and use of the Internet in SMEs.

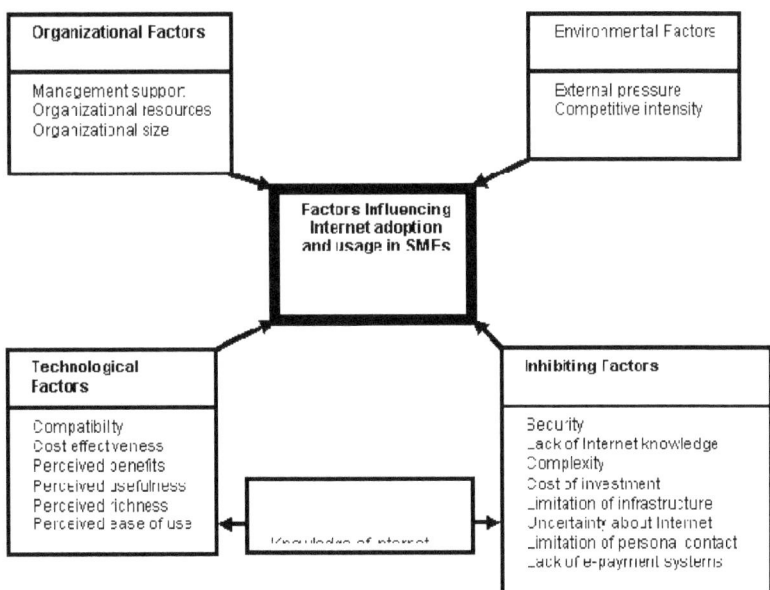

Figure 1: SME internet adoption and usage model (source: fieldwork 2006)

5 Evaluation of interpretive research in terms of data

With regard to data, Myers (1997) suggests a significant mass of data must have been collected for significant insights to emerge. The combination of different data techniques provided a significant quantity of data that enabled significant insights to emerge. It provided a sufficient range of examples of how and why SMEs adopted and used the Internet in business. The study provided sufficient citations and quotes in each of the cases used and this provided an important way of ensuring internal validity in the study. The diversity of SMEs backgrounds in this study provided a considerably broader context and process of Internet usage in business. It also provided rich insights into the human, social and organisational aspects of information systems adoption and use.

Myers (1997) suggests that a good piece of interpretive research should represent multiple viewpoints and alternative perspectives. Multiple viewpoints and alternative perspectives occurred in this study through the inclusion of adopters of the Internet and non-adopters. When the participants were selected, it was decided that both SMEs that used the Internet and those that did not use the Internet in business be selected for this study. The inclusion of SMEs with different level of Internet use and those that did not use the Internet in business enabled the researcher to gather different viewpoints from the participating SMEs and it provided different viewpoints on the factors that influence adoption. Therefore, given the diversity of backgrounds of the SMEs selected for this study, both the context and the process of Internet usage differs considerably, thus providing a broad social context.

Another issue Myers (1997) considered is whether sufficient information about the research method and the research process has been presented. The application of the specific research method chosen for this study, which was based on interpretive paradigm and used qualitative case study, was discussed in the methodology section above. The interpretive approach shows that the whole arena of social relations revolves around shared meanings, interpretations, and the production and reproduction of cultural and social reality by humans. It motivates investigations into how humans enact a shared social reality through understanding human behaviour from their point of view of the world. Considerable attention was devoted to the research process, in terms of both the philosophical underpinnings of the research method as well as the practicalities of conducting the study. Details of this have been provided in Lawrence (2002), which outlined how the data was gathered, when and where the research took place, how the research was developed over time, and how the data was analysed.

Myers (1997) concludes that the most important question relating to the quality of the contribution concerns the significance of the findings for both researchers and practitioners. This study has several important strengths in addition to having been designed explicitly to develop a theory of adoption and usage of Internet in SMEs. The study adopted a strategy of methodological triangulation that yielded both qualitative and quantitative evidence intended to facilitate the interpretation of results.

6 Contribution of interpretive research

The contribution of this study can be judged from a number of perspectives. The research has presented a broader picture of how SMEs currently use the Internet to carry out tasks, and the factors that influence their decision to adopt it in business.

A number of recent developments indicate that the factors influencing the decision to adopt IT is one of the most important issues facing many organisations, particularly SMEs. The UK Labour government published a white paper on the uptake of the Internet in SMEs in response to growing global competition of information technology, particularly the Internet. The importance of Internet in organisation continues to be important today than ever before. The white paper (entitled 'Information Highway') relates specifically to the role and importance of SMEs to the economy. It reinforces the importance of SMEs participation in global trade and for researchers in examining the role of the Internet in SMEs business. This present research is therefore both relevant and timely. The findings make a significant contribution to the understanding of the factors that influence SMEs decision to adopt and use the Internet in business.

Research conducted in the UK into adoption of the Internet in SMEs has tended to focus on Internet usage. Factors influencing the decision to adopt the Internet in SMEs have not attracted the attention of the research community. This trend is consistent with the research focus in other countries. Within the context of the UK this study breaks new ground as it focuses exclusively on SMEs decision to adopt and use the Internet.

The factors influencing large organisations decision to adopt and use the Internet are significantly different to the factors influencing SMEs. Findings from the relatively substantial amount of research conducted into adoption of IT in large organisations may not be relevant for an understanding of SMEs decision to adopt similar technologies which have a range of different functional characteristics. The findings from this study go some way towards addressing this imbalance in the research focus. The study is also useful for researchers interested in understanding factors that influence the adoption of information systems in organisations; or it may be used in studies within and across organisations by researchers who are interested in understanding the diffusion of information technology and the determinants of technology adoption.

The findings from this study can also act as a guide to help decision-makers take advantage of the Internet for business and it can help practitioners and researchers understand its growth in the marketplace. The study provides researchers and business planners with information on the growth and development of the Internet in the UK, and allows them to compare and contrast developments in the UK with the growth of Internet in North America and other European countries.

Another significance aspect of this study is the development of an Internet adoption model based on theory-driven case study that explains the factors that influence or inhibit SMEs decision to adopt and use Internet in business. The model shows technological, organisational and environmental factors as important constructs that explains IT adoption and usage in organisation.

Drawing on the rich data of SMEs' experiences, the study generated a grounded understanding of the factors that influence adoption and use of the Internet in SMEs. This grounded theory is valid empirically because the theory-building process is so intimately tied with evidence that the resultant theory is consistent with empirical data. While many believe that building theory from a limited number of cases is susceptible to researchers' preconceptions, the author argues persuasively that the opposite is true. The iterative comparison across cases, methods, evidence, and literature that characterises such research leads to a constant comparison of conflicting realities that tends to "unfreeze" thinking. The process has the potential to generate theory with less researcher bias than theory built from incremental studies or armchair, axiomatic deduction (Orlikowski, 1993).

The grounded theory developed in this study added substantive content to the understanding of the factors that influence SMEs decision to adopt and use the Internet, such an understanding has been absent from the research and practice discourses on the use of the Internet in SMEs. The approach followed here focused specifically on developing such an understanding, thus bringing a fresh set of issues to the already-researched topic of the Internet. The study integrates grounded theory with the more formal insights available from the innovation literature, developing a more revised general theoretical model that allows researchers and practitioners to explain the adoption and use of the Internet in organisations.

7 Implications of research findings

The study has shown the areas SMEs used the Internet most and how they currently used it to carry out tasks in their business. It has presented the results of a grounded theory analysis into the adoption and use of the Internet and a deeper understanding of the main factors responsible for SME decision to adopt and use the Internet in business. It has developed an enriched theoretical model for conceptualising the adoption and use of the Internet in SMEs. The study results indicated that technological, organisational and environmental factors influenced adoption and use of the Internet, while barriers to Internet adoption hindered adoption. The findings and framework articulated here have important implications for both researchers and practitioners.

7.1. Implications for research

From an academic researcher's perspective, the findings suggest that innovation adoption theories should not only account for technological factors (innovation characteristics), but also organisational and environmental factors should be included in IT adoption and use in organisation. Although the adoption of the Internet in SMEs has been led by Internet attributes, however, the case result has shown the importance of organisational and environmental factors in SMEs decision to adopt and use the Internet in business.

The existing theories such as technology acceptance model (Davis, 1989) and diffusion of innovation theory (Rogers, 1983) were developed with the concept of static individual computing environment in mind. As such, in today's rapidly changing IT environment, they do not provide adequate explanations of an organisation's IT usage behaviour (Kang, 1998). Further, there has been little or no previous study done to examine the applicability of these models to the SME context.

The technology acceptance model (Davis, 1989) posits that both perceived ease of use and perceived usefulness correlate with system use. The model's two constructs are limited to technological attributes of usefulness of computer technology and the ease of use of the technology. The model, with its assumption of users being motivated primarily by job performance expectations from IS use, may be considered as a model of compliance. In this model, the users are motivated to use the IS to gain specific rewards. However, the model is influential in the contribution to the enduring line of IT adoption and diffusion research. It has proved useful for understanding the factors involved in organizational adoption decision making.

The same criticism goes to diffusion theory (Rogers, 1983) that considers innovation characteristics for adoption of innovation. However, diffusion theory provided a useful perspective on the adoption of innovations and diffusion in organisation. Fichman (1992) argues that conclusive results were most likely when the adoption context closely matched the contexts in which diffusion theory was developed for example, individual adoption of personal-use of technologies or when researchers extended diffusion theory to account for new factors specific to the IT adoption context under study. There are other factors to consider when organisations are adopting any technological innovation, such as the organisational characteristics (e.g. resources) and environmental factors (external pressure); these factors emerged as important in the adoption of the Internet in SMEs.

An alternative model that extended the technology acceptance model and diffusion of innovation has been proposed see Lawrence (2002) based on the findings from a theory-driven case study. The proposed theoretical model redressed the inadequacies of these models by developing a more enriched adoption model that considered not only the technological characteristics, but also the organisational as well as the environmental factors. The diffusion of innovation of Rogers (1983) and technology acceptance model of Davis (1989) have been expanded by incorporating, both technological organisational and environmental factors. Within the proposed model, each of these factors was shown as having an influence on the decision to adopt and use the Internet in SMEs. The models were extended to an SME context, whereas most previous research has used these models in large firms or on college students (Igbaria et al, 1997; Davis, 1989).

Empirical validation and elaboration of these concepts in other settings are clearly needed. The theoretical model was generated by only examining few cases, albeit in depth. More empirical grounding and comparisons will sharpen and enrich the concepts developed here and yield more complex understanding of the phenomenon. It is also necessary to investigate different contexts where the Internet has been introduced. While the SMEs studied here differed significantly on environment, strategy, size and structure, they still only represent few organisational types.

More organisations need to be examined to ascertain whether the proposed concepts and model are relevant in other situations. In this way, the analytic generalisation posited here, that other organisations' experiences with the Internet would resemble the patterns detailed above will be tested and elaborated. While more empirical work is necessary to elaborate and verify the theoretical model, it is believed that a useful starting point has been made. Understanding the factors that influence adoption of the Internet allows researchers to explain why SMEs introduce Internet technology in their business.

7.2. Implications for practice

There are many characteristics of the Internet that are useful to SMEs in particular and organizations in general. The Internet is non-proprietary and offers gains in both effectiveness and efficiency and it has the potential to change the nature and diversity of interpersonal interactions and how business is conducted (Fulk et al, 1986) as well as the organisation itself (Rogers, 1986).

A growing issue in organizations is the overuse of paper for hard copies. Paper copies must be stored physically, which incurs great cost, and environmental concerns are beginning to weigh heavily on organizations, leading to pressure to reduce paper consumption when possible. Although FAX transmissions are fast, they still consume paper, and costs rise quickly if the transmission is a long one over great distances. On the other hand, the Internet is fast and through its asynchrony, eliminates the need for communication to take place at the same time. The asynchrony of the Internet helps to reduce "telephone tag". It also lessens the impact of geographical distance between customers, suppliers and business partners and through its email function provides directness between sender and receiver. Due to automatic time and date stamping, email messages, if saved, can serve as useful audit trails and organizational histories.

The study has also identified key factors that influence adoption and use of the Internet in SMEs. The results point out that compatibility of the Internet and their relative advantages (in terms of operational and strategic benefits potential) are important facilitators of adopting the Internet in business. This suggests that SMEs contemplating using the Internet should explore and set up appropriate mechanisms to become more clearly aware of the technology. Industry-based associations and trade publications may be a few mechanisms to generate in-depth awareness of the Internet. Interaction with peer firms in the industry and their experiences may motivate SMEs to adopt and use the Internet. Such efforts would also help them to engage in initial experimentation that can significantly aid their own learning process and better understand the degree to which the Internet would be compatible with existing environments and work practices. The results also point out that management support and commitment is a crucial element in adopting and using the Internet in SMEs.

The study findings indicated that efforts should focus initially on greater management support. Education and training programs should aim to increase awareness of the Internet and emphasise the benefits of using it in the organisation. The theoretical model developed and presented here suggests that before the implementation of a technology such as the Internet, mangers in the organisation should articulate their intentions with respect to the technology and assess its usefulness and the resultant organisational consequences of the technology. A better understanding of these factors may enable practitioners to formulate strategies for improving the adoption and usage of the Internet in organisations.

The theoretical model developed here meets the criteria of practical applicability proposed by Glaser and Strauss (1967). It fits the substantive area of study. The concepts and relations posited as central are intimately related to the arena of the Internet adoption and usage. The theoretical model is sufficiently general to be applicable to a range of situations around the adoption and use of the Internet in particular and IT in general.

It is readily understandable by practitioners, and should consequently provide some useful guidance in the organisations introducing the Internet. By providing practitioners with some insight into the context and the factors that influence the decision to adopt and use the Internet, the theoretical model serves as a basis from which the IS practitioner can assess and manage what is typically a poorly understood, complex, and dynamic situation (Orlikowski, 1993).

The theoretical model generated from the empirical findings has shown that the technological, organizational and environmental factors as well as the context in which the Internet is used, played an important role in shaping the adoption of the Internet in SMEs. It has provided valuable insights for practitioners, detailing the factors that influence the decision to adopt and use the Internet in a business environment. The study has suggested that practitioners will be better able to adopt the Internet in business, if they understand how these factors influence its adoption and usage.

While all research methodologies have strengths and weaknesses, the use of the grounded theory approach for the case study analysis here was particularly appropriate, generating a set of insights, concepts, and interactions that address the main factors involved in adopting and using the Internet in business, elements to date largely overlooked in the adoption literature (Orlikowski, 1993). The study has made it clear that the success of adoption of an innovation in organization is dependent on a large number of factors. Managers should be aware of their potential impact on the adoption and diffusion of an innovation and of their interdependency. Applying the model of Internet adoption in organizations, as presented here, can enhance such an understanding.

8 Further research

This study is cross-sectional in nature, and the focus of the present study is on the adoption and usage of Internet in SMEs, which limits the ability to examine the processes involved in Internet adoption. The research has drawn conclusions about the adoption and use of the Internet in SMEs and has laid a foundation on which further longitudinal studies could be undertaken. It has identified technological, organisational and environmental factors and barriers that facilitate or hinder adoption of Internet technology. A longitudinal study tracing the factors during the various processes of adoption can address this limitation. Alternatively, instead of focusing on organisations, it may also be useful to examine the adoption of the Internet by individuals. Comparison can then be made between individuals and organisations in terms of factors influencing the adoption of the Internet, for example, characteristics such as purpose of use and usage behaviours or patterns. Additional research could be conducted to determine if other kinds of technological innovations are affected by these factors.

The study has developed a theoretical model of Internet adoption and use in SMEs. Two of the main strengths of this model are its parsimony and the derivation of its factors from the empirical case study. Although the case-based investigation of the theoretical model has provided insights into the factors influencing adoption and use of the Internet in SMEs, further empirical study is needed to assess the validity of the theoretical model proposed in this study in order to develop an appreciation of the relative contributions of the model's constructs.

Because this is one of the earliest attempts to build a theoretical approach to modelling SME adoption and use of the Internet, the researcher believes that the theoretical model and propositions can form the basis of larger scale studies to examine the validity and applicability of the model and improve and refine it. As with any other simple model, there is a danger that additional significant factors have not been included in the model. Researchers who believe that additional variables play a critical role in the adoption of the Internet could use the constructs developed in this study in their own studies to better estimate the influence of each factor.

A cross-sectional study such as this is useful in identifying the patterns of relationships among the relevant factors, but large-scale longitudinal research design is essential particularly, it would allow researchers to measure the explanatory factors that emerged from the case study before the adoption of the Internet and more objectively assess the impact of the Internet on the organisations. Finally, the researcher suggests that the model be applied in the context of larger organisations as well. Such empirical testing will allow the identification of the necessary modifications to the model to enlarge its generalisability and isolate the differences in the factors that influence the adoption decisions of both SMEs and large organisations.

9 Conclusions

The central concern of this study has been to gain insight into current Internet usage in SMEs and the factors that influence their decision to adopt it in business. This study, which was based on empirical data, examined Internet usage as it is actually used in SMEs. The study has developed a model that considered the technological, organisational and environmental factors that explained the adoption and use of the Internet in SMEs. The author has argued both theoretically and where possible using empirical evidence, why these categories helped to better understand and explain Internet adoption and usage in SMEs. The results provided significant support to past findings in innovation and IS literature.

The study was presented in a descriptive form and chronicles the perceptions and experiences of SMEs adoption and use of the Internet in business. Zeller (1991) suggests that studies with an interpretive perspective don't report out "data", they report "scenes" that is accounts of researchers' engagement over time with participants in their surroundings (Zeller, 1991 cited in Miles and Huberman, 1994). In addition, Hammersley (1992) argues that "an account is valid or true if it represents accurately those features of the phenomenon that it is intended to describe, explain or theorise". The study has presented the current picture of how SMEs used the Internet in practice and the factors that influenced their decision to adopt the Internet in business. It has told story of Internet adoption and use from the perspective of the SME cases examined.

The conclusions of the study were based on the analysis of the SMEs studied and not on a population. It is not the goal of an interpretive study to make generalisations from the examined SMEs, but rather to offer understanding or insights about the adoption and use of Internet in SMEs. A rich, thick description of the case allows readers to make decisions regarding transferability of the research (Merriam, 1988). This study has presented significant progress in Internet usage and toward explaining the factors influencing the adoption of the Internet in SMEs. The findings provided theoretical and practical insights into the adoption and use of the Internet in SMEs. The study has contributed to the existing body of research on IT usage in general and Internet usage in particular. Finally, the research reported here contributes to what is hoped will be a continually expanding body of empirical evidence that can increase knowledge of Internet technology usage in business.

References

Barker, N., Fuller, T., and Jenkin, A., (1997), *Small firms experiences with the Internet,* Proceedings of the 20th ISBA National conference, Belfast, Northern Ireland

Benbasat, I., Goldstein, D. K., and Mead, M., (1987), *The Case Research Strategy in Studies of Information Systems,* MIS Quarterly, volume 11, number 3, September, pp. 369-385.

Boland, L. A., (1985), *Reflections on Blaug's Methodology of Economics: Suggestions for a Revised Edition,* Eastern Economic Journal, Eastern Economic Association, vol. 11(4), pages 450-454, Oct-Dec.

Boland, L. A., (1979), *A Critique of Friedman's Critics,* Journal of Economic Literature, American Economic Association, vol. 17(2), pages 503-22, June

Cavaye, A.L.M., (1996*), Case Study Research: A Multi-faceted Research Approach for IS,* Info Systems Journal, 6, 227-242.

Chua, Wai Fong, (1986), *Radical Developments in Accounting Thought,* The Accounting Review, 61 (1986), 601-632

Davis, F. D., (1989), *Perceived Usefulness, Perceived Ease of Use, and User Acceptance of Information Technology,* MIS Quarterly (13), pp. 319-340.

Dey, I, (1993), *Qualitative Data Analysis: A user-friendly guide for social scientists,* Routledge, London

Eisenhardt, K.M., (1989), *Building theories from Case Study Research,* Academy of Management Review, volume 14, number4, pp. 532-550

Fichman, R. G., *(1992), Information Technology Diffusion: A Review of Empirical Research,* in Proceedings of the Thirteenth International Conference on Information Systems, J.I. DeGross, J. D. Becker, and J. J. Elam (eds.), Dallas, TX, pp. 195-206.

Fulk, J., Monge, P., Contractor, N. & Singhal, A., (1986), *Cultural assumptions that influence implementation of communication technologies,* Vikalpa, 11, 287-299

Gable, G.G., (1994), *Integrating case study and survey research methods: an example in information systems,* European Journal of Information Systems, volume 3, no. 2, pp. 112-126

Galliers, R.D., (1992), *Choosing Information Systems Research, in Information Systems Research,* Galliers, R., (ed.), Alfred Waller Ltd, Oxfordshire.

Glaser, E.G., and Strauss, A.L., (1967), *The Discovery of Grounded Theory: Strategies for Qualitative Research,* Weidenfeld and Nicplson, London, England

Hammersley, M., (1992), *What's wrong with ethnography? Methodological explorations,* Routledge, London

Igbaria, M., Zinatelli, N., Cragg, P., and Cavaye, A., (1997), *Personal computing acceptance factors in small firms: A structured equation model,* MIS Quarterly, September

Kang, S., (1998), *Information Technology Acceptance: Evolving with the Changes in the Network Environment,* Proceeding of IEEE 31st Hawaii international conference on system science, Hawaii

Kaplan, B., and Duchon, D., (1988), *Combining Qualitative and Quantitative Methods in Information Systems Research: A Case Study,* MIS Quarterly, December, pp. 571-586.
Klein, H.K., and Myers, M.D., (1999), *A Set of Principles for Conducting and Evaluating Interpretive Field Studies in Information Systems,* MIS Quarterly, (23:1), pp 67-93.
Lawrence, J.E., (2002), *The Use of Internet in Small to Medium-Sized Enterprises,* PhD thesis, Information Systems Institute, University of Salford, UK.
Martin, P.Y., and Turner, B.A., (1986), *Grounded theory and organisational research,* Journal of Applied behavioural science, vol.22 (2), pp. 141-157
Merriam, S. B. (1988). *Case study research in education: A qualitative approach.* San Francisco: Jossey-Bass.
Miles, M. B., and Huberman, A. M., (1994), *An Expanded Sourcebook: Qualitative Data Analysis,* Sage Publications Inc., Thousand Oaks, California
Miles, M. B., and Huberman, A. M., (1984), *Qualitative Data Analysis: A sourcebook of new methods,* Sage Publications Inc., Thousand Oaks, California.
Myers, M., (1997), *Interpretive research in information systems,* in J. Mingers and F. Stowell (eds.), Information systems: An emerging discipline, McGraw Hill, London, 239-266
Orlikowski, W.J., (1993), *CASE tools as organisational change: Investigating incremental and radical changes in systems development,* MIS Quarterly, vol. 17, pp. 309-340
Orlikowski, W.J., and Baroudi, J.J., (1991), *Studying Information Technology in Organisations: Research Approaches and Assumptions,* Information Systems Research, 2:1, pp. 1-28
Poon, S., and Swatman, P.M.C., (1999), *An exploratory study of small business Internet commerce issues,* Information and management, January, 35, pp. 9-18
Rogers, E. M, (1986), *Communication technology: The new media in society.* New York: Free Press
Rogers, E.M, (1983), *Diffusion of innovation,* 3rd edition, Collier Macmillan Publishers, London
Strauss, A.L, and Corbin, J., (1990, 1998), *Basics of Qualitative Research: Techniques and Procedures for developing Grounded Theory,* Sage Publications Ltd, London
Strauss, A.L, (1987), *Qualitative Analysis for Social Scientists,* Cambridge University Press, Cambridge
Walsham, G., (1995), *Interpretive case studies in IS research: Nature and Method,* European Journal of Information Systems, pp. 74-81
Walsham, G., (1993), *Interpreting Information Systems in Organisation,* John Wiley & Sons Ltd, Chichester, England
Yin, R. K., (1994), *Case Study Research, Design and Methods,* Sage Publications, Newbury Park

Strategies for Gaining Access when Doing Fieldwork: Reflections of two Researchers

Satirenjit Kaur Johl and Sumathi Renganathan
Universiti Teknologi PETRONAS, Malaysia
Originally published in EJBRM (2010) Volume 8: Issue 1.

Editorial Commentary
Researchers are usually keen to have access to real-life case studies for their projects, but all too often gaining access to such sites is fraught with difficulties. This paper offers a useful overview of this critical aspect of field research. The authors outline two different sets of experiences, and relate these to some of the models proposed in the literature. The key lessons, however, can only really be derived from using accounts such as these as a warning that although field research is critical in all subjects, it is also fraught with difficulties requiring ingenuity, consideration of alternatives, and compromises.

Abstract: One of greatest pitfalls in conducting research successfully is the inability to obtain access to the research field. Obtaining access to the research field can vary to a considerable extent, depending on the kind of cases being investigated. In fact, researchers often spend considerable amount of time on this task. However, many researchers do not even describe their access to the research field in their research reports. The main aim of this paper is to share the experiences of two researchers in gaining access to fieldwork practice. We believe that the issues we discuss based on our experiences in gaining access would benefit other qualitative researchers. We also hope that comparing the experiences of two different researchers in two very different research fields would help highlight issues which are often neglected in doing qualitative research. In this paper, we present our comparison of the different approaches we used in the various stages in gaining access. We discuss our strategies in gaining access using a four stage model: pre-entry, during fieldwork, after fieldwork and getting back. Finally, we present a basic framework for gaining access successfully which other researchers can use, and also critically analyze our experiences in using the two different approaches, formal and personal, in gaining access in our respective research projects.

Keywords: gaining access, ethnography, gate keepers, fieldwork, mixed method

1 Introduction

The success of a qualitative research project as many researchers would agree depends greatly in the researcher's ability in gaining access successfully to a particular research field. However, gaining access into a research field is hardly discussed explicitly by researchers in their writings once the research project has been completed, except in ethnography based research. It is as if gaining access is a "taken for granted process" that all researchers have to fulfil as part of their research endeavour. In this paper, we argue that anyone embarking on a research project should not dismiss this important task of gaining access to a research field as just a simple and straightforward task. In fact, by sharing our experiences in this paper, we emphasize important details and strategies which could benefit other researchers in assuring successful access to their research fields.

The main aim of this paper is to share our experiences in gaining access into two different research fields. As both of us are from two different disciplines, we believe that by comparing and contrasting our experiences, this paper will contribute to existing literature on gaining access in doing fieldwork especially in qualitative based research. This paper will first present a brief background of the two research projects we were involved in. Next, by combining Laurila's (1997) and Buchanan's (1988) classification, we introduce a four-stage model: pre-entry, during fieldwork, after fieldwork and getting back. Using this four-stage model, we present our comparison and contrast of the different approaches we used in gaining access into our respective research fields. Finally, based on our critical examination of our experiences in gaining access, we offer a basic framework which we believe would benefit other qualitative researchers.

2 Gaining access to fieldwork

Researchers engaged in qualitative based research will definitely agree that successful access to a research site during fieldwork would greatly ensure the success of a research project. According to Bryman (1988), obtaining access is a major obstacle in doing research in an organization. Furthermore, different types of research sites can pose different kinds of challenges for researchers to successfully gain access. In this section, we present different issues discussed by researchers from various disciplines in gaining access for research.

In the tourism field, Okumus et al (2007) reflected on their experiences in gaining access into international hotel groups. According to them, although detailed planning facilitated their access into the participant organizations, at times they had to rely on sheer luck to have gained access especially when they encountered variables which were not within their control as researchers. They also highlighted the role and importance played by the gatekeepers in facilitating their entry into the international hotel groups. Furthermore, they also discussed at length their experiences in establishing rapport and trust, being well versed in the hotel group's internal dynamics and being aware of relevant ethical issues which all contributed to the success of gaining access for their research.

Coleman (1996) based on his experience doing extended fieldwork in Japanese and American bioscience laboratories explored the complexities related to gaining access into professional work organizations. According to Coleman (1996; 334), by "identifying and serving the needs of the professional work organization studied" researchers can increase and improve their chances of obtaining access. Therefore, Coleman suggests that researchers should offer to disseminate their research findings to the professional communities who participated in their study and at the same time publish the findings to gain academic recognition.

In the field of management research, Laurila (1997:407), based on her fieldwork experiences in an established Finnish firm, argues for researchers "to utilize critical events that can balance the inherently uneven relationship between themselves and the managers". Furthermore, by examining crises in established firms she explored how critical events can be utilized to obtain formal access and create individual rapport with managers as informants. Laurila also discussed three ways in obtaining research access: formal access, personal access and fostering individual rapport.

According to Laurila, formal access is achieved through negotiated terms between the researcher and the organisation. Thus, researchers having this form of access must be prepared to adapt to the changes imposed by the organization. Personal access refers to access gained through contact with individual organizational actors. This involves researchers creating various forms of relationship with individual informants. Fostering individual rapport refers to researchers equipping themselves with relevant knowledge of the organization to establish good rapport between researchers and informants.

While Laurila (1997) classified different ways of gaining access, Buchanan et al (1998) classified different stages a researcher gains access into the research site in ethnographic research. Buchanan et al's (1998) model consisted of four stages in gaining access: *getting in, getting on, getting out* and *getting back*.

In the first stage of getting in, Buchanan et al (1998:56) recommends an "opportunistic approach". Thus, researchers are advised to allow an appropriate duration of time, exploit known relationships, explain the purpose of research using non-threatening language, address participants' reservations positively and offer to share the final report on the findings of the research. In the second stage of getting on, the social skills and the interpersonal communication skills of the researcher is stressed. This is to ensure that good rapport is established between the researcher and the informant. In the getting out stage, it is recommended that researchers fulfil obligations which have been agreed with the research participants to ensure future access is not denied. Finally, in the getting back stage, researchers need to ensure that they leave the research site in a favourable manner to ensure easy negotiation if re-entry is required.

The above literature on gaining access mainly explored different researchers' experiences encountered during fieldwork at various research sites. In addition to this, a number of authors have also discussed strategies and drawbacks of gaining research access as part of fieldwork methodology (Bryman and Bell, 2003; Gummesson, 2000; Burgess, 1984; Shenton and Hayter, 2004). For instance, Bryman and Bell (2003:319) cite Milkman (1997) as securing access to the General Motors automobile assembly plant by promising "to produce 'hard' quantitative data to management, through survey research". Another familiar access strategy is 'hanging around' (Bryman and Bell, 2004: 319) whereby Bryman and Bell described researches such as Beynon (1975), Casey (1995) and Parker (2000) as lingering and spending a lot of time until noticed as part of their strategy in gaining access into their respective research sites.

In another example, Burgess (1984) described his access to the school site where he conducted his fieldwork as an ongoing negotiation and renegotiation process in different stages with different members of the school. Therefore, having gained access to organizations does not guarantee easy access to individual informants in those organizations. On the other hand, Shenton and Hayter (2004:223) also warn researchers that "gatekeepers who deny researcher access to their organizations [can] also effectively prevent him or her from approaching all potential informants within them" unless researchers are able to gain alternative means.

Thus far, the literature discussed confirms the complexities researchers experience in gaining access for research. As researchers from two different disciplines, we also acknowledge that issues related to gaining access vary depending on both the type and field of the research being conducted. However, we hope that sharing our experiences in gaining access into our respective research sites will benefit other fellow researchers.

3 Background of the Two Research Studies

In this section we briefly discuss the context and methodology of the two research projects this paper is based on. Both research projects are in the field of Social Science. Research Project 1 (Table 1) is based on a doctoral study in Business and Management (Johl, 2006) and Research Project 2 is based on a doctoral study in Education (Renganathan, S., 2005).

3.1. Research Project 1

The first researcher explored the relationship between corporate governance and corporate entrepreneurship activities among the FTSE 100 companies. This study used a mixed method approach for testing propositions, triangulating and elaborating the relationship between corporate governance and corporate entrepreneurship activities in firms.

Table 1: Comparing background information of Research Project 1 and 2

Research Project 1	Research Project 2
Mixed-method approach (qualitative – quantitative – qualitative); Questionnaires, interviews, secondary data (annual reports); Social science – Business and Management discipline.	Mixed-method approach (quantitative – quantitative); Questionnaires, interviews, observations; Social science – Language and Education discipline.

Two qualitative studies were undertaken to ascertain the nature of corporate entrepreneurship and corporate governance. This, along with other evidence, enabled the development of a corporate entrepreneurship index and a corporate governance index. A quantitative analysis was then undertaken, based on the FTSE 100 companies to ascertain the nature of any relationship between the two indices. Qualitative case studies were then used through an interview process to gain a deeper understanding of the issues involved.

This study collected data in three stages. In stage one an exploratory study was conducted to obtain the perception of corporate entrepreneurship and to determine the understanding and familiarity level of this concept. The second phase of this study used the quantitative approach to measure the entrepreneurial and governance levels of the companies. Two indexes were developed to measure the corporate entrepreneurship and corporate governance levels of the FTSE 100 companies. Finally, in Stage three the qualitative approach was used to ascertain consistent patterns in the results identified earlier as well as to elaborate the quantitative findings.

3.2. Research Project 2

In this research, the researcher explored the social practices of learning and using English among university students in a private university in Malaysia (Renganathan, S., 2005). The private university uses English language as its medium of instruction, and thus, the research explored the use of English as a social practice among the university students. This research adopted an "ethnographic perspective" (Green and Bloome, 1997) and the relevant data were obtained from surveys, interviews and observations. These data were used to explore students' perceptions of using English in their everyday lives both inside and outside the language classrooms in the university.

The second researcher also used a mixed method approach. However, the qualitative aspect of the research had more weighting as compared to the quantitative. Data for the research were collected in three stages. In Stage 1, through a pilot study, the researcher gathered information from the students in the university through survey questionnaires. The researcher intended to identify relevant issues that will require in depth investigation in the following stages. Thus, in Stage 2, the researcher carried out interviews with some of the students and two of their language lecturers, gathered information from a larger population of students through surveys in the form of questionnaires, and observed some of the language classes. Finally, in Stage 3, the researcher carried out follow-up interviews with some of the student participants in Stage 2 of the research and interviewed the rest of the language lecturers in the university.

4 Strategies in Gaining Access

4.1. Pre-Entry to the Field

In this section, we describe and compare (Table 2) how both researchers using different types of access employed relevant strategies in gaining access to their respective research sites.

Table 2: Comparing Pre-Entry access of Research Project 1 and 2

Research Project 1	Research Project 2
Formal access	Personal Access
Online-directory, telephone calls (to public relations manager), e-mail (questionnaire attached), e-mail (cover letter with official letter head attached);	Informal e-mails, telephone calls to familiar people;
Fix appointments based on interviewees availability;	No formal appointments were made;
Researcher felt obligated due to infringement on interviewees' time;	Colleagues felt obligated to help;
Need to emphasise benefits of research to the organization;	Benefits of research is taken for granted by the organization;
Issues of anonymity and confidentiality assured.	Issues of anonymity and confidentiality assured.

4.1.1. Research Project 1

The first researcher used a formal way of obtaining access in organizations. The Northcote Website: http://www.northcote.co.uk, an online directory of public listed companies in the U.K was used to identify the population of the FTSE 100 companies. Listing 100 top companies in the country, the latest version (2004) at the time of the research was used to obtain their addresses and contact numbers. A number of ways were used to gain respondents' co-operation and motivate them to respond (Oppenheim, 1992) and in identifying the most appropriate person within the firm that would be able to participate in answering the questionnaire. Firstly, telephone calls were made as a preliminary notification to the companies in explaining about the research project and to identify the most appropriate person prior to e-mailing the questionnaires. The telephone calls were made to the company's Public Relations Manager to determine who would be the most appropriate person in the corporation that would be able to participate in answering the questionnaires according to his/her best knowledge. This strategy was utilised with the intention of maximising the response rate. Also, this approach helped to identify a contact person within the firm who could then be referred back to in order to obtain any further information about the organisation. After locating the most appropriate person within the firm, e-mails were then sent that contained a cover letter stating the research objectives and requesting participation. This was designed and attached as a file with the e-mail and questionnaires (Bell, 1993; Cohen and Manion, 1994; Oppenhiem; 1992). A similar letter was also e-mailed to each of the case study participants. Although the cover page of the questionnaire contained an introductory statement to indicate the purpose of the study (Sudman & Bradburn, 1982), it was considered important that respondents understood and accepted the aims of the study and hence, willingly imparted information (Foddy, 1993). Also, it was crucial to seek legitimate access to avoid the participants from being bias to non-response (Oppenhiem, 1992).

Respondents were promised anonymity in terms of revealing information as their name and contact numbers would not be revealed publicly. This helped to gain their trust and confidence in terms of revealing information. In addition, to obtain the requested information as legitimate and to garner respondent trust (Foddy, 1996), it was essential to promise confidentiality to the respondents. Oppenhiem (1992) argued that it is crucial for all surveys to be treated as confidential in the sense that only researchers have access to them and steps were taken to ensure that no information about identifiable persons or organisations was published without permission. Both the survey and case study respondents were also promised a copy of the results in due course (Cohen & Manion, 1994). Also, the respondents were provided with a named contact in the event of a query and finally the letter ended with a note of thanks (Sudman and Bradburn, 1982).

There being no interviewer to provide additional information, the length of the cover letter in the e-mail questionnaire might be longer than the introduction to a personal interview (Sudman & Bradburn, 1982). However, the length of the cover letter was limited to one page in order to prevent respondents from skimming and ignoring it completely. The letter used the official letterhead of the University of Nottingham Institute for Enterprise and Innovation as a channel in building contacts and network with the organisations. This was expected to be significant in securing widespread co-operation (Johl, 2006; Oppenheim, 1992). In addition, telephone calls and e-mails were used to fix appointments with the interviewees based on their time availability.

4.1.2. Research Project 2

In the second research project, the researcher used "personal access" (Laurila, 1997) and established individual rapport to get the relevant information for the study. In this research project the researcher was a staff member who was on study leave from the organisation where the field work was carried out. Thus, the research site was familiar to the researcher and thus the researcher employed various familiar ways to gain access to the research site.

Entry to the field was established through informal emails, and phone calls to familiar people in the organisation (the university). The researcher was familiar with the university's semester system, thus it was easy to determine suitable time to gain the relevant information from the research site. Furthermore, the researcher was a member of staff, thus, the researcher's requests were often easily met. In addition, because of the researcher's familiar identity within the research site, access to relevant information was mostly based on trust. Some of the interviewees for the research were the researcher's colleagues. Thus, none of these colleagues declined to be interviewed. In fact, the researcher believes that her colleagues even felt obligated to help her with the research.

The issue of confidentiality was also very important because the researcher was a member of the staff. The researcher was aware that the interviewees, especially those who were colleagues, would not be comfortable disclosing information which can be considered "private" or "sensitive" to another member of staff. Thus, the researcher promised that the information obtained would be confidential and only pseudo names will be used in the writing of the research. As for the students, they were given a confidentiality letter, which promised to treat all information obtained in the interviews confidentially.

4.2. During Field work

In this section we compare the issues we experienced and discuss the strategies we employed during our fieldwork at the respective research sites.

Table 3: Comparing issues and strategies in Research Project 1 and 2

Research Project 1 (formal)	Research Project 2 (personal)
Dressed formally	Dressed casually
Adapting from Asian culture to Western culture;	Share same cultural practices, values and languages;
Addressed interviewees formally using surnames – vice versa;	Encourage interviewees to use researcher's first name;
Familiarizing with British accent;	Well-versed in interviewees' mother tongue language;
Permission obtained to tape-record interviews.	Permission obtained to tape record interviews.

4.2.1. Research Project 1

During the field work, the first researcher dressed in a formal way in order to gain the trust and confidence from the interviewees. This was considered to be very pertinent as the researcher interviewed individuals who are from the top management team of the corporation and it is important to set a good impression to these individuals. Also, the researcher's background is from the Asian culture therefore she had to learn and adjust to the Western culture in order to blend in and to be accepted as knowledgeable in their business practices. This was pertinent to gain the trust and willingness of the interviewees to reveal information without any hesitation. In addition, the researcher had to familiarize herself with the British accent in order to communicate effectively with the interviewees. The interviewees were addressed formally by using their surnames as it was the first time the researcher was meeting them. All respondents permitted the conversations to be tape-recorded. The interviewees expressed their views openly. This is because the researcher was able to make them feel comfortable by assuring them about confidentiality and anonymity in revealing information.

4.2.2. Research Project 2
The researcher's familiarity with the research site also facilitates the information gathering process. The research was carried out in a multilingual, multi ethnic population. Thus, the researcher's familiarity with the interviewees' cultural practices, values, and languages helped greatly in obtaining the relevant information for the research. The second researcher purposely dressed casually especially when interviewing the students to avoid emphasising power relations in interviewing students in an educational setting (Scot and Usher, 1999). According to Scot and Usher (1999), respondents in an interview will give responses based on the setting and role they are positioned in. Therefore, they stated that an education researcher may find the interviewees responding as they would to a teacher in relation to their role as a student. Furthermore, the students were also encouraged to call the researcher using her first name which is uncommon in an educational setting where the research was carried out. These were purposely done to encourage the students not to strictly see the researcher in the role of a lecturer.

Using the languages which were familiar to the interviewees was also an advantage. The researcher did not share the same mother tongue language as the interviewees. In fact, many of the interviewees preferred to be interviewed in their mother tongue language. Thus, it was crucial for the researcher to be familiar with the interviewees' mother tongue language in order to obtain the relevant information.

4.3. After Fieldwork
Table 4 below, summarises our experiences after leaving the research sites once we have collected the relevant data for our respective research.

4.3.1. Research Project 1
The case study interviews were recorded and then transcribed after each interview session. This permitted greater flexibility in analysis and provided a better grasp of the underlying meanings. A primitive classification system was created which was continually revised as more data was assimilated.

Table 4: Comparing after fieldwork practices of Research Project 1 and 2

Research Project 1 (formal)	Research Project 2 (personal)
Transcribed each interview session;	Transcribed verbatim each interview;
Analysed using 2 steps: within case analysis and across case analysis;	Used QSR Nudist software to assist analysis;
Used conventional method – to establish unique patterns;	Informal appreciation;
E-mailed a formal thank-you note immediately;	Results were not revealed to the organization.
As promised, sent a copy of the result (report) to the respective organization.	

The data was searched for patterns, and regularities which formed the basis of the initial categories into which units of data could be placed. The explanation building process was iterative and based upon the propositions that were developed. This study did not utilize any qualitative data analysis package (for example, NVivo or QSR NUDI.ST software) which allows rich text documents to be coded and thus formulate models of underlying categories and constructs. This was because the research study involved a relatively small number of interviews and the use of primitive classification systems was considered to be a sufficient and convenient way of analysing the data. The data was analysed in two steps: within case analysis, followed by across case analysis (Eisenhardt, 1989). As a first step, detailed case study write-ups were generated. Although primarily descriptive, they helped to cope with the high volume of data, while at the same time enabling familiarity with each case as a stand-alone entity. This, in turn, allowed the unique patterns of each case to emerge by comparing the similarities and differences across cases thus allowing the generalization of patterns across cases.

Immediately after each interview session, a formal thank you note was e-mailed to the interviewee. This is to ensure good rapport is being built with these individuals and to ensure if any further information is required form these individuals they would be willing to share it. Also, as promised a copy of the results were provided in a report form to the respective individuals.

4.3.2. Research Project 2

The researcher left the research site to analyse the data obtained from the interviews and observations carried out in Stage 2. All the interview data were transcribed verbatim. The interview data in the students' mother tongue language were retained and only necessary excerpts were translated for the research report.

The analysis of the interview transcripts for this research was facilitated with the use of the QSR NUDI.ST programme. QSR NUDI.ST is a computer programme which assists the data analysis of qualitative data. This programme was very helpful in coding sections of the transcribed interview texts, and enabling easy retrieval and search of coded texts segments, words, and phrases.

Using QSR NUDI.ST, the researcher established a preliminary list of coding categories by going through each interview transcript. The initial coding categories reflected a combination of themes and issues that were closely related to the research questions as well as categories of expressions that the interviewees themselves used. The coding categories formed different levels of generality in order for retrieval of information at various levels. From the preliminary list the researcher identified eight coding categories that best fit the whole data.

4.4. Getting Back

In this section, we discuss the options we had on whether there was a need to return to the research sites again.

4.4.1. Research Project 1

The researcher built a good rapport with the interviewees and thus, would not have faced many obstacles if there was a need to get back to the research site to obtain further information. In the event, the researcher was not required to do so as she has had sufficient information.

Table 5: Comparing the choices of returning for Research Project 1 and 2

Research Project 1 (formal)	Research Project 2 (personal)
• Established good rapport, easy to return to the research field; • Sufficient information gathered to complete research; • Need not return to the organization.	• Familiar with the research site, easy to gain access again; • Insufficient data collected, this required to get back again to the research site.

4.4.2. Research Project 2

After the analysis of data obtained at Stage 2, the researcher realised that further information was needed. Thus, the data at Stage 3 was collected a year after obtaining information from the students at Stage 2. Although, it was easy for the researcher to go back to the research site again, it was difficult to contact all the students who took part in the interviews at Stage 2. However, with the help of some of the administrative staff, the researcher managed to get in touch with some of the students. The purpose of this interview was to clarify certain issues and information which emerged during the analysis of data obtained at Stage 2.

5 A Framework for Gaining Access Successfully

Based on the discussion above, we provide a basic framework (Figure 1) which a qualitative researcher can use in gaining access either using the formal or informal approach as discussed in this paper. We believe this framework can provide a basis for other researches to utilize in gaining access to their respective research sites.

6 Critical Analysis of Using Two Different Approaches in Gaining Access

Gaining access to the field is considered crucial in ensuring success in conducting research. As discussed in the earlier section there are two ways of gaining access: formal and informal. The first researcher used a formal approach in gaining access whereby the researcher was not familiar to the field which can be considered as a drawback. However, the researcher was able to benefit using this approach due to the following reasons:

- A formal structured way was used in approaching the respondents. The first researcher was very sensitive in terms of the respondents' availability. She fixed appointments according to the interviewees' convenience. This was very much appreciated by the interviewees and they were very cooperative during the interviews.
- The first researcher is not familiar to the field. Therefore, she has no preconceived ideas about the organization. Thus she was not biased towards the information given by the interviewees;
- The first researcher comes from different cultural background and country where business practices differ from that of her research site (United Kingdom). However the interviewees took extra effort and

were patient enough in providing detailed explanation about their business practices;
- The first researcher had no prior relationship with the interviewees. Therefore, the answers given to her were not influenced by any form of prior relations between the researcher and the respondents. In fact. The respondents were very frank in giving their views and opinion;
- As a formal approach was used in gaining access to the companies the interviewees kept to the appointments seriously without any cancellation as they would need to set a good impression of their company and themselves;
- The letters that were sent to the respondents bore University Nottingham letter head and were endorsed by the researcher's supervisor who holds a prominent position in the university. This gave an impression of the importance of the research project and therefore the interviewees paid extra attention and gave full cooperation to the researcher.

On the other hand, the second researcher used the personal approach in gaining access to her research site. Although existing literature supports that if the researcher is familiar with the research site, obviously gaining access would be easier as compared to an outsider. However, a critical analysis of the researcher's access to her research site showed that although as an insider it is much easier, it should not be taken for granted.

- As the research site was familiar to the researcher, appointments and schedules were often changed. This is because the interviewees, especially the researcher's colleagues, and the researcher could easily accommodate one another at short notices without jeopardizing the relationship between the researcher and participants.
- The researcher was familiar to the research site under investigation, thus, it was extremely important for the researcher to consciously acknowledge her own personal feelings towards the research. The researcher also paid careful attention not to influence the interviews and observations with her own preconceived ideas.
- The researcher shared many of the values and cultural practices of the participants. The researcher is even well versed in the participants' mother tongue language. During the interviews, the participants made a lot of assumptions that the researcher would be able to

easily understand their explanations. Thus, sometimes there were awkward situations where the participants were asked to explain explicitly the meanings underlying their explanations.
- The researcher had known the participants, especially her colleagues, before embarking on her research. Thus, there is always the possibility that the participants' responses during the interviews are influenced by the relationship the participants share with the researcher.
- Since the researcher made informal appointments, often they were not taken seriously by the interviewees. There were quite a number of last minute cancellations and changes. Some interviewees did not even turn up at the agreed time.
- During fieldwork at the university, the importance of the research was only acknowledged by the researcher. The participants and the university merely assisted the researcher. None of the participants or members of staff from the university questioned any of the researcher's actions during her fieldwork.

Leading Issues in Business Research Methods

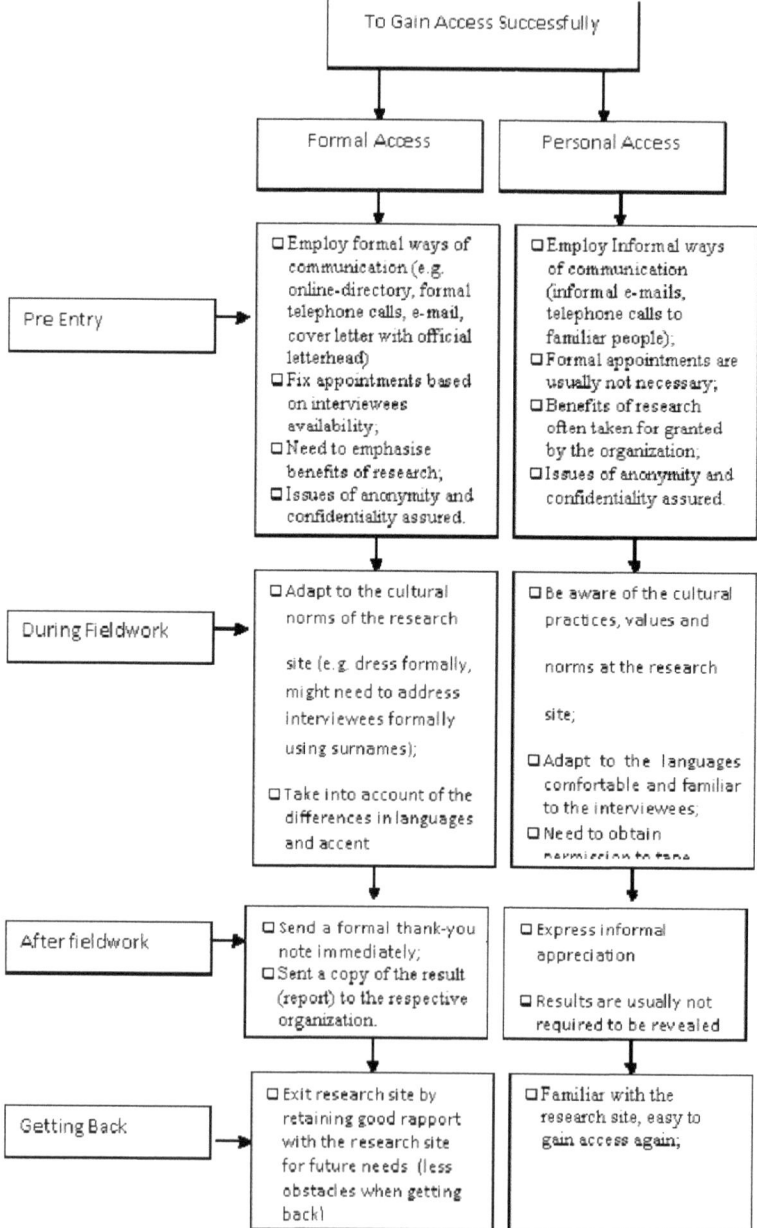

Figure 1: A Framework for Gaining Successful Access

7 Conclusions

In this paper we have shared our experiences especially on the various strategies we used in obtaining access to the two different research sites in our respective research projects. We discussed specific issues which were salient in gaining access using the four stage model: pre-entry, during fieldwork, after fieldwork and getting back.

The first researcher found that choosing the right strategy in gaining access to the field is considered to be paramount in ensuring a high response rate. This is demonstrated in her research as she was able to obtain a high response rate of 42%. Also, all the six interviewees for the case study that were contacted after the questionnaire session were all agreeable to be interviewed. As for the second researcher, she found that planning was very important in gaining access to obtain the relevant information for her research. However, the second researcher also believes that it is also equally important to be flexible and adaptable to the changes which occur at the research site.

Different researchers would encounter and experience different types of issues in gaining access to their research sites. However, it is only through the sharing of the researchers' experiences in gaining access that important issues can be highlighted and discussed for the benefit of other fellow researchers. It is hoped that the various issues and strategies we discussed in this paper would benefit other researchers in gaining access in doing field work for their own research projects.

References

Bell, J. (1993) *Doing your Research Project: A Guide for First Time Researchers in Education and Social Science: 2nd Edition*, Buckingham, Open University Press.
Bryman, A. (1988) *Doing Research in Organisations*, London: Routledge.
Bryman, A. & Bell, E. (2003) *Business Research Methods*, New York: Oxford University Press.
Buchanan, D., Boddy, D. & Mc Calman, J. (1988) *Getting In, Getting On, Getting Out and Getting Back,* In Bryman, A. ed. Doing Research in Organisations, pp. 53-67, London: Routledge.
Burgess, R. G. (1984) *In the Field: An Introduction to Field Research*. London: Allen and Unwin.

Cohen, L. & Manion, L. (1994) *Surveys in Research Methods in Education: 4th Edition*, London: Routledge.

Coleman, S. (1996) Obstacles and Opportunities in Access to Professional Work Organizations for Long-Term Fieldwork: The Case for Japanese Laboratories, *Human Organisation*, Vol. 55, pp. 334-343.

Eisenhardt, K.M. (1989) "Building Better Theories from Case Study Research", *Academy of Management Review*, 14, pp. 532-550.

Feldman, M., Bell, J. & Berger, M. (2003) *Gaining Access: A Practical and Theoretical Guide for Qualitative Researchers*, California: AltaMira Press

Foddy, W (1996) *Constructing Questions for Interviews and Questionnaires: Theory and Practice in Social Research*, Cambridge, Cambridge University Press.

Green, J., & Bloome, D. (1997) Ethnography and ethnographers of and in education: A situated perspective. In J. Flood, S. Heath, & D. Lapp (eds.) *A handbook of research on teaching literacy through the communicative and visual arts.* (pp. 181-202). New York: Simon & Shuster Macmillan.

Gummesson, E. (2000) *Qualitative methods in management research*, 2nd Ed., Sage: London.

Johl, S.K. (2006) *Corporate Entrepreneurship and Corporate Governance: An Empirical Analysis*, Unpublished Doctoral Thesis. University if Nottingham, UK.

Laurila, J. "Promoting Research Access and Informant Rapport in Corporate Settings: Notes From Research on a Crisis Company." *Scandinavian Journal of Management*, 13.4 (1997): 407-18.

Okumus, F., Altinay, L. & Roper, A. 2007, "Gaining access for research: reflections from experience", *Annals of Tourism Research*, vol.34, no.1, pp.7-26.

Oppenheim, A.N. (1992) *Questionnaire Design, Interviewing and Attitude Measurement:* New Edition, London: Continuum.

Patton, M.Q. (2002), *Qualitative Evaluation and Research Methods*, 3rd ed., New

Renganathan, S. (2005) *The use of English as a social practice: A study of Malaysian ESL students.* Unpublished Doctoral Thesis King's College University of London, London.

Scott, D. & Usher, R. (1999) *Researching education: data, methods and theory in educational enquiry.* London: Cassell.

Shenton, A. & Hayter, S. (2004) Strategies for gaining access to organizations and informants in qualitative studies. *Education for Information*, 22, 223-231.

Sudman, S. & Bradburn, N.M. (1982) *Asking Questions: A Practical Guide to Quetionnaire Design*, San Francisco: Jossey-Bass.

Taking Stock of Research Methods in Strategy-as-Practice

Ramya T Venkateswaran and Ganesh N Prabhu
Indian Institute of Management Bangalore, India
First Published in EJBRM (2010) Volume 8 Issue 2

Editorial Commentary

In this brief paper the authors seek to develop some ideas about forms of investigation that can be encompassed by the term 'action research' – i.e. 'go out and do'. In fact they use the somewhat more constrained phrase 'go out and look' in characterizing 'strategy-as-practice' research. In fact as the authors demonstrate clearly in the discussion of their 'four major research issues' it is not possible simply to 'go out and look'. What constitutes 'strategy' is itself an issue, as is the 'unit of analysis' to be considered once one has adopted some view of the nature of strategy itself.

The paper provides an account of this nascent approach, and makes some interesting links to other fields, such as software engineering that links practices to performance. Taken together with the action research perspective this implies that strategy-as-practice research demands imaginative and innovative insights by researchers. This may make it difficult to break in to traditional research enclaves, but on the other hand may provide a basis for developments in research practices that extend to the business and management research community as a whole.

Abstract: Strategy-as-practice research provides understanding of a complex phenomenon in language rich and holistic process terms, rather than statistically significant but limited variance terms. It requires mapping individual and organisational activities in the process of strategizing. This article assesses four research issues in strategy-as-practice research and their impact in advancing this field: challenges in bounding the scope of the research question, issues with the unit of analysis, difficulties in defining the dependent variable of outcomes and finally the challenge in specifying a particular level of analysis, all of which present complexities in the design of data collection. We suggest two broad alternative approaches that have the potential to push the frontiers of methodology to greater rigour in strategy as practice research. First, quantification methods that can capture practice can be a valuable tool, a paradigm that has been ignored in much of strategy-as-practice research. Second, better process data may be revealed by organizations that voluntarily initiates a consultation process with a researcher as it benefits by doing so, so we suggest that clinical research methods, that include such intervention, provide better understanding of the phenomena of strategizing. We make a case for why these methods must be considered for acceptability in strategy-as-practice research.

Keywords: strategy-as-practice, research methods, strategy research, clinical research, review

1 Introduction

Research methods are an 'intricate set of ontological and epistemological assumptions that a researcher brings to his or her work' (Prasad 1997 quoted in Mir and Watson 2000). Strategy-as-practice research subsumes a plurality of interests and research methods mainly with the lens of sociology (Jarzabkowski 2004; Whittington 2007). It draws upon sociological and philosophical developments related to practice theory, such as the well known works of Bourdieu, de Certeau, Giddens, Schatzki, Sztompka and others (see Jarzabkowski 2004 for an overview). Johnson et al. (2007) believe that the pragmatist tradition of philosophy, in highlighting the importance of the practical, is winning attention (Egginton and Sandbothe 2004 quoted in Johnson et al. 2007) in recent years. Basically, strategy-as-practice simply requires one to "go out and look" so as to find ways to capture such activity as it occurs, so that it can be examined closely and understood, similar to a 'direct research' approach proposed by Mintzberg (1979). Epistemologically, most strategy-as-practice studies have taken different positions, ranging from post-positivist to interpretive (Johnson et.al. 2007). Strategy-as-practice research provides understanding of a complex phenomenon in language rich and holistic process terms, rather than statistically significant but limited variance terms. The orientation towards 'action research' complicates research conclusions due to the close proximity between the observer and the observed (Johnson et al.

2007). This article assesses four major research issues in strategy-as-practice research and their impact in advancing this field.

2 Scope of the research question

The first issue is the broader scope of strategy-as-practice research – studies of the strategizing process must go beyond the organisation (Whittington 2003, Jarzabkowski and Spee 2009) as it is influenced by policy makers, competitors, consultants and business schools as well as organisational members adapting practices from other organisations whose strategies they analyse, critique, enact, develop or change (Whittington 2003). Also strategic practice could be bottom-up or emerging from middle managers, consultant, senior executives, intrapreneurs and even members outside the organization, thus encompassing a plurality of actors. Johnson et al. (2007) explain that there is a move from the relatively unitary perspectives that have characterised strategy research in terms of levels of analysis, explanatory variables and theoretical perspectives, to greater plurality. Hendry and Seidl (2003) admit that strategy, as an activity, is not well defined, with the result that the empirical net is cast impracticably wide.

3 Unit of analysis

The scope of the research question directly impacts the second issue – ambiguity in the unit of analysis in strategy-as-practice research. The unit of analysis refers to the precise object of the research, the entity about which one is trying to draw conclusions. Thus the focal unit of analysis could be very narrow (e.g. individual strategy retreats, workshops, managers, meetings, discourses, conversations etc.) or it could be broader (strategic decisions, strategic issues etc.). Hendry and Seidl (2003) have introduced the notion of 'strategic episodes' where an episode is a sequence of events with a structured beginning and ending during which normal communicative practices are suspended and alternative communicative practices are explored. Similarly, analysing strategy off-sites and away-days as rituals could also provide interesting units of analysis (Bourque and Johnson 2008).In strategy-as-practice research, the unit of analysis has ranged from strategic episodes – such as strategic planning meetings, to implemented strategic decisions over a limited period of time – such as an acquisition, to the evolution of the firm's strategy over a long period of time – such as international expansion. To decide what is and what is not included under the entity of strategizing, is an open-ended task. The emerging consensus in strategy-as-practice research is to look at 'a practice' as a unit of analysis but lack of clarity on what constitutes 'a practice' may lead to such research being labelled a 'study of everything'. Johnson et al. (2007) quote Wildavsky (1973) that if strategizing is everything, including any activity that might contribute to the orientation of the organization, then maybe it's nothing. Since such an approach is extremely ambiguous, the emphasis on activity suggests a unit of analysis being defined in micro terms. Chia and Mackay (2007) argue that it is the theoretical unit of analysis that must be revised. Instead of individuals and organizations and their processes, activities and practices, they argue that it is practices and the transmitted regularities associated with them that draw the attention of strategy-as-practice researchers.

Even recognising only one unit of analysis in a study may pose challenges according to Johnson et al. (2007). Langley (1999) studied the role of formal analysis in strategic decision making and was confronted with the difficulty of identifying the two main units of analysis: what constituted 'an analysis' and a 'strategic decision', and how could these be clearly identified from other analysis-like instances or other decisions, and hence she had to draw up a set of criteria for the study. Hence, apart from deciding on the logical unit of analysis, bounding the unit of analysis operationally is also a challenge (Johnson et al. 2007). Two possibilities arise here. One is to adopt positivist perspectives that can provide a clear and well bounded unit of analysis. This would mean drawing up a list of exclusion criteria to bound the operational unit of analysis. The issue with such positivist approaches is that they typically tend to take a reductionist direction, because of the efforts to isolate focus on narrowly defined objects and eliminating any ambiguity. Therefore this deprives us of the opportunity of capturing the richness of the whole process. The second approach is to adopt interpretive or ethnographic approaches. These approaches, while certainly offering to capture the richness, may end up leaving the unit of analysis ambiguous. Johnson et al. (2007) cite Van Maanen (1995: 139) in representing the essence of this tradeoff, 'to be determinate, we must be indeterminate': the research itself must reflect the ambiguity present in the empirical situation. A middle range tactic is advocated by Johnson et al. (1999) wherein one may explicitly admit the possibility of variation in the study and incorporate it within the research design. This basically means that the researcher will have to provide an explicit report of the extent to which several issues are interrelated.

4 Dependent variable

The third issue in strategy-as-practice research is the choice of the dependent variable or the outcome of strategizing process. The study of 'outcomes' (performance) has traditionally been a dominant theme in strategy research. There has also been an increasing attention called towards better focus on outcomes within strategy-as-practice (Jarzabkowski and Spee 2009). However outcomes in strategy-as-practice research cannot be firm level performance alone, as is common in strategy research, as the strategizing process also directly impacts the individuals, groups, institutions and practice communities involved – each of whom may be seeking different types of outcomes. Thus the 'straightjacket' of performance measurement prevalent in the traditional strategic management literature is deliberately avoided by strategy-as-practice, given the focus on multiple levels.

For instance, Ambrosini et al. (2007) have looked at the outcomes from micro-level activities in strategy-as-practice. Organizational performance is considered at a disaggregated level with a plurality of dependent variables. The strategy-as-practice perspective argues for explaining the performance of people as they interact and enact institutional and organizational practices. Such disaggregated dependent variables include levels at the individual, group, tools, systems, episodes as well as the contribution that these variables make towards strategic outcomes (Johnson et al. 2007). However the notion of outcomes is still not fully mature, and appears to be closer to the concept of praxis.

Some of the outcome related questions that are currently discussed by strategy-as-practice researchers in the strategy-as-practice website (accessed on 9-May-2009) are: What outcomes may be consequential to the firm at all levels of an organization? (see Jarzabkowski et al. 2007)? How could we study outcomes at a more micro level without losing focus of wider social factors within which such outcomes emerge? What other outcomes could there be in addition to those listed in Jarzabkowski and Spee (2009)?

5 Level of analysis

This leads to the fourth issue in strategy-as-practice research – specifying the level of analysis. While articles are increasingly developing the theoretical level of strategy-as-practice research, comparatively little has been written on the methodological level with the exception of Balogun, Huff and Johnson (2003). They explain that the growing need for researchers to be close to the phenomena of study, to concentrate on context and detail, and simultaneously to be broad in their scope of study, attending to many parts of the organization, clearly creates conflict. Johnson et al. (2007) explain that strategy-as-practice may be concerned with more plural levels of analysis, and importantly, the relationship between them. "It not only goes beneath organization-level processes to investigate what goes on inside organizations; it also goes above these processes to interrogate how the practices and tools originate from a wider business environment outside the firm" (Molloy and Whittington, 2005 quoted in Johnson et.al. 2007). Hence both contexts and the people who enact them are of interest to strategy-as-practice researchers. This is difficult as such research must cover multiple levels of analysis to be adequately holistic in scope and sufficiently nuanced in insight. The linkage of level of analysis through to strategic outcomes is an important component of practice research, as the ultimate need is to be able to link the outcomes of strategising activities by various practitioners within the firm, to more macro organisational, institutional and, possibly, even broader social contexts and outcomes (Jarzabkowski and Spee 2009). Outcomes of studies are likely to depend on the analytical focus and unit of analysis. Based on current strategy-as-practice research, Jarzabkowski and Spee (2009) distinguish between personal/individual, group, strategising process and organisational as well as institutional outcomes. How strategists' actions construct particular outcomes; as well as how differences in what strategists do can be explained through variations in the outcomes that are observed.

6 Data collection

Balogun, Huff and Johnson (2003:197) argue that 'today's large, multinational, and highly diversified organizational settings require complementary methods providing more breadth and flexibility'. They suggest three particularly promising approaches (interactive discussion groups, self-reports, and practitioner-led research) that fit the increasingly disparate research paradigms now being used to understand strategizing and other management issues. Interestingly, they also stress the importance of working with organizational members as research partners rather than passive informants. At one level the solution appears to be about innovation of methods, but if we pursue to its logical conclusion the argument that issues of depth, breadth, relevance and diversity are inter-linked, then it becomes apparent that we actually need to re-conceive the way we conduct research. Johnson et al. (2007) also call attention to the physical artefacts or objects in strategy as practice as such, such a power point presentations, flip-charts, other texts, photographs. Even the physical arrangement of participants at a strategy offsite meeting and their body language could be highly useful for understanding strategizing. Strategy-as-practice research provides rich scope in including the 'respondent' as a research partner, rather than only as a subject of research, as the respondent is often an experienced strategist who has a more nuanced understanding of the phenomena and the organisation's domain than the researcher. An indepth knowledge of practice may be acquired only through participation, even by becoming a practitioner (Johnson, et al. 2007). Some academics are also strategy consultants, but their knowledge may again be unconscious. A potentially valuable approach suggested is to find a 'master' and become an 'apprentice'. Balogun, Huff and Johnson (2003) focus in particular on the importance of working with organizational members as research partners rather than passive informants. Johnson et al. (2007) also cite a work by Stronz (2005) who videotaped naturally occurring strategy implementation meetings over a period of several months. Based on the video data and an 'action science framework', she then chose excerpts from the meetings to present to the implementation team members and further interview them. This captured both strategizing as it happened, as well as the recall value of interviewees as they reviewed their reactions. Such research can benefit by designing effective methods to capture this nuanced understanding. However one must be aware of the pitfalls of such action research approaches that may cause issues of methodology acceptance. Three risks are well known – the risk of contamination (where the researcher ends up influencing the phenomena), risk of going native (researcher getting socialised and hence failing to maintain an external perspective) and the risk of political alignment (researcher getting used as a tool by some faction). While research methods currently used in strategy-as-practice are largely borrowed from ethnography and anthropology, where the researcher is trained to avoid these three risks, practice studies need to ensure sensitivity to these risks as well, The literature on process consultation such as Schein (1995, 1999) or on making sense of the organizational 'mess' as advocated by Ackoff (1981, 1999) provide valuable directions in this regard. Such literature provides researchers with practical tips and highlights appropriate techniques on data gathering that can minimise biases due to these risks. For instance, Ackoff (1999) explains that the person who should prepare the reports on organizational status should be chosen to have an optimal number of years of experience in the organization to reduce biases and yet know the context sufficiently, Schein (1995) distinguishes between pure, diagnostic, action-oriented and confrontative modes of inquiry with members of the organization that corresponds to different levels of intervention. Such an approach provides support for active sense making processes from intra and inter-individual perspectives. We believe that there is scope for better process data being revealed by an organization that voluntarily initiates a consultation process with the researcher as it directly benefits by doing so as described in Schein (1999).

7 Quantification and variance theorizing

Apart from descriptive contributions from rich qualitative datasets, or process theorizing drawn out of understanding of phenomena based on temporal evolution, a third but relatively unexplored possibility is that of middle range theories that link strategic practices to some form of outcome. The outcomes relevant for micro-strategy may remain at a micro or meso level. Eisenhardt's (1989) study of decision making strategies and its relation primarily to decision speed and corporate performance is held up as an exemplar. The systematic way of replicating findings across eight cases provides a strong basis for a credible theory, providing analytical generalisability. Johnson et al. (2007) also explain that there is room for other nomothetically driven work that relates practices to their context.

While it is argued that qualitative data is essential to understand the 'doing' of strategy, Johnson et.al. (2007) allow a role for quantification primarily towards summarizing and categorizing observations. They also warn about the dangers of quantification that hide the detailed understanding acquired about the actual "doing" of strategy. Balogun, Huff and Johnson (2003) argue that that 'deep' data gathering around the unique characteristics of organizations, rather than their generic attributes, is needed. At the same time, however, there is a need for research designs that give priority to breadth. In a globalizing world, strategizing research must reflect large-scale strategizing activities in several places simultaneously.

We suggest that it is possible to draw inspiration from works in domains like software engineering that seek to link practices to performance. For instance, Cusumano, MacCormack, Kemerer and Crandall (2003) have reported the wide range of software development practices and the differences in practices and performance levels around the world. Their article reports descriptive results from a global survey of completed software projects that show international differences in the adoption of software development practices. Similarly, Cusumano and Kemerer (1990) did a comprehensive literature review that analyzes existing comparisons of Japanese and U.S. practice in software development and summarize the major proposed differences in performance. Similar studies could be attempted about strategizing practices in organizations across the world - promising insights into strategizing processes as the field matures and as practices are more or less identifiable in a relatively standard manner.

On similar lines, Whittington and Cailluet (2008: 243) highlight quantitative research possibilities "strategic planning remains a pervasive and influential phenomenon in the world, perhaps more so than earlier. Since 1996, Bain & Co's survey of management tools has regularly reported strategic planning being used by around 80 per cent of its responding companies, and in 2007 (as in many years before) found it the most popular tool of all, with an eleven-year record of 88 per cent of companies using it. Accenture describes the rise of the 'the Chief Strategy Officer', with supporting departments, in large multinational companies around the world. Job advertisement analysis shows a significant increase in the number of formal strategy roles in the United Kingdom during the 1990s, with a major increase in the public sector especially." They argue that if strategic planning is taking new forms and entering new domains it deserves scholarly attention (Whittington and Cailluet 2008: 243).

8 Methodological innovations

Jarzabkowski, Balogun and Seidl (2007) consider it necessary to consider the methodological implications of different theoretical approaches. However, little empirical work conducted in the strategy-as-practice perspective has developed innovative methodology specific to the perspective, with the exception of anthropological (e.g. Johnson et al., 2007) and ethnomethodological (Samra-Fredericks, 2003) approaches. There is therefore an opportunity for methodological innovations in the area of strategy as practice. One inspired direction that we were suggested to explore was in Schein (1995, 1999, 2004). Schein (2004) used clinical research to study organizational culture, where the data comes voluntarily from the members of the organization because either they initiated the process and had something to gain by revealing themselves, or if the researcher/consultant initiated the project and if they had something to gain from cooperating with him/her. The clinical model makes two explicit fundamental assumptions – one that it is not possible to study a human system without intervening in it, and two one can fully understand a human system by trying to change it. In this regard, clinical research and ethnography differ sharply as ethnography generally aims to leave the system as intact as possible. Schein (1995) makes a clear distinction between formal data driven action research on the one hand and client driven clinical inquiry on the other hand. Action research as defined by researchers involves the client in the data gathering but is driven by the researcher's agenda. Action research as defined by the clinician involves the helper consultant in the client's inquiry process and the process is driven by the client's needs. What makes the clinical method more powerful than other methods, is that if the researcher/consultant is helping the organization, they have the licence to ask all kinds of questions, hang around and observe almost in an ethnographic fashion, all this with due consideration of the risks involved of going native, contamination and political alignment as may be addressed from the extensive literature on ethnographic methods or anthropology. Another profitable direction to obtain such data is highlighted by Bednar (2000), who examines constructive dialogue as a means of gaining access to the existing but unreleased individual and group competencies. Bednar (2000) mirrors Schein (1999) in recommending an interventional approach that regards individual perspectives while focussing on situations, and engages the actors in reflecting on their experience when problem-solving is involved. Strategy-as-practice may like to consider a clinical research approach as it is in alignment with what strategy consultants do.

9 Implications for research

The notion of strategizing spans a wide scope that goes beyond the organization boundaries and what constitutes strategizing remaining undefined, at several levels, the challenges in research design are numerous, Connecting micro level activities to macro level outcomes is a key challenge going forward in strategy-as-practice research. Large, multinational and diversified organizations require complementary methods providing more breadth and flexibility. While descriptive and process studies are the dominant paradigm in strategy-as-practice research, we suggest that quantitative studies is one much ignored approach that may provide greater insights. Using practitioners who are repositories of tacit knowledge more actively in research may provide significant benefits. Therefore another approach that we propose is that of clinical methods, inspired from process consultation techniques of Schein (1998). This potential approach has the promise to balance several tradeoffs in the field between richness of data and the traditional challenges in ethnography. Strategy-as-practice research has untapped scope for creative researchers to innovate on research methodology and possibly even to reconceptualise how research itself is conducted.

10 Conclusions

Although it has its beginnings in the late 1990's, the strategy-as-practice field is yet to come of age, and the track record of its presence at the Academy of Management suggests that it is still viewed as a nascent body seeking to establish itself. While there could be several challenges to its grounds for legitimacy, research methodology is one enormous point that deserves attention. This article has explained the four challenges in strategy-as-practice research. First, defining the scope of the research question is an issue given that the definition of strategy itself is not unambiguous and strategizing can happen in many ways in and even outside an organization. Second, the theoretical unit of analysis of individuals and organizations and their processes, activities and practices must be revised. Third, the notion of performance measurement prevalent in the traditional strategic management literature is purposely avoided by strategy-as-practice, instead organizational performance is considered at a disaggregated level with a plurality of dependent variables. Fourth, the level of analysis merits attention as strategizing activity spans individual, group, organization, institutional and practice community levels.

Beyond enumerating these challenges, we have also proposed new avenues that can further the frontiers of strategy-as-practice research, particularly on the methodological front. After summarizing the tradeoffs in data collection, we propose a relook at quantification or variance theorizing as a potential methodology for studying practice at a macro level. We derive inspiration from fields such as software engineering, where macro level studies of practices have provided valuable insights. Another exciting possibility is clinical research whose established methods have the promise to provide the right level of access and richness to strategy-as-practice studies.

Acknowledgements

We thank Deepak K Sinha for suggesting the scope of clinical methods in strategy-as-practice research.

References

Ackoff, R. L. 1999 *Re-creating the Corporation: A Design of Organizations for the 21st Century*, Oxford University Press, USA.

Ackoff, R. L. 1981 *Creating the corporate future: Plan or be planned for*, John Wiley & Sons Inc.

Ambrosini, V., Bowman, C. and Burton-Taylor, S. 2007 Inter-team coordination activities as a source of customer satisfaction'. *Human Relations* 60: 59–98.

Balogun, J., Huff, A.S. and Johnson, P. 2003 Three responses to the methodological challenges of studying strategizing. *Journal of Management Studies* 40:197–224.

Bednar, P. M. 2000 A contextual integration of individual and organizational learning perspectives as part of IS analysis. *Informing Science* 3(3): 145-156.

Bourque, N. and Johnson, G. 2008 Strategy workshops and 'away-days' as ritual. In Hodgkinson, G. and Starbuck, W. (eds), *Oxford Handbook of Organizational Decision Making*. Oxford, UK: Oxford University Press: 552–564.

Chia, R. and MacKay, B. 2007 Post-processual challenges for the emerging s-as-p perspective: discovering strategy in the logic of practice'. *Human Relations* 60: 217–242.

Cusumano, M.A. and Kemerer C. F. 1990 A quantitative analysis of U.S. and Japanese practice and performance in software development'. *Management Science*, 36(11), 1384-1406.

Cusumano M.A., MacCormack A., Kemerer C.F. and Crandall B. 2003 'Software development worldwide: The state of the practice'. *IEEE Software* 20/6: 28-34.

Eisenhardt K. 1989 'Building theories from case study research'. *Academy of Management Review* 14: 532–550.

Hendry J. and Seidl D. 2003 'The structure and significance of strategic episodes: social systems theory and the routine practices of strategic change'. *Journal of Management Studies* 40: 175–196.

Jarzabkowski, P. 2004 'Strategy as practice: recursive, adaptive and practices-in-use'. *Organization Studies* 25: 529–560.

Jarzabkowski P. and Spee A. 2009) 'Strategy-as-practice: A review and future directions for the field'. *International Journal of Management Reviews*, 11(1): 69-95

Jarzabkowski P., Balogun J. and Seidl D. 2007 'Strategizing: the challenges of a practice perspective'. *Human Relations* 60: 5–27.

Johnson, G., A. Langley A., Melin L. and Whittington R. 2007 *Strategy as Practice: Research Directions and Resources*, Cambridge University Press.

Langley, A. 1999 'Strategies for theorizing from process data'. *Academy of Management Review* 24: 691–710.

Mir, R. and Watson, A. 2000 'Strategic management and the philosophy of science: the case for a constructivist methodology'. *Strategic Management Journal* 21(9): 941–953.

Mintzberg H.1979 'An emerging strategy of direct research. *Administrative Science Quarterly* 24: 582-589.

Samra-Fredericks, D. 2003 'Strategizing as lived experience and strategists' everyday efforts to shape strategic direction'. *Journal of Management Studies* 40: 57–82.

Schein, E. H. 1995 'Process consultation, action research and clinical inquiry: are they the same?' *Journal of Managerial Psychology* 10(6): 14-19.

Schein, E. H. 1999 *Process consultation revisited: Building the helping relationship*, Addison-Wesley Reading, MA.

Schein, E. H. 2004 *Organizational Culture and Leadership*, Jossey-Bass.

Whittington, R. 2003 'The work of strategizing and organizing: for a practice perspective'. *Strategic Organization* 1: 119–127.

Whittington, R. 2007 'Strategy practice and strategy process: family differences and the sociological eye'. *Organization Studies* 28:1575–1586.

Whittington, R. and Cailluet, L. 2008 The crafts of strategy. *Long Range Planning*. 41(3): 241-247.

Using Focus Groups in Studies of ISD Team Behaviour

Colm O'hEocha[1], Kieran Conboy[1] and Xiaofeng Wang[2]
[1]Business Information Systems Group, NUI Galway, Galway, Ireland
[2]Lero, the Irish Software Engineering Research Centre, Limerick, Ireland
Originally published in EJBRM (2010) Volume 8 Issue 2.

Editorial Commentary

In this account of the use of focus groups the authors provide an illustration of the ways in which such an approach can be applied, analysed and evaluated when employed in the context of a fairly contentious and sensitive issues. They outline some of the benefits and disadvantages of focus group research, and then apply various frameworks to their findings.

The basic operations of the focus group approach are described, and the findings are then discussed in terms of three approaches to validation. The paper thus offers readers an insight into the basic processes of focus group research, as well as indicating the possible ways in which any findings might be presented and evaluated. The authors point out that focus group research can provide rich and wide-ranging data in a fairly short time; which can be beneficial if the material is used and evaluated carefully. On other hand the quality and reliability of the outcomes from the focus groups themselves is highly dependent on the skills of the researcher(s) in ensuring appropriate forms and levels of participation and discussion.

Abstract: This paper discusses an innovative focus group approach used to study an Information Systems Development (ISD) environment. The research had to cope with the application of a broad framework, untested in practice, seeking to elicit potentially highly sensitive opinions and judgments in a highly pressurised, time-restricted environment. The researchers' design of the case research is discussed, in particular the use of focus groups. Through a description of how these were conducted some of the novel aspects of the data collection technique used to address the specific issues mentioned above are illustrated. This is followed by an exploration of various frameworks proposed in the literature for evaluation of focus groups in particular, and interpretive research in general. Future work proposed includes the evaluation of this research using a set of 7 criteria proposed in the literature based on critical interpretive epistemology.

Keywords: focus group, information systems development, evaluation criteria

1 Introduction

The research team in this study was tasked with assessing the agility of a proprietary method in a globally distributed systems development organisation. Rather than trying to assess agility by establishing the compliance of implementation with the defined method, we examined each implementation using a conceptually well-established agile assessment framework (see Conboy 2009). The assessment objectives were (i) to establish the agility afforded by the proprietary method as implemented in the organisation ('method-in-action'), and (ii) to identify major issues with the adoption and generate recommendations to address these.

This assessment was highly complex. Significant time restrictions were in place. A previously untested, broad, multi-faceted framework, consisting of highly complex and multidimensional constructs was to be used. There were no accompanying set of prescriptive questions, and the researchers had to address the potential for poor judgement, unsupported anecdotal statements, and statements arising from ulterior motives. The study also involved potentially sensitive and controversial data, and data was difficult to collect in some cases where ISD team members were geographically dispersed.

All of these issues required careful consideration when designing the focus groups approach for this research. Thus, the objectives of this paper are to describe the research approach used and discuss how it could be evaluated in terms of efficiency and effectiveness. In the following sections, the objective of this research is discussed and focus group theory is outlined, including a discussion of its use in various fields. We then describe the key elements of the ISD study we conducted, to demonstrate the complex nature of the study, and elaborate the focus group fieldwork conducted with a summary of the modifications to the focus group approach used in collecting data. This is followed by an evaluation of this modified data collection technique using evaluation criteria specifically proposed for focus groups, and reflection on possible improvements. We then discuss the need for a more holistic evaluation using other potential evaluation criteria which address the whole research method, including focus groups, in a comprehensive and rigorous manner. Finally, future work, including the application of such a broad research evaluation framework, and conclusions are discussed.

2 Research objectives

There are many reasons for specifically relaying experiences of focus group research in Information Systems (IS) and for evaluating their effectiveness in this discipline. As discussed below, focus groups have not been used extensively in IS research, despite apparent suitability. They are advocated for descriptive, explanatory and exploratory studies, leverage common concrete situations and groups which are common in work teams in general, and can provide deep and specific insights into complex sociological situations such as teams. They also allow investigation of ambiguous or multi-dimensional topics and a large quantity of data to be collected even where time or researcher access is limited.

As well as all the advantages of the approach, the literature also recognises potential drawbacks. These include difficulties in directing topics for discussion while not imposing the researchers interpretation on the group, effects of group dynamics on the data collected and the lack of prescription in how the technique should be applied. While the literature contains some general 'rules of thumb' (Morgan 1997), such direction remains quite ambiguous and ill-defined compared to other techniques such as surveys (Kidd and Parshall 2000). For example, Morgan (1997) suggests that when conducting focus groups, the researcher "should use a relatively structured format with high moderator input". This in itself is quite a loose prescription, but the true ambiguity is revealed when Morgan suggests that "this guideline will vary depending on how exploratory, descriptive or explanatory the research objective".

In the current study, several significant modifications were made to the focus group technique described in the literature. These were designed to increase the efficiency of the method given the broad set of specific topics to be covered and the severe time restrictions. Modifications included describing each sub-topic to be addressed on an A1 poster stuck to the walls of the room, and collecting data primarily through notes written by members and stuck to these posters. This allowed the capture of inputs from multiple participants simultaneously and in a nominally anonymous manner. These modifications are discussed in more detail later in the paper.

Given the limited use of focus groups in IS research, the vagueness of details on its implementation in a specific context, the significant potential weaknesses in the method and the modifications to reported usage in this study, the researchers felt an evaluation of the technique was warranted. This paper describes such an evaluation, where the method as here implemented is reviewed with respect to criteria defined in the focus group literature. It is then argued that evaluation of the focus group data collection technique alone is insufficient where there is an impact on other areas of the research method, such as analysis. Therefore, alternate evaluation criteria are discussed and proposed for further work.

To illustrate the conceptual basis of the paper, the general focus group literature is reviewed in the next section before we introduce the specific extended focus group approach we employed in our ISD study and the evaluation of it.

3 Focus group research

Focus group research emerged from work performed by Paul Lazarsfeld, Robert Merton and colleagues at Columbia University in the early 1940s, It is defined as a "research technique that collects data through group interaction on a topic determined by the researcher"(Morgan 1997) and involves a group of participants and one or more moderators. The core theoretical elements of focus groups include topical focus, group interactions, in-depth data and a 'humanistic' character (Stewart, Shamdasani et al. 2007).

The focus element derives from participants of the group having a 'particular concrete situation' in common (Merton and Kendall 1946) but is also affected by the moderators direction of the groups discussions. In the present study, all participants shared common membership of an ISD project team. In terms of group interaction, small group dynamics can greatly affect the data collected and can lead to increased depth and reflection over individual interviews. In this case, since the topic being investigated related to the team as well as individuals, the group aspect of the technique is considered important in increasing the depth of data collected, as discussions stimulated reflection and helped surface opinions and other inputs that might otherwise not have been forthcoming. Finally, the technique supports an emphatic and open interaction with participants, where discovery of meaning is valued over measurement.

There are many advantages and disadvantages of the technique highlighted in the literature. Focus groups allow the researcher to obtain substantially more data from a group in a short amount of time than one-to-one interviews (Morgan 1997). Insights and less accessible data can emerge which may not otherwise come to the surface (Morgan, 1997). This is especially true where participants may not know much about the research topic and require a group discussion to stimulate them to make a contribution, or what is referred to as "introspective retrospection" (Merton and Kendall 1946). In addition, Bloor, Frankland et al (2001) suggest that focus groups allow participants to "articulate those normally unarticulated normative assumptions". Other researchers (Kitzinger 1994; Kidd and Parshall 2000) draw attention to the importance of this differentiator of focus groups from other forms of collective or focused interviews.

Ideally, group interaction will lead to "collaborative construction" but it can lead to effects such as conformity of views as dominant characters or roles in a group cause others to 'tow the line' (Morgan 1997). Small group dynamics come into play, which can stymie minority or controversial opinions. Conversely, the group setting can lead to polarisation into one or more sub-groups or 'factions' (Sim 1998; Barbour 2007). Opinions expressed may reflect those of a particular group context rather than an aggregation of the opinions of the individuals (Stewart, Shamdasani et al. 2007). Additionally, more 'subtle' input that might emerge in a less 'public' context can be missed. While the moderator has less control over a group and less access to individual opinions, the setting of the topic of focus by the researcher can also influence the range and depth of input gathered and may not reflect topics considered important or interesting to participants (Merton and Kendall 1946). Focus groups do not allow observation of groups in more 'natural' contexts and are primarily restricted to discussions rather than other forms of interaction (Morgan 1997). Data collected is confined to participants' opinions and reportage of experiences and therefore is highly subjective (Wilkinson 1998).

Focus groups are suitable for exploratory, descriptive and explanatory research but, as implied by the definition above, is particularly suited where the researcher wants to focus on specific topics while leveraging group interaction. The method has also been advocated for "formative evaluation, for programme improvement" (Patton 1990) which matches the use in this study (Hines 2000). Focus groups could be considered to lie between dyadic interviews and direct observation: while allowing the researcher to direct attention to specific topics as allowed by interviews, they also facilitate group discussion as per observation. A significant benefit of focus groups is the ability to get a lot of data from a group in a short amount of time (Morgan 1997; Stewart, Shamdasani et al. 2007).

Despite being a valid data collection approach, and extensively used in other disciplines such as marketing and health service research, an examination of the IS literature shows that focus groups as a method of research are under-utilised in the field, with very few IS studies adopting the approach to date (Sobreperez 2008), and none specifically within the domain of ISD as far as we are aware. Where focus groups have been used in IS studies, they are usually in contexts where focus group studies are more widely used such as health (Eysenbach 2000; Koppel, Metlay et al. 2005) and marketing (Pitt, Watson et al. 1995). Some other research in IS has used focus groups but only as a minor supplementary data collection technique (Reich and Benbasat 2000). More indirectly related to IS, related fields such as Library and Information Science have reportedly used Focus Groups extensively (Kerslake and Goulding 1996).

In the following section we discuss the use of two conceptual frameworks in the study of the agility of ISD teams. This is followed by a description of the case research conducted in a company using these frameworks before discussion of how the quality of such research can be evaluated.

4 Extended focus group approach in an ISD study
Here we describe the research approach adopted for this study, and how the focus groups were conducted in the field.

4.1. The ISD study: Assessing agile development methods
In assessing ISD methods, measuring compliance to defined practices is common. However, this fails to take account of contextual factors specific to a work context. The novel approach used in this research considers the

true contribution of each method practice to agility itself, rather than compliance to a defined agile method. For this we used a 'conceptual framework' for agility which defines the underlying aspects of an agile team such as creativity and simplicity. Therefore, the agile methods in use could be assessed effectively regardless of the particular practices each project did or did not implement, or indeed how the project implemented each practice. This approach allowed effective comparison of the three projects using three different agile implementations – in effect allowing us compare 'apples and oranges'. Therefore the assessment involved answering the three following questions illustrated in Figure 1 High level research design Figure 1 for each project.

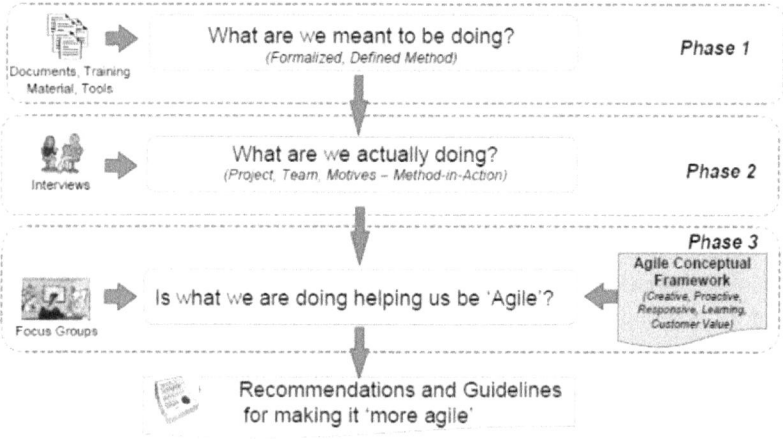

Figure 1: High level research design

The defined method was established through analysis of the documentation and training materials provided by Pennysoft describing the various practices. Then a set of interviews with team leaders from each of the projects established the method-in-action (Fitzgerald, Russo et al. 2002). Research has shown that work methods are never implemented exactly as defined, varying by project, team and organizational context (Madsen, Kautz et al. 2006). Agile methods generally acknowledge this explicitly, citing the 'tailoring' of methods to ensure effectiveness in specific situations. Therefore, it is not good enough to assume the practices have been implemented in a textbook manner – it's essential to understand where implementations are similar and where they differ from the documented method and across projects.

The method-in-action for each of the three projects studied were found to be quite different. Different sets of practices were used, and each of these were used differently. Each project method was examined in terms of the following which derive from the method-in-action framework (Fitzgerald, Russo et al. 2002):

- Development context: The nature of the business and technical project drivers, stakeholders, project history, criticality, complexity and so forth.
- Team context: Characteristics of the project team including size, diversity, experience, skills, geographical distribution and motivation.
- Rational and political roles: The role of the ISD method on a particular project, both in terms of explicit and rational use (reduce cost, increase quality, etc) and political use, such as team reputation, showcasing fast development ability, etc.

Once the method-in-action was established, the third phase involved a half-day focus group session with each team to establish how each practice supported or inhibited agility.

Agility in work is not a new concept, and originated long before software development was established as an industry. From a foundation of organizational agility, and with reference to agile software development, the core contributory concepts of agility have been identified (Conboy 2009). Creativity, proaction, reaction, learning, cost, quality and simplicity are the foundations of agility and were used to study how the work methods used in these projects affected team and organizational agility. The agile concepts we used derive from the following definition of agility (Conboy 2009):
The continual readiness of an ISD method to rapidly or inherently create change, proactively or reactively embrace change, and learn from change while contributing to perceived customer value (economy, quality and simplicity), through its collective components and relationships with its environment.

In the focus group sessions, described further below, each agile practice employed by each project was evaluated for the following:

- Their agility in terms of creativity, proaction, reaction and learning from change
- Their perceived customer value of cost, quality and simplicity

Using these concepts allowed characterization of each project method in a consistent manner, regardless of the details of how they had implemented agile. Table 1 below gives a description of each concept to guide how they can be considered in relation to each ISD practice.

Table 1: Agile concepts used in the agility assessment

Concept	Description
Creativity	The ability to create inventions or solve problems using an original, novel, or unconventional approach. This involves creativity among all stakeholders, sharing of ideas and knowledge and continuous improvement in the team and processes.
Proaction	Taking steps in advance of change, which pre-empt the change, or acting in anticipation of future problems, needs, or changes. This requires early identification, estimation and prioritization of risks and planning for contingencies.
Reaction	Responding to situations, or changes that have taken place, including communication of changes requested and rapid interpretation and empowered response to such changes and their impacts.
Learning	Knowledge or skill acquired or modification of a behavioral tendency by experience (as exposure to conditioning). This requires both dissemination and absorption of knowledge.
Cost	The total cost of the solution including time spent by stakeholders, skill and experience levels required by the team, capital and operational costs and lost opportunity costs.
Quality	The quality of the solution in terms of delivery (bugs), the business value delivered, and the quality of the experience for various stakeholders
Simplicity	Maximizing the work not done by ensuring the processes, tools and metrics are easy to use, all solution features implemented are needed and used and the design is as simple as possible to deliver current functionality.

Agility analysis involved a half-day focus group session with each team to establish how each practice supported or inhibited agility. Focus groups were selected as the primary data collection technique for the current study due to their efficiency in gathering a lot of data from a group of informants and their ability to improve the range and depth of input. However, to address some of the shortcomings mentioned in the previous section, Several novel extensions were made to the method. Participants were encouraged to provide input in the form of written notes as well as through recording and analysis of group discussions. Therefore, the discussions allowed group (and sub-group) exploration of the topics before participants gave written input, but the post-its also facilitated individual input without discussion. The discussion was also highly focused, covering each agile practice in turn. Input was solicited for each practice covered to avoid 'gaps' where certain topics would not have input. Therefore, the less defined, 'non-directive' moderator strategy often advocated for focus groups was not followed. Additionally, participants were not randomly selected from a homogenous population as normal; for practical reasons they included several roles (which could be considered to have opposing interests, priorities and motivations) and were selected by the participants rather than randomly. Further details of the novel aspects to these focus groups are described in the next.

4.2. Conducting focus groups in Pennysoft

Here we describe the context of the data collection followed by the technique used across three ISD teams. This includes modifications to the focus group approach such as the use of ISD method practices on posters to act as an interview guide, the use of written input by participants as the primary data input method, and the 'self-coding' of such input by attaching the notes to the appropriate poster under a particular agile concept.

Pennysoft (referring to the case study organization which is not identified for confidentiality reasons) is a global financial services firm with approximately 45,000 employees worldwide. Up to 10,000 of these are IT personnel developing systems to support the business, distributed across multiple sites in the US, Europe and India. A formal 'waterfall' development method has been used extensively across the company for several years. A newly developed proprietary method incorporating many principles and practices from agile methods such as Scrum is currently being piloted in several sites. Three such trial projects located in an Irish office were studied as part of this research between July and September 2009. All were part of distributed teams, but with the majority of analysis, development and test based in Ireland. One was a 'green field' project with some US members and a small, inexperienced team of five. The other two were larger (10-20) with US and India based members and were part of larger enterprise wide programs.

A single, 3 hour focus group was then held for each project, with a representative sample of half or more of the team selected by project management. In one case, two participants based in India used a videoconference link and contributed written input using instant messaging. From 3 to 6 researchers filled the roles of moderators, note takers, discussion facilitators and logistical support, and several audio recorders were placed about the room. Each session began with an overview of the research project objectives and the format of the group session. This was followed by an introduction to the agile conceptual framework, including description and examples of how a practice might impinge on creativity, quality and other aspects that affect agility. Then 5-10 minutes was spent on considering each practice in turn (a total of about 2 hours). This was followed by 30 minutes for further discussion of emerging topics, ambiguities and so on. At the end of each session, informants were invited to submit any further, possibly confidential, input directly to the researchers outside the focus group setting.

Before the group session, each development practice as used in the project was described briefly as a set of bullet points on an A1 poster, all of which were hung on the walls of the meeting room. The posters also included a column for each agile concept (see Figure 2) where participants could stick post-it notes with their input on how that concept was affected by the practice concerned. Additionally, two A1 posters were displayed describing the agility constructs. Pens and post-it notes were made available around the room. During the session, the moderator moved from practice to practice, describing each briefly to refresh informants memories and inviting updates or corrections about the practice in verbal or written form. The moderator then encouraged discussion between informants and invited written input. Researchers also captured verbal input from discussions and added these to the posters using a different coloured post-it.

Periodically, the importance of specific, concrete examples was emphasised in preference to abstract opinions and feelings. As informants stuck post-its to the posters the researchers selected particularly vague or particularly interesting examples and read them out to the group. Immediately following each focus group the post-it notes were coded to record the practice and concept to which they applied and the content was typed up into data tables for use in the analysis. Group discussions, which took place during the session, were later transcribed from the audio recordings. The initial analysis was allocated to four researchers with each working on a set of practices, sometimes jointly. Due to time and resource constraints, formal coding and other data analysis techniques were not used. Following the analysis each section was reviewed by at least two academic reviewers and one industrial reviewer (all of whom had also been involved in the focus groups) with extensive discussions and revisions leading to a comprehensive report for the company.

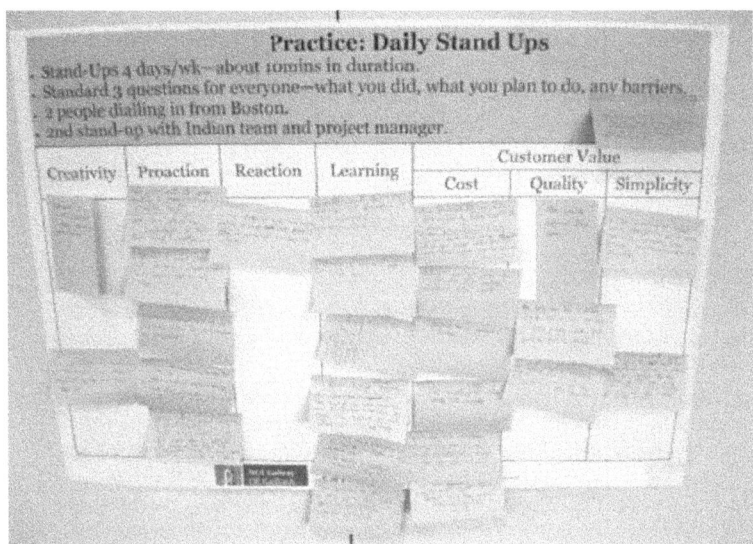

Figure 2: Poster sample with post-it note contributions

Table 2 summarises the specific extensions and modifications made to the focus group method as described in the literature.

Table 2: Novel extensions to focus group data collection technique

Captured Written Participant Input	Written input was regarded as the primary data input method, rather than group discussions as usual in focus groups
Self-Coding of Participant Input	Participants decided what practice, and which agility concept, with which they would associate each written post-it by placing it appropriately on the wall posters.
Substantial Anonymity of Written Input	Written input was substantially anonymous – there was no identification on the post notes, though it would be possible through hand-writing etc for participants to determine the author of a note if they tried.
Concurrent Independent Input by Participants	Participants were free to write notes on practices not currently the focus of the group – at times participants were considering and giving input on a range of different practices at the same time.

Reduced Capture of Group Discussions	Usually in a focus group there is one discussion underway at any time, and it can therefore be captured in full by the researchers. In this case, there were several concurrent discussions by subsets of participants – some but not all such discussion was captured.
Possible increase in 'thoughtful' interpretation by participants	Rather than discussions providing the data for the research, where initial thoughts and preconceptions might be captured, the written input could be regarded as the output or conclusion of such discussion. It therefore may include consideration of others opinions and a more thoughtful & considered input.
Loss of attribution & other context in written input	The post-its did not identify the individual, role, time written, discussion under way or other contextual data which would be available for normal focus group data.
Restricted time/space for writing low inference descriptors	Written input was restricted due to: the short time given each topic limited space on post-its relatively slow speed to write rather than speak input Therefore, opportunity to give illustrations and examples was limited.
Highly Structured interview guide based on Method-In–Action analysis.	The sessions were based on a set of practices pre-determined by the researchers through document reviews of the defined method and interviews with the project manager for each team.
Highly directed topics to minimise gaps in data	There was a conscious effort to ensure each practice received a minimum level of input – this may have reduced time spent on more important topics (as judged by participants) and placed too much emphasis on topics not considered significant.
Heterogenous participants with different team roles/status	Focus group literature calls for randomly selected, homogenous participants to arrive at deep insights into particular topics. Although the concrete situation (the project) was common to all participants, significant heterogeneity was evident based on the diverse team roles involved. Also, participants were determined by project management and were not randomly selected.

5 Evaluating focus group research

There is extensive literature on the design and moderation of focus group research (Merton, Fiske et al. 1990; Kitzinger 1994; Morgan 1997; Barbour 2007; Stewart, Shamdasani et al. 2007; Krueger and Casey 2009). However, there are few criteria defined for evaluating such research designs. Nor can these researchers find examples of the evaluation of focus groups as a data collection technique. In this section we first consider two sets of evaluation criteria for focus groups, and report an evaluation of the current study using one of the criteria sets. Then we discuss other potential evaluation frameworks proposed for interpretive research in general which, it is argued, provide a more holistic view of the quality of the research as a

Leading Issues in Business Research Methods

whole, rather than the specific focus group technique used for data collection.

5.1. Focus group evaluation criteria

The first framework, proposed by Sim (1998), proposes three critical constraints to focus group research as follows:

Table 3: Focus group research evaluation criteria (Sim 1998)

Issues on consensus and dissent	Participant discussion and "argumentative interactions" (Kitzinger 1994) are central to focus groups (Sim 1998). Yet research into group dynamics indicate that apparent consensus may merely reflect dominant personalities, or majority views and may not be shared by less articulate subjects, or participants in the minority. Similarly, dissent and polarisation into factions may have more to do with group dynamics than with the actual views held. Getting participants to write down their views in advance, a technique used in this study, may help in reducing such effects (Albrecht, Johnson et al. 1993).
Strength of Opinion	The emphasis and time spent discussing certain viewpoints in a group setting do not necessarily represent the true strength of feeling of the participants. Therefore, using focus groups to gauge strength of opinion cannot be considered valid. They cannot be considered a verbal form of such surveys (Asbury 1995) quoted in (Sim 1998) .
Generalisation	Generalisation is a common objective in positivist quantitative research, and normally takes the form of empirical generalisation allowing findings from the study of a representative sample to be extrapolated to the population with a certain degree of statistical confidence. But generalisation in qualitative research is more problematic since findings are normally situated in a certain context. However, theoretical generalisation is still possible whereby findings can be "transferred" from one context to another which has a similar context (Sim 1998).

An alternative set of four criteria is proposed by Merton, Fiske et al. (1990). These are range, specificity, depth and personal context, and each is described briefly in table 4.

Both these evaluation frameworks are derived from focus group literature and relate directly to the design and conducting of focus groups as a data collection technique. The following section describes the application of one of these to the study conducted in Pennysoft.

Table 4: Focus group research evaluation criteria (Merton, Fiske et al. 1990).

Range	It is recommended that a broad range of topics be discussed, possibly including some not foreseen by the researchers. This approach is supported through "nondirective" moderation of the group (Merton and Kendall 1946) and ensures participant input reflects what is important or interesting to the participant rather than to the researcher. Directed research questions and prompts invariably reflect the "framework" of the researcher and may imply certain interpretations and suggestions.
Specificity	Capturing input in terms of experiences and perspectives rather than just opinions is advocated by Merton and Kendall (1946). This helps prevent discussion drifting to generalities and reflects Yin's (1994) call to focus on "low-inference descriptors". However, this advice has been contested in the literature with the argument that the participants may be best placed to interpret events or experiences and that this approach may actually reduce researcher bias (Hines 2000). An improved technique is to elicit both specific input but also the participants interpretation or opinion.
Depth	This relates to the extent of self-revelatory input gained from participants, rather than merely descriptive input. It is important that a 'feeling context' is established to elicit input which provides more insight than statements describing what happened or was experienced. This can be easier where participants are intimately involved in the topic as in this study.
Personal Context	The personal and social context can be associated with the role played by the individual, such as project manager or developer, their skill and experience and their affinity with the team. Additional individual circumstance may also play a part, such as previous experiences with agile practices and with other project stakeholders (Morgan 1997). Although there are contrary views (Krueger and Casey 2009), most literature (Merton, Fiske et al. 1990; Kitzinger 1994; Sim 1998) calls for homogenous groups selected randomly from a population. Although different roles and experiences will bring different insights to a group discussion, one of the strengths of a homogenous group is that the differences and convergences can be more easily identified and can lead to deep insights (Sim 1998).

5.2. Evaluation of the extended focus group approach

We evaluated the extended focus group approach using the criteria of Merton, Fiske et al. (1990), selecting this based on its prominence in the literature and more extensive operationalisation details provided.

Range – It is recommended that a broad range of topics be discussed, possibly including some not foreseen by the researchers. In the current study, one of the moderators had worked in the organisation previously, had conducted the dyadic interviews and was very familiar with the various projects, methods and participants. The previous senior position of this researcher in the organisation may have led to a certain directed effect in participants, and comments or questions may have inadvertently carried more weight than appropriate.

Planning for focus groups normally include preparation of an interview guide, which contains typical questions, areas for inquiry and hypothesis (Merton and Kendall 1946). However, given the importance of free flowing discussion in a focus group, such guides must be used carefully – the researcher should be familiar with the domain of inquiry and be attentive to both the explicit and implied content of the discussion. This allows them avoid re-covering topics already discussed or inadvertently cutting short a member by switching topic at an inappropriate time. In this case the guide was expressed as a set of ISD practices as used by the particular group in their project, along with the conceptual agile framework. Each practice was addressed in turn with strong delineation as the discussion moved from one to the next. However, the agile concepts were addressed all together for each practice and allowed free flowing discussion. Due to the written input method used, participants were also free to write down input to practices not currently the focus of the moderators and rest of the group. The researchers feel that this structure allowed sufficient flexibility for individuals and sub-groups to address topics as they saw fit, while ensuring all practices used by the team were given minimum attention and input.

A common criticism of focus group research is that conversations between participants are largely ignored both in reportage and analysis (Wilkinson 1998). Although several extended discussions were transcribed and included in the analysis, undoubtedly the main data collection mechanism considered was the written input. Therefore, more careful attention to group discussions could significantly improve the range of data collected, and its depth.

Specificity – Capturing input in terms of experiences and perspectives rather than just opinions is advocated by Merton and Kendall (1946). In this study, the moderators actively encouraged the use of specific examples by participants in illustrating their opinions, and even articulated examples from other projects to encourage description of specific instances. This approach supports "retrospective introspection" (Merton and Kendall 1946) which increases the specificity of input. However, the use of post-its with limited writing space and constraints on time most likely restricted the contribution of specific input and may, indeed, have biased written responses towards the more abstract and subjective.

Depth – Achieving depth of input requires an emotionally and politically 'safe' environment for participants. Sensitive issues may not emerge in a group that is not sympathetic. Such 'safety' was achieved in some part by using written notes as the primary method of accepting input from participants – such notes were nominally anonymous. However, since each participant posted their notes, in their own handwriting, on the wall posters it could not be considered entirely secure in this respect. The emphasis put on specificity and detailed examples from the stimulus situation also helped in achieving depth.

Personal Context – The personal and social context of participants is an important factor in interpreting input. In the current study, a representative sample of members from across the ISD teams were selected – these differed in roles, skills, and experience among other factors. However, all had intimate knowledge and experience of the project and the practices used and were homogenous in that respect. Since the study was evaluating the agility of the team as a whole rather than a certain role within the team, it was felt this was the most appropriate way to constitute the groups. However, participants were selected by the project manager of each team and a certain bias may have been introduced in terms of representation.

In considering the effect of personal context on the research method, it is clear that this is particularly important in the data analysis stage. To facilitate this, quotations and other input should to be attributed accurately to individual group members (Sim 1998). This facilitates effective coding and pattern detection during data analysis (Kidd and Parshall 2000). In this study, a significant opportunity for improvement is to devise a mechanism to allow attribution of both written and verbal input. However, this must be integrated with an approach that also provides broader context to the input – which places each written contribution in terms of the questions or discussion which prompted it. Although the placing of post-its at certain places on each poster provides some such context, this cannot be considered entirely reliable.

5.3. Evaluation criteria for qualitative research

Although the evaluation described above allowed us to draw several improvements of the approach we have used, the evaluation criteria employed are akin to "rules of thumb" for conducting focus groups. This is because there is no theoretical or conceptual grounding of these criteria – they are not based on any evaluation criteria more widely used in qualitative research. In addition, they are proposed for evaluating the focus group aspects of research rather than the overall research method. As such, their ability to establish the impacts of such data collection on the quality of research is limited. Therefore such criteria are not sufficient to appraise the efficiency and effectiveness of the overall approach. Further evaluation with respect to quality criteria well-grounded and commonly used in qualitative research will help address these shortcomings and highlight other aspects of the approach that can be improved. In this subsection we provide a review of several potential evaluation criteria.

In terms of the evaluation of more general interpretive research, validity and reliability are two most important facets of the quality of qualitative inquiry (Yin 1994, Silverman and Marvasti 2008). Hammersley (1990) provides two straightforward definitions of validity and reliability respectively: "by validity, I mean truth: interpreted as the extent to which an account accurately represents the social phenomena to which it refers" (p. 57); and "reliability refers to the degree of consistency with which instances are assigned to the same category by different observers or by the same observer on different occasions" (p. 67). A more detailed and complex set of criteria have been argued for (Miles and Huberman 1994, Yin 1994), which further deconstruct validity and reliability. It is important to acknowledge at the outset, however, that particular philosophical underpinnings or theoretical orientations and resulting methodological commitments for qualitative inquiry will suggest different criteria for judging validity and reliability (Patton 2002). Furthermore, as the popularity of interpretive research in IS has increased, a debate has developed as to how to evaluate its quality. Here we provide an summary review of the major contributions to this debate to provide context for the selection of evaluation criteria the authors believe most suitable to assess the extended focus group data collection method used in our research.

Interpretive research in IS has gained considerably in popularity since 1991 when it constituted a very small proportion of published IS research (Orlikowski and Baroudi 1991; Walsham 2006). Early interpretive research used quality criteria borrowed from the well-established positivist tradition which broadly assesses validity and reliability at various levels of granularity and specificity. Texts on qualitative and case study research offered operationalised versions of these (Miles and Huberman 1994; Yin 1994) and were adopted by interpretive researchers (Johnson, Buehring et al. 2006). However, there has been an increasingly active debate in the literature over the appropriateness of such criteria, based as they are in positivist philosophical assumptions (Johnson, Buehring et al. 2006). By failing to guide research design and execution appropriately, and in undermining the perceived quality of such research, the pervasiveness of these well-established but not-universally optimal criteria are seen to limit the effectiveness of interpretive research.

Recognition of this weakness has led to three distinct responses in the literature. One argues that the epistemological underpinnings of interpretive research argues against the use of established, standardised or imposed criteria at all (Bochner 2000). The application of criteria is seen as constraining the freedom and limiting possibilities of the research, and indeed resisting the change which characterises the progressive nature of research itself. The use of "personal standards" is instead advocated to ensure quality of research. This approach to judging research is reflected in the view of interpretivism as a 'craft' (Seale 1999) and criteria to evaluate it as restricting the freedom and creativity of the researcher to operate in the "new rubric of poetic social science" (Bochner 2000).

A second response, and seemingly the most popular in the literature, is that of extending existing criteria for validity and reliability by sub-categorisation. Several works have contributed variously alternative, complementary and overlapping proposals. These result in validity being extended from the three most popular forms of construct, internal and external validity to increasingly specific forms such as 'successor', catalytic', 'voluptuous' and 'ironic' (Altheide and Johnson 1994) . Similarly, reliability can be disaggregated into more specific concepts such as 'quixotic', 'diachronic' and 'synchronic' (Kirk and Miller 1986).

Leading Issues in Business Research Methods

A third approach to creating evaluation criteria for interpretive research is to propose alternates which are not based explicitly on validity and reliability. In a recent paper Geoff Walsham, an authority on interpretive methods in IS research, excludes any mention of the words validity or reliability when describing how the quality of such methods should be evaluated (Walsham 2006). Instead he refers to two alternate schemes which propose variously the use of authenticity, plausibility and criticality (Golden-Biddle and Locke 1993) or the seven principles based on anthropology, phenomenology and hermeneutics which have gained prominence in recent years (Klein and Myers 1999). However, there remains considerable ambiguity in how these should be applied, with one study (Cepeda and Martin 2005) looking at the quality of case studies applying the seven principles in addition to, rather than instead of, Yin's (Yin 1994) tests for validity and reliability. Regardless, K&M are frequently cited by IS researchers to justify or validate their research approaches (e.g., Pan et al. 2006, Dhillon and Torkzadeh 2006, Bjørn and Ngwenyama 2009).

Table 5: Interpretive research evaluation criteria (Klein and Myers 1999)

Range	It is recommended that a broad range of topics be discussed, possibly including some not foreseen by the researchers. This approach is supported through "nondirective" moderation of the group (Merton and Kendall 1946) and ensures participant input reflects what is important or interesting to the participant rather than to the researcher. Directed research questions and prompts invariably reflect the "framework" of the researcher and may imply certain interpretations and suggestions.
Specificity	Capturing input in terms of experiences and perspectives rather than just opinions is advocated by Merton and Kendall (1946). This helps prevent discussion drifting to generalities and reflects Yin's (1994) call to focus on "low-inference descriptors". However, this advice has been contested in the literature with the argument that the participants may be best placed to interpret events or experiences and that this approach may actually reduce researcher bias (Hines 2000). An improved technique is to elicit both specific input but also the participants interpretation or opinion.
Depth	This relates to the extent of self-revelatory input gained from participants, rather than merely descriptive input. It is important that a 'feeling context' is established to elicit input which provides more insight than statements describing what happened or was experienced. This can be easier where participants are intimately involved in the topic as in this study.

Personal Context	The personal and social context can be associated with the role played by the individual, such as project manager or developer, their skill and experience and their affinity with the team. Additional individual circumstance may also play a part, such as previous experiences with agile practices and with other project stakeholders (Morgan 1997). Although there are contrary views (Krueger and Casey 2009), most literature (Merton, Fiske et al. 1990; Kitzinger 1994; Sim 1998) calls for homogenous groups selected randomly from a population. Although different roles and experiences will bring different insights to a group discussion, one of the strengths of a homogenous group is that the differences and convergences can be more easily identified and can lead to deep insights (Sim 1998).

A lack of satisfactory conclusions or universally accepted criteria for judging interpretive research indicates that this debate may continue for some time to come (Guba and Lincoln 1994; Johnson, Buehring et al. 2006). Although the two sets of evaluation criteria for focus groups proposed (Sim 1998; Merton, Fiske et al. 1990) confront specific aspects of that data collection technique, they do not consider the wider interplay between data collection, analysis, research design and other factors impinging on the quality of the research. The authors therefore favor a framework addressing the complete research method. Given that the epistemological nature of the research is critical interpretive, criteria with a basis in positivism were not considered as relevant as those explicitly grounded in interpretivism. The most comprehensive and established evaluation framework specific to critical interpretive research is therefore chosen (Klein and Myers 1999). The seven principles described in the framework also include descriptions of and references to various studies which are assessed by the authors using one or more of the principles. However, a search of the literature has not revealed any previous studies involving the formal operationalisation of all of the principles.

6 Conclusion

Given the severe time and resource restrictions, and the extensive scope and lack of prescription of the research task, the focus group approach was highly successful in gathering large amounts of data from each ISD team. The use of written, semi-anonymous input and a highly structured format created specifically for each team, together with multiple researchers with deep knowledge of the projects were critical. However, the several novel extensions to the focus group data collection technique described here justifies a comprehensive evaluation of the research method. In this paper the authors discuss several evaluation frameworks found in both focus group and qualitative research literature. We outline the current debate concerning the evaluation of focus groups specifically, and interpretive research in general. In proposing the use of a comprehensive evaluation framework which addresses the whole research method rather than specifically focus groups as the data collection method, the authors recognize such a framework should not be based on assumptions of positivist epistemology. Although not widely applied in the literature, the 7 principles proposed by K&M, being founded on hermeneutics, phenomenology and anthropology, are designed specifically for the evaluation of critically interpretive research. Future work will include the operationalisation of these 7 principles as a set of self-reflective questions, and the application of these to the research described in this paper. It is expected that this work will lead to a set of guidelines for the use of focus groups as a useful data collection technique for IS researchers, and a new framework for the evaluation of interpretive IS research more generally.

References

Albrecht, T., G. Johnson, et al. (1993). "Understanding Communication Processes." in *Focus Groups. Successful Focus Groups: Advancing State of the Art*. D. L. Morgan. London, Sage.

Altheide, D. L. and J. M. Johnson (1994). "Criteria for Assessing Interpretive Validity." in *Qualitative Research. Handbook of Qualitative Research*. Sage, Thousand Oaks, CA: 485-499.

Asbury, J. (1995). "Overview of Focus Group Research." *Qualitative Health Research* **5**: 414-420.

Barbour, R. (2007). *Doing Focus Groups*. London, Sage.

Bjørn, P. and O. Ngwenyama (2009). "Virtual team collaboration: building shared meaning, resolving breakdowns and creating translucence." *Information Systems Journal* 19(3): 227-253.

Bloor, M., J. Frankland, et al. (2001). *Focus Groups in Social Research*. London, Sage.

Bochner, A. P. (2000). "Criteria Against Ourselves." *Qualitative Inquiry*, 6(2).

Cepeda, G. and D. Martin (2005). "A review of case studies publishing in Management Decision 2004-2004." *Management Decision* **43**(6).

Conboy, K. (2009). "Agility From First Principles: Reconstructing The Concept of Agility in Information Systems Development." *Information Systems Research* **20**(3): 329-354.

Dhillon, G. and G. Torkzadeh (2006). "Value-focused assessment of information system security in organizations." *Information Systems Journal* 16(3): 293-314.

Eysenbach, G. (2000). "Consumer Health Informatics." *British Medical Journal* **320**: 1713-1716.

Fitzgerald, B., N. Russo, et al. (2002). *Information Systems Development: Methods in Action*. London, McGraw-Hill.

Golden-Biddle, K. and K. Locke (1993). "Appealing work: an investigation of how ethnographic texts convince." *Organization Science* 4(4): 595-616.

Guba, E. G. and Y. S. Lincoln (1994). Competing paradigms in *qualitative research*. *Handbook of Qualitative Research*. N. K. Denzin and Y. S. Lincoln. Thousand Oaks, Sage: 105-117.

Hammersley, M. (1990). *Reading Ethnographic Research: A Critical Guide*. London: Longmans.

Johnson, P., A. Buehring, et al. (2006). "Evaluating qualitative management research: Towards a contingent criteriology." *International Journal of Management Reviews* 8(3).

Hines, T. (2000). "An evaluation of two qualitative methods (focus group interviews and cognitive maps) for conducting research into entrepreneurial decision making." *Qualitative Market Research* **3(1)**.

Kerslake, E. and A. Goulding (1996). "Focus groups: Their use in LIS research data collection." *Education for Information* **14**: 225-235.

Kidd, P. and M. Parshall (2000). "Getting the Focus and the Group: Enhancing Analytical Rigor in Focus Group Research." *Qualitative Health Research* **10**: 293.

Kirk, J. and M. L. Miller (1986). Reliability and Validity in *Qualitative Research*. Newbury Park, CA, Sage Publications.

Kitzinger, J. (1994). "The methodology of Focus Groups: the importance of interaction between research participants." *Sociology of Health & Illness* **16**(1).

Klein, H. and M. D. Myers (1999). "A Set of Principles for Conducting and Evaluating Interpretive Field Studies in Information Systems." *MIS Quarterly* 23 No. 1(March): 67-93.

Koppel, R., J. Metlay, et al. (2005). "Role of Computerized Physician Order Entry Systems in Facilitating Medication Errors." *Journal of the American Medical Association* **293**(10).

Krueger, R. A. and M. A. Casey (2009). *Focus Groups: A Practical Guide for Applied Research*. Thousand Oaks, CA, Sage.

Merton, R. K., M. Fiske, et al. (1990). *The focused Interview*. New york, Free Press.

Merton, R. K. and P. L. Kendall (1946). "The Focused Interview." *American Journal of Sociology* **51**: 541-557.

Miles, M. B. and A. M. Huberman (1994). *Qualitative Data Analysis: An Expanded Sourcebook*. Thousand Oaks, CA, Sage Publications, Inc.

Morgan, D. L. (1997). *Focus Groups as Qualitative Research*. Newbury Park, CA, Sage Publications.

Orlikowski, W. J. and J. J. Baroudi (1991). Studying Information Technology in Organizations: Research Approaches and Assumptions. *Information Systems Research*. 2: 1-28.

Pan, G., S. L. Pan, et al. (2006). "Escalation and de-escalation of commitment: a commitment transformation analysis of an e-government project." *Information Systems Journal* 16(1): 3-21.

Patton, M. Q. (1990). *Qualitative Research and Evaluation Methods* 2nd Ed. Newbury Park, CA, Sage Publications.

Patton, M. Q. (2002). *Qualitative Research and Evaluation Methods* 3rd Ed. London, Sage Publications.

Pitt, L. F., R. T. Watson, et al. (1995). "Service Quality: A Measure of Information Systems Effectiveness." *MIS Quarterly* **19**(2 (June)): 173-187.

Reich, B. and I. Benbasat (2000). "Factors that Influence the Social Dimension of Alignment Between Business And Information Technology Objectives." *MIS Quarterly* **24**(1).

Seale, C. (1999). "Quality in Qualitative Research." *Qualitative Inquiry* 5(4).

Silverman, D., & Marvasti, A. (2008). Doing Qualitative Research: A Comprehensive Guide. *Nursing Research* (Vol. 44). Sage Publications, Inc.

Sim, J. (1998). "Collecting and analysing qualitative data: issues raised by the focus group." *Journal of Advanced Nursing* **28**(2): 345-352.

Sobreperez, P. (2008). "Using Plenary Focus Groups in Information Systems Research: More than a Collection of Interviews." *Electronic Journal of Business Research Methods* **6**(2).

Stewart, D., P. Shamdasani, et al. (2007). *Focus Groups Theory and Practice*. London, Sage.

Walsham, G. (2006). "Doing Interpretive Research." *European Journal of Information Systems* 15: 320-330.

Wilkinson, S. (1998). "Focus Group Methodology: a review." *International Journal of Social Research Methodology* **1**(3): 181-203.

Yin, R. K. (1994). *Case Study Research: Design and Methods*. Thousand Oaks, CA, Sage Publications.

www.ingramcontent.com/pod-product-compliance
Ingram Content Group UK Ltd.
Pitfield, Milton Keynes, MK11 3LW, UK
UKHW022211230426
12048UKWH00016BA/788